D0210960

Wisdom With Understanding is Better Than Rubies

Lurine Karon Greenberg
Fine Arts Collection

BEATEN, SEARED, AND SAUCED

BEATEN, SEARED, AND SAUCED

On Becoming a Chef at the
Culinary Institute of America

JONATHAN DIXON

Clarkson Potter/Publishers
NEW YORK

For Jane and Peter Dixon
And for Nelly Reifler

All rights reserved.
Published in the United States by Clarkson Potter/Publishers, an imprint of the
Crown Publishing Group, a division of Random House, Inc., New York.
www.crownpublishing.com
www.clarksonpotter.com

CLARKSON POTTER is a trademark and POTTER with colophon
is a registered trademark of Random House, Inc.

Library of Congress Cataloging-in-Publication Data
Dixon, Jonathan.
Beaten, seared, and sauced / Jonathan Dixon. — 1st ed.
p.   cm.
1. Dixon, Jonathan.   2. Cooks—United States—Biography.
3. Culinary Institute of America.   I. Title.
TX649.D59 A3   2011
641.5092—dc22   2010040145
[B]

ISBN 978-0-307-58903-3

Printed in the United States of America

Design by Stephanie Huntwork
Jacket photographs © Jetta Productions; David Atkinson (chef);
Rubberball/Mike Kemp (egg)

1   3   5   7   9   10   8   6   4   2

First Edition

ACKNOWLEDGMENTS

THANK YOU TO DAVE Larabell, my agent. Thank you to Rica Allannic, my editor. I owe both of you a huge debt of gratitude.

And thank you to everyone who directly impacted this entire experience: Adam Kuban, Gail Rundle, John J. Singer Jr., Barbara Ryan, Anna Dixon Lassoff, Dave Lassoff, Sam and Niloufer Reifler, Jenefer Shute, Susan Daitch, Lauren Cerand, Lesley Porcelli, Deborah Finkel, Adam Walker, Gerard Viverito, Robert Perillo, Irena Chalmers, Ben Smith, Lee Greenfeld, Chesley Hicks, Lacy Shutz, Ian Bickford, Dwayne Motley, Laura Wallis, Jay Cooper, Jill Olson, Elizabeth Albert, Erik Satre, Andrew Lindsay Cohen, Sarah Prouty, Ryan Carey, all the Pownal WW crew, and Bob Miller.

And of course, Dan C., Margo G., Stephen P., Bruce P., Micah M., Rocco P., Gabi C., Jessica S., Max S., Brian T., Carol J., Jackie Y., Mike O., Diego F., Greg L., Jeremy D., Kevin S., Zach L., Natasha M., Sam G., Sammy S., Gio A., Mike B., Sasha G., Jeff S., Sitti S., Evan B., Dimitri K., Joe C., and Leo R.: gracias to all of you.

I want to acknowledge Michael Ruhlman's excellent book, *The Making of a Chef,* which looked at the day to day workings of the Culinary Institute of America's curriculum with a more microscopic, objective eye than I achieved in mine. My goal was to supplement Michael Ruhlman and not to supplant him.

1

My throat felt tight. My hands were slick. My heart kept up a high rhythm, so fast the beats almost collided. Because of nerves, I'd had three hours of sleep.

I was just a few weeks away from my thirty-eighth birthday.

We'd been staying with my girlfriend Nelly's parents in Rhinebeck, New York, about twenty minutes up the road from the Culinary Institute of America. Last night, I'd turned the lights out at eleven and lay in the dark, twitching and tossing through a long pileup of minutes and hours. At four a.m., I got out of bed, made coffee, and sat outside watching dawn stir and listening to a riot of birdsongs. At five, I started Nelly's car and drove off.

For an hour, I'd been sitting in the student parking lot, listening to the Grateful Dead, weighing the situation: the fact of this day, the fact of the next two years. I was certain other people too had made decisions before that seemed ordered and right, seemed logical and good, and then felt suddenly disastrous and badly considered. They had screwed up, and screwed up supremely, had been blind all along to a plan's inherent, obvious flaws.

We'd packed up the better part of all our books, our furniture, all the little totems of our life, and trekked from Brooklyn to the Hudson Valley. I'd turned down a job offer. A stranger was in our apartment for the next six months. My savings account was paltry, and I'd just bought a decrepit pickup truck, which was being made less decrepit by a mechanic for a good chunk of what little remained in the bank.

At one point, I'd realized that walking away would cost me only the $100 registration fee I'd paid the school to enroll in their Associate of Occupational Studies (AOS) in Culinary Arts program. The tuition was, at this juncture, fully refundable.

I knew that Nelly thought this was a little crazy. She'd spent some of her early years in Poughkeepsie and knew exactly what it meant to attend the CIA. She was excited I'd be doing it. But a good part of the day-to-day finances—money for electricity, gasoline, groceries—was going to be her purview. She is a writer, and shouldering that burden would be rough. I knew that a few of our friends also thought this was a little crazy and—more—irresponsible. I was borrowing tuition money, and I'd be paying it back. You didn't do that at thirty-eight.

I saw people moving off in the distance. They wore white chef's jackets and checked pants and carried notebooks, textbooks, and knife kits. Others wore suits. Everyone, I noticed, walked quickly and intently. Without knowing them, without seeing their faces, I felt inferior. My fingers felt incapable; my mind felt shaky. I did an inventory. My discipline seemed slack and my concentration delicate. I wasn't, perhaps, all that smart. My memory for figures and facts would certainly fail me. It didn't feel as if I belonged here.

The school, a few hundred yards from where I was in the parking lot, loomed like a set piece out of *Citizen Kane*. The main building, its biggest building, Roth Hall, the one taking up most of the campus real estate, was a former Jesuit monastery. It rose up for five stories, all dark aged stone, stained glass, and ivy. It felt permanent and pitiless, significant.

A new group of students begins at the CIA every three weeks. Every three weeks there must be someone racking themselves just like I was. I had almost an hour to kill before I was supposed to present myself, along with all the other students starting that day, in the school's Admissions Office.

The sky was overcast and it was cold out. Bob Weir was singing about Mexican prostitutes and venereal disease at the precise moment I decided to start the car, drive away, and go explain to Nelly, her parents, my parents, my sister, my grandfather, my friends—to everyone—why I decided this was just a bad idea.

I'd be almost forty when school was finished. This was escapism. This was indulgence.

I had given a lot of thought to what I was going to do after I graduated. The results—the specifics—were inconclusive, but I knew I wanted to cook for the rest of my life and I wanted to do it for other people. By definition, I wanted to be a chef. I did not know how I'd bend the definition of that word to suit me. But I wanted to be a chef and I was here in the parking lot of the school that taught you how to become one.

I liked the idea of cooking on the line in a restaurant. I liked the notion of being anchored to a burning stove in a rush and whirl of activity, of making food strangers would eat. If it was good, you earned their admiration, and that was attractive too. But being a cook under those circumstances will not fill your wallet, and it's physical. I was fit, I was still strong. But cooking involves serious time on your feet, a real commitment of the body. Eventually, I might need to be realistic. I didn't know.

I knew I would never own a restaurant. To do so would most likely sap any assets I might someday acquire, and cause my heart to rupture and stop. I'd drive myself to an embolism obsessing over how to save two pennies on a bushel of spinach, worried sick that my staff was robbing me blind behind my back.

I would never be Daniel Boulud. I would never be Ferran Adrià.

I would never be on TV. I knew the camera would never love me enough.

But I loved food, and I loved cooking.

It would be two years gone, two years of strain, two years getting older—all without any guarantees. I had an aptitude for cooking, but as far as I knew, I'd never shot off sparks of brilliance. My parents, my friends, dinner guests—everyone liked my food when they ate it. Or said they did.

A few weeks before, I'd reread Denis Johnson's *Already Dead*. There was a line I'd always liked, right at the beginning when one of the characters is cruising the back roads off California's Highway 1, that said, "You might throw a tire and hike to a gas station and stumble unexpectedly onto the rest of your life, the people who would finally mean something to you, a woman, an immortal friend, a saving fellowship in the religion of some obscure church." Or cooking school.

We are what we nurture. I'd nurtured writing. I hadn't nurtured cooking. But I felt it there in me, and I was here to coax it out and see how it flourished.

People amble through their lives with the serious weight of lost years on them, looking for moments like this. I watched the students in their uniforms for a while longer. Then I got out of the car and walked toward the Admissions Office to stumble onto the rest of my life.

THE ADMISSIONS OFFICE WAS a nicely turned-out room of gentle carpeting, only-just-tasteful couches, and brooding light. About seventy people were already there.

In my mind's cineplex, I think I had envisioned the other students— soon to be my peers—as people of unequaled intensity. Their knowledge would be encyclopedic. Already excessively competent, they were here to hone and refine, to make food sing. I had worked my way through most of the titles on the CIA's recommended reading list that had been sent out several months prior. I was dipping into Escoffier's *Le Guide Culinaire*—the foundation of classic French cuisine—every day. I wanted to try and catch up. The competition, I'd assumed, would be fierce in the school kitchens.

The scene in the Admissions lobby was very different from the film in my head.

These faces were still puffy with baby fat. They were gritted with acne. A dozen or so stood in small clusters. I overheard a few conversations. Most of the kids lived on campus and had arrived to settle in several days earlier. A few had been up late the night before, drinking. Someone had been sick in the shower. One young man wondered aloud several times when we'd get our knives.

But the majority of them stood alone. There was a general sway of exhaustion and disquiet in the air; I wondered how many had slept as poorly as I had. A few people in the crowd began to stick out. Their faces were older. Not quite in my age range, but definitely closer to me than to eighteen. They seemed to be scanning the room and looking a little bit wary. Way apart from the crowd I saw two people standing together who were definitely in my age group. They probably had an involved story of how they got here and why they came. But I couldn't bring myself to cross over to where they stood. I leaned against the wall and stared at my feet. I didn't really know how to begin telling my story.

Except for the knot of people in the room's center, few others were talking at all. Maybe they didn't know how to tell their stories either.

At 7:00 a.m. on the nose, we were led into an adjoining room, a small auditorium with a video monitor and a few hundred seats.

A squat, thick woman of potent seriousness gave a speech on the Institute and the rigors of its program, about how hard we were going to work, about how much it would change us, how skilled we'd be at the end. It was exactly what I wanted to hear, but terrifying to be told. She went over the schedule of classes for the next semester and the one following. The calendar was broken up into blocks, the first one a quartet of academic classes that lasted six weeks (five classes if you had to take the basic writing course, which I had tested out of). Afterward, there were twenty-four weeks of practical classes, broken into eight three-week blocks. At that point, every student left the school to do an eighteen-week externship, working for minimum wage, or nothing, in a restaurant somewhere around the country or world. Upon completion of the externship, you returned for the second part of the program, which meant six more weeks of academics, and another twenty-four weeks of practical classes. A lot of the kids were fidgeting as she talked.

She called a list of names, mine included, and told us to speak with the school nurse, who was at a table by the door. We needed to schedule a hepatitis-A vaccination and a tetanus booster. Then we were sent upstairs to set everything right with the bursar.

The wait in line for the bursar was long, but I spent it watching the others. We'd been sent sternly worded notices about the school's dress code—dressy pants, collared shirt, no sneakers, no jeans, no facial hair. The hair on your head must be of "natural color." No lengthy sideburns, and no earrings for the men. No nose rings for anyone. Most of the males in line—including me—looked as if we had hit the same sale at Old Navy. We looked like stereo salesmen, or golfers. Everyone had the same polo shirts in the same small spectrum of solid colors. Everyone's khakis had the same cut. Some people had apparently missed the memo, though. As we stood in line, an administrator of some sort approached each of the scofflaws and explained that they'd have to change or shave. One young kid, with a huge bush of a beard hanging off his thin face, made arrangements with a complete stranger to go back to the stranger's dorm room and shave.

Very few of the people in line were talking. That vibe of angst and fatigue just seemed to mute the moment. One by one, we made our way to the bursar. Afterward, we were ushered through a door and down a long hallway to a tailoring station where we were measured for our uniforms. Then we were set loose for a few hours until lunch. I filled the time touring the campus.

When you're on these grounds, it's hard to not be impressed. This was certainly intentional. They went at the planning and landscaping with grandeur in mind. The place is situated a couple miles north of Poughkeepsie, in Hyde Park, on a bluff overlooking the Hudson River, high enough so that every building catches the sunlight. Right across from the Admissions Building was a structure modeled to look like an Italian villa. It was done up in yellow stucco, with a red tiled roof, and hemmed in on two sides by evergreen trees. Inside was the school's Italian restaurant, open to the public and staffed by students. The road in front of it was made to look like a cobblestone street. Behind and below the villa, at the bottom of a slope, lay meticulous rows of dozens of herbs. I walked the rows and periodically reached down to rub the leaves between my fingers and smell the oils on my skin. Maybe because of the neatness of the garden, or because of the surroundings, they had an authority in their scent, as if these were not herbs like those you bought or even grew on your own.

Across from the gardens was the library. We'd been told that morning that the Conrad Hilton Library housed the second-biggest collection of cookbooks in the country, and I wanted to see what the second-biggest collection of cookbooks looked like. I went inside, made some inquiries, and was told that the cookbooks were on the second and third floors. When I went upstairs, I saw dozens and dozens of rows of shelves, dense with books from floor to top. I went at random through the stacks, walking more and more quickly—every book Elizabeth David ever wrote, everything by Jane Grigson. Michel Guérard's books were here, Alain Ducasse, Paul Bocuse, arcane books on Serbian gastronomy and Native American cooking, endless numbers of books on Chinese cooking from every region; the collection went on and on and on. For the first time that day, anxiety gave way to anticipation. I wanted to learn everything that was in here, everything available. I wanted to turn my mind into a repository and I wanted to fill it. I had never once in my life pondered Serbian cooking, but right then I wanted to make myself an expert. After an hour, I forced myself back outside.

Next to the library stood a plaza with a view of the river. The plaza was small but looked imperial, broken up into a geometry of trimmed grass, a fountain, trellises, and gazebos. The water was off, but it had apparently been on earlier. Puddles lay on the surface and some of the students, out of uniform, dressed for the summer weather, ran and splashed. These grounds were beautiful, everything devoted to food. It was like Disneyland for cooks.

We'd been told to report for lunch at eleven thirty, in the same complex as the Admissions Office, where the Banquet and Catering (B&C) class is taught. To get to the banquet room, you walk down a long hallway that passed the B&C kitchen. For the benefit of visitors, there are large windows looking in, and I stopped to watch the students at work. These students were on the tail end of their second year. Their faces did not carry baby fat. They didn't have the lazy radiance of the kids I'd mingled with a few hours ago. The acne was a little more stubborn, apparently, but, still, I noticed they all moved with purpose and focus. They were cutting up tenderloins of beef, attending to big steaming pots, working some decorative tricks over plates of desserts. No one was bumping into each other; no one seemed panicked. They simply flowed through the two or three minutes I stood watching.

A young woman appeared right in front of me on the other side of the glass, wearing the standard white chef's coat, checked pants, and a paper toque on her head. She had a box of tools open on a tabletop and was searching through it. She looked up and straight at me. I could see her take in the clothes I was wearing. I saw her notice the name tag. She smiled and raised her eyebrows at the same time, then pursed her lips like she was suppressing a laugh and quickly looked down and away. If a thought bubble had formed over her head, I was imagining that it would have read, *You poor little fucker. All awkward in your khakis, with that stupid name tag. You just have no idea*—no idea—*what's coming.*

As the other new students arrived at the Banquet dining room, a long line formed at the door. One of the Banquet students, dressed in dark pants, a dark vest with a faintly ridiculous almost-psychedelic-patterned fabric on the front, and a tie, acted as the maître d', and escorted people to random tables. There were eight places at each table. We were in for some forced socializing. I didn't actually mind; we were all going to have to talk to each other at some point.

Lunch was allotted an hour's time on the schedule and consisted of three courses: appetizer, entrée, and dessert. Bread with the meal came from baking kitchen classrooms. Everything else had been produced in the B&C kitchen.

When I sat down at the table—I was the eighth person—I looked at everyone else and gave a cursory greeting. Everyone—about an equal mix of male and female—smiled and nodded and recommenced a long stare at the tablecloth or out the windows that ran along one side of the room.

The silence was awkward. It stretched itself out until I, too, was staring with great concentration at the tines of my fork. Then it became absurd. I chortled a little to myself and looked up.

"Wow, this is stupid," I said. Everyone looked surprised. I turned to the woman on my left. "Where are you from?"

She flinched, smiled, and then said, "Hershey."

"As in, Pennsylvania?"

"Mmm-hmmm." She sipped her water.

"What's your name?"

She pointed to her name tag. *Britney.*

"So Britney," I said, "are you culinary arts or pastry?"

She mumbled something.

"I'm sorry?"

She mumbled again.

"What?"

"She said, 'pastry,'" another woman chimed in. Her name tag read *Tara.* She turned to Britney. "Are you coming here from college or high school?"

Britney paused for a long time. "I just graduated from high school two days ago, on Saturday. I got my diploma, went home, got into the car, and drove up here. I didn't want to spend the summer in Hershey because I was getting into too much trouble and my parents wanted me to come here instead of juvie."

Silence descended again, but this time, I just let it go unbroken.

Eventually the appetizer arrived, and everyone grew a little more animated. We were right then seeing a portion of our future on the plates. It was a vol-au-vent with mushrooms, a puff-pastry cylinder filled with sautéed mushrooms in a Madeira cream sauce. We all waited until each had been served, put napkins in our laps, and tasted it. Today, the future tasted pretty decent.

We'd been told earlier that all students are allowed two meals a day. For new students, during the first six weeks, one of those meals could be in any of the school's different kitchens—the Asia kitchen, the Americas kitchen, the Mediterranean kitchen—but one meal had to be in the B&C room. This was where we'd get the first look at what we were supposed to be doing at the Institute. The meals, as we'd discover, were often ornate, complex: foie gras profiteroles; seared duck breasts with green peppercorn and pineapple gastrique. Occasionally the food was sublime; occasionally it was horrible. You couldn't help but take mental notes, writing critiques in your head. There were things to try and emulate, things to avoid. These meals were cooked by students just on the cusp of their graduation. It was no coincidence that the newcomers were forced to eat here night after night.

After the appetizer and before the entrée, the silence evaporated. I'd been watching Tara a little bit while we were eating because I discovered something strange about her, mainly that I suspected she was a lunatic. Her eyes pinwheeled, and she'd jump and agitate in her chair. She cracked her knuckles over and over. Her lips were perpetually set as if she'd give a raspberry at any second, and every movement of her hands and arms and head had something frantic to it. She simmered with a very peculiar energy. She caught me looking at her.

"Okay, then," she said. "Tell us where *you're* from."

"I grew up in New Hampshire, but I've been living in Brooklyn for a long time."

She slapped the table with her hand and said, "I'm from Brooklyn."

"Where?"

"Cobble Hill."

Right near my apartment.

"I live on Atlantic Avenue, right off Court Street," I said.

"You're kidding! We're neighbors!" Tara turned to the guy next to her. "We're neighbors." She turned back to me. "Well, we'll have to get together sometime in the city."

The entrée arrived. Roasted beef tenderloin, pureed potatoes, sautéed green beans. The future was tasting simple, but still pretty damn good.

IF YOU PAID ANY attention at all to the CIA's public persona, you knew who Tim Ryan was. A graduate of the school, he became the youngest-ever Certified Master Chef (a title bestowed on experienced cooks who pass a rigorous test of skills, technique, and creativity); a popular instructor; and, in his early forties, the president of the Institute. That's just the short list. He was also on the US Culinary Olympics team, honored by dozens of culinary societies, on and on and on. In the realm of food he is a serious overachiever. He is known to be a no-nonsense but extremely kind sort of person. He also has a reputation as someone best not crossed.

And he'd been in the news lately.

Two months before I was set to start at school, someone e-mailed me an article from the *New York Times,* detailing the clash between certain student groups, the teachers' union, and Ryan. Slipping standards. Bad equipment. Overcrowded classes. Cozying up to corporate food entities. And my favorite: the use of premade frozen waffle fries for the Quantity Food Production class. Nelly and I both laughed hysterically when we read that.

The teachers' union had given him a vote of "no confidence." The students had created Facebook pages.

The corporate toadying and, yes, the waffle fries gave me pause. I decided to call the CIA and ask about it. I spoke with a woman in the Student Affairs Office who was surprisingly candid.

"I really can't say that I feel academic standards have fallen," she said. "The same chefs are still teaching the exact same curriculum we've taught for years. They aren't deviating. Those people—with all their experience and training—are the ones you'll be studying with. No one from Sysco is going to be teaching you in the classroom. And yes, we have relationships with corporations. We're a nonprofit institution. We rely on benefactors and donations. So, yeah, we have the

Conrad Hilton Library and the Colavita Olive Oil Center. But does Mr. Hilton's name mean that the second-largest collection of cookbooks anywhere in the country is any less valuable? And furthermore, let me address the question of frozen waffle fries. Let's say that you're working in an industrial cafeteria, or a hospital or a prison or on an army base. Are you going to have the time to cut thousands of servings of waffle fries from scratch? No, you're not. But when you do get those frozen fries, we want to show you how to prepare them so they're as good as they can be. However good that is.

"Listen, Jonathan, if you want to drive up here, or take the train, we'll pay for your gas or your ticket. You can come and spend an entire day, or two days if you want, in one of the kitchens. And if you still have any concerns, we can sit and talk about them."

I thought she was so up-front that I decided to take her word for it. I also found out later that, for cost-cutting purposes, some members of the board of directors had been pressuring Ryan to eliminate seriously costly items like foie gras or truffles from the curriculum recipes. Ryan wouldn't budge. If the recipe—deemed to be of such stature and classicism that it should be learned by every student—called for foie gras, then there was going to be foie gras available.

A student I met early on told me that I'd see Ryan twice during my entire time at the CIA: on the first day when he spoke to all the incoming students, and when I graduated.

When I walked into the auditorium, where he'd address us shortly, there was a large video monitor down front with the words "Your attitude determines your altitude" projected on it.

I sat midway down the sloping rows of seats. We waited just a few minutes and a man came out to tell us that we were about to be addressed by Dr. Ryan. Then another man came out to do an actual introduction. And then Ryan emerged.

He is a handsome guy, distinguished, with the sort of thicker build that men in their fifties seem to grow into. He wore a blue blazer, a blue shirt, and a starkly green tie. He was also immediately charismatic. I found myself watching intently as he conferred with a few people around him and strapped on a microphone.

I became aware again, as I looked around, of just how young so many of these people in the room were. I realized the attitude/altitude slogan was probably part of a talk geared toward people who hadn't yet worried about paying for electricity and rent.

"Good afternoon," Ryan began. He got a muted response.

"That was terrible," he said. "Let me hear you: Good afternoon."

This time he got the shouts and bellows. I felt faintly uncomfortable.

The next ten minutes were pretty much what you'd expect—he spoke about the high standards in the classrooms, the high rate of people who don't continue because of the pressures of it all. He told us that the school only selected a very limited number of applicants. Thinking of Britney, I was a little dubious.

"There are eighty of you in this entering group," he said. "This time, only eight of you have degrees so far. Of those eight, we have a number of career changers." I slid down in my seat.

He went on: "What careers are they changing from? We have a law school student. We have a telephone sales rep. We have a magazine writer and a professor." Two students across the aisle conferred with each other, slightly disbelieving, at that professor thing. It did sound a little off. He listed a few more occupational switches. And then began one of the strangest speeches I'd ever heard.

On the video monitor, the letters "CPA" appeared.

"CPA," Ryan began. "Does anyone know what those letters mean? 'CPA' stands for this: carrot-peeling attitude. Does anyone know what that means? Anyone know what it means to have a carrot-peeling attitude? No? Let's say you landed an externship at the French Laundry out in Napa Valley with Chef Thomas Keller. Everyone knows who he is, right? Now, if you get an externship there, what do you think you're going to be doing when you start?"

This was about the sixth time I'd heard Keller mentioned that day. His name was used pretty much as a synonym for unparalleled excellence, and it was invoked all the time as the program went on. The Muslims may have ninety-nine names for God, but at the CIA, there was pretty much just one: Keller.

"If you were an extern at the French Laundry, your first job would most likely be peeling carrots. A lot of carrots. Now, some externs would think this was beneath them. They'd think that spending weeks peeling carrots at the French Laundry was a waste of time. But, if you have a carrot-peeling attitude, this isn't true. If you have a carrot-peeling attitude, there's no such thing as a waste of time. If you have a carrot-peeling attitude, you're going to make it your business to be the best carrot peeler the French Laundry has ever had. Why should you be discouraged if you're asked to peel carrots, day after day? This is an opportunity.

"Try and see how many carrots you can peel in a day. And then the next day, try and break that record. Now, each time, you'll want to go see whichever chef is supervising you and say, 'Chef, I know you're busy, but could you come and look at my carrots?' He or she will always—always—take the time to look at your work if you show that kind of carrot-peeling attitude."

You could hear the faint whispers of disbelief and, I thought, a little bit of scorn. People covered their mouths with their hands and spoke asides to their neighbor. They exchanged glances. Undeterred, Ryan, who had obviously given this speech before, continued.

"So now you want to keep trying to break that record. How do you track your progress? You make a chart. You have the days of the week labeled, you have the number of weeks you're going to be there, and you fill in how many carrots you did each day. And you ask your chef, each day, to come and look at your carrots. Hang that chart above your station in the kitchen. And each time you break your record . . ." For one second, it seemed as if he was steeling himself. "Each time you break that record, you put a gold star for that day."

The place erupted in audible incredulity.

"No, no—" Ryan said, holding up a hand. "Sure, you'll get some good-natured ribbing from your coworkers"—there were loud hoots and catcalls—"but they'll *respect* you. They will! They'll respect you!"

The guy next to me turned. " 'Good-natured ribbing'?"

I thought of some of the cooks I'd encountered in my life. "I guess either that or a good-natured shanking between the ribs," I said.

Ryan went on. "And by the end of your externship, maybe you'll have your entire chart covered with stars. And who knows—maybe, because you've shown so much dedication, maybe you'll be invited to walk across the road from the French Laundry with Chef Keller and go to the garden they keep there. And maybe you'll be invited to help Chef Keller pick carrots for that evening's service. Wouldn't that be something? Picking carrots with Thomas Keller?

"You'll be the best carrot peeler they've ever had. You'll peel carrots better than anyone else. The journey is the destination, people, the journey is the destination. And you'll be able to use that attitude no matter what job you have in the kitchen. And if you do have that attitude, you can become the best at anything you want to do."

The guy was, admittedly, a really good speaker. But the idea of anyone over the age of twelve being so meek and submissive as to ask a supervisor whether it was okay to put a gold star on a chart made me squirm. I got the point. I think everyone did. But you'd really have to be a special kind of sniveling bootlick to plumb that depth of obsequiousness.

That acronym, CPA, still showed on the monitor. And then we were dismissed.

Done for the day, I went back to Roth Hall and began walking down the hallways. I needed to see what was going on in the kitchens. I wanted to look at the students while they worked. I wanted to look closely at their faces and see if I could recognize something reflected back to me, a portent or omen that might indicate I wouldn't fuck this up.

The hallways were dim like tunnels, the colors of the floors and walls both dark, and the ceiling was high above, almost in shadow.

Along the hallways were the kitchens, bright portals visible through glass windows in the doors, humming with motion, but quiet inside, nearly silent. I stopped at one. In the dimness, it almost had the force of a revelation, light and movement from another world. It was another world. It would, I found myself understanding, be my world too.

The kitchen walls were all yellow tiles; the floors, red tiles. There were workstations arranged strategically throughout the room, and a number of ranges, ovens, and sinks. The instructor was walking among the students as they worked. He'd stop and hover, dig among their chopped vegetables, hold pieces between his fingers, and shake his hand for emphasis, dropping them back onto the cutting boards. Some students were at the ranges, attending pots and sauté pans. The instructor walked to a pair of them and spoke. The students stopped what they were doing. The fire burned unsupervised under the pans; steam rose up from whatever was inside. They nodded at him and he kept talking. The steam was coming up thicker. I saw the students— one young male and one young female, brown hair coming out from under the back of her toque—eyeing the pan. The instructor walked away, and they scrambled to take the pan from the heat. The instructor took a few steps backward, keeping his front to the students, and said loudly to the group that they had thirty minutes left. He pivoted and was facing me. He was tall and thin, with a heavy mustache streaked with gray. I saw him see my name tag and he smiled and made a nod with his head and then swooped away to stand behind someone else at their station.

I fixated on one student who was chopping what looked like parsley; his knife came up and down, up and down, with violence and speed, and the metal caught the light in the room and the knife seemed to glimmer. He worked with complete purpose, and I felt something that was like a cousin to admiration and envy both. I watched him, feeling that sensation for another minute or so, until it was time to get to the parking lot, start the truck, and drive home.

2

I DROPPED OUT OF kindergarten, and I had no friends until I was six. I knew how to talk to adults, but not to others my own age. I was a tiny kid—bait for bullies. And the world was just about at an end.

We'd moved from some remote burg in the White Mountains of New Hampshire down to a small town bordering Massachusetts. We lived next door to my grandparents. This was during the autumn when I was five, and, because of the move, why I never finished kindergarten. I was reading already, so I was set to start first grade the following September. There were no other kids around; my sister was a toddler and therefore useless. I spent the year with books and playing by myself in my own fantastical hazes. I counted Charlie Bucket, heir to Willy Wonka's chocolate factory, as a good friend. I took a seat around the Cratchit family's Christmas table. Laura Ingalls was my first girlfriend.

Right before we moved, I'd undergone one of the great rites of passage. My parents took me to the drive-in and we saw *Bambi*. After Bambi's mother was shot, our car was one of many queuing up at the exit with a weeping, hysterical little kid in the backseat. Around that time my mother had been supposed to die. She was bitten by an infected mosquito and contracted viral encephalitis, which cooks the brain and leaves you dead or comatose. I was called into her hospital room to say good-bye but I didn't quite get it; I kept asking for soda. I thought we'd be back the next day—which we were; my mother pulled through. It messed her up for the next decade, but she lived.

But the end of time was hovering over us. My parents are people of faith, and their faith is in a branch of conservative Christianity. They believe in the Bible, and they try to live it. They also believe that the end of things is soon, sooner than anyone thinks, a coming cataclysm. I lived haunted by the idea that time was short, that the mountains would melt, the dirt of the earth would burn, the sea would boil. There would be fire and blood and dying in the night, with wars raging and sicknesses eating alive the wicked of the world. Vivid sunsets sometimes scared me because they made the sky look molten. There were battles being fought in Cambodia, then Afghanistan and later in Beirut, in Latin America. I was sure that the momentum of the fighting would someday swing right into my backyard.

The town next to us, Nashua, New Hampshire, was home to the FAA's Air Traffic Control Center for the Northeast. I was told that across the world, nuclear missiles were poised and aimed right at it. I assumed if it happened, if a missile was launched, we'd never know what hit us.

My mother loved my sister and me with everything she was. I knew this even as a kid and sensed that no one could ever love me like that again. And when the cataclysms and disasters split the skies into splinters, there would be no one to love me at all.

My parents are devout, but they aren't Bible thumpers; they never spoke in tongues, and they were compassionate. They were interesting. They were interested.

My mother studied archaeology, and my father is an artist. He has a vested interest in human expression and every Saturday morning, he would take a few albums from his collection and give them to me: the Rolling Stones, Dylan, Hendrix, *The White Album*. I never got tired of hearing his story of seeing Hendrix perform in a gymnasium on Long Island.

When I was a boy, I remember an afternoon alone in the house, when I crouched in front of the stereo speakers in the living room, playing "Gimme Shelter" over and over and over. It was the sound of the beginning of the end of the world. I was trying to prepare myself.

Almost every great memory I have of my childhood is set at one dinner table or another.

Discounting religion, we were as Anglo-Saxon as families get. My favorite days were Sunday afternoons at my grandparents'. We'd eat big dinners of roasted meats and potatoes and gravies and vegetables. My mother made beautiful Yorkshire puddings. My father made the gravy and we'd all sit—my parents, my sister, my grandparents, and usually one of my mother's sisters—for hours at the table, from late afternoon until past dark. Everyone laughed a lot. Outside, leaves blew in the wind; wood sparked and flamed in the fireplace. Right then nothing was ending. Everything was as it should be.

As I got older, I still spent most of my time by myself. But I also started spending a lot of time with my mother in the kitchen, watching and absorbing. She explained some of the basics: how to cut butter into flour to make biscuits; how to cream butter and sugar to make cookies; how to fry an egg. I applied myself and learned quickly. We always had a steady supply of cookies on hand, or biscuits, and we ate a lot of my fried eggs.

My mother let me move on to roasting chickens and pieces of beef. She gave me her Yorkshire pudding recipe, and my father showed me how he made his gravy, pouring boiling water over the drippings in the bottom of a pan, making a paste of flour and cold water, stirring it into the liquid, simmering it and skimming.

I was in love with every moment spent in that kitchen, over the old electric stove, its glowing metal coils bent and listing. I loved every inch of the white countertop and its divots and burns.

When I wasn't cooking, I was reading, and this fueled my cooking even more. I wanted to taste what my book friends tasted. Bilbo Baggins and company roasted a leg of mutton on a spit over an open flame; I made do with a leg of lamb in the oven. Mrs. Ingalls made corncakes with molasses for her family so I tried that, too (the corncakes were okay; with the molasses, they tasted awful). I read and reread *A Christmas Carol* and, one Christmas way before my voice changed, I roasted a goose. Before the age of thirteen, I did at least half the family dinners every week. My parents bought me a cloth toque that I proudly wore every time I worked in the kitchen. I must have looked ridiculous.

WHEN I WAS A teenager, a girl I was in love with played me all sorts of underground music. The first few cacophonous Sonic Youth records, Black Flag, the Bad Brains, Einstürzende Neubauten. I fell for this stuff in all its extremes—music for a personal apocalypse. I became obsessed with the Grateful Dead. I had no idea what anyone was talking about when they described the Dead as full of warmth and peace. I had never heard music that dark, dazed, and knowing. It was on a nice continuum to everything else I listened to—a more measured chaos.

If you believe, as I once did—as I was taught—that everything will come to a sudden end, what point is there in being ambitious? This was not the message, I think, my parents wanted to send. But I was not ambitious. Life pulled me with it; I did not steer.

I left New Hampshire for college in Boston, and I was stunned by the divergence. In that space between everything I'd known growing up and what was inflicting itself on me now, my mind went dark and it filled with snakes. There was rain in everything, and everything was cold. I had never imagined that even the bricks of a building's wall could be hostile. I barely graduated.

I went to New York, looking for the rest of my life. The city was immense and dizzying and hypnotic. The rest of my life seemed mostly to be two steps ahead of me. I couldn't catch it. I just let the wind push me.

Each night, I made a ritual of cooking dinner for myself. I hated going out. My mother had a quick and easy dish I used to love: chicken breasts breaded, sautéed, served with a wine and mushroom sauce, rice, and broccoli. I made it several times a week, because it tasted like I was home. But it never tasted that way enough; maybe it was not enough wine, too much wine, the wrong bread crumbs, or maybe too much lemon in the sauce.

If you walk on almost any block in New York City, you can catch your own reflection in the window of a restaurant. They're innumerable and most aren't very good. But I suspected that in some of them, there were geniuses in the kitchen who could take the same ingredients I used and work miracles with them, who could make perfectly every time the dishes that haunted my palate. It never occurred to me that they had *learned* how to do it, or that I could learn, or that they could create dishes I'd never had before that might haunt me in the same way.

If I had a date, if I was making friends, if I was seeing old friends, I cooked for them. I never felt fluent in the real language we speak to each other in, the one by which we assemble ourselves in the company of, for the benefit of, other people. I spoke my mind and myself with food. I didn't do that with any of my jobs.

For a while I was a foot messenger. I was a receptionist. I was a proofreader. I became a host at a restaurant.

I was a nanny. I had a five-year-old kid in my charge. His mother was suffering from cancer. I picked him up from school, helped with homework, cooked him dinner, took him to movies. I talked to him when he was so terrified he didn't know how to live. His mother got well, he got older, and I moved on.

I wrote music and book reviews for papers like the *Boston Phoenix* and *New York Newsday*. I wrangled some assignments from the *New York Times*. I wrote the first, and it was published. I wrote the second. The editor would go through everything I did, word by word, changing most of them as we went. Every time, my piece would be gutted. For a writer, this was the best place you could ever be. I was among people whose words changed the world. But it was too much. I couldn't do it. I didn't belong there. I never would. I folded; I didn't finish the remaining pieces. The deadline came and went. After a while, the editor stopped asking for the stories. I never quite finished feeling ashamed at the failure.

I did layout at magazines. I took reservations at a jazz club. I cleaned apartments. I wasted a decade.

The world didn't end, but depression had eaten away my twenties. Just before I was thirty, I fell into a job at Martha Stewart Living Omnimedia, as a staff writer. I took writing seriously, and I took this job seriously; I'd lost a lot of time to the black dogs in my head and I wanted to grow up and function well, like others did, and I wanted to live well.

While I was at Martha I first heard about the Culinary Institute and began to really understand the concept of cooking school. Most of the kitchen staff there, and a significant number of the people writing about food, had gotten a culinary education. I shared an office with another writer, Laura Wallis, who would become a close friend, and we began spending some time looking at the websites of cooking schools—the CIA, various schools in and around Manhattan—just idly daydreaming. *If we ever get rich,* we said, *we'll go to cooking school.*

I was not Martha Stewart material. People liked me, editors liked me, but I wasn't one of them. Everyone was promoted ahead. I survived three rounds of layoffs. I still never moved. I was writing all over the company: the website, the merchandise catalog, the magazines, the newspaper column. I never moved. After a couple of years, I gave up. I didn't quit, I just stopped caring. I came to work in T-shirts and work boots. I never shaved. I lasted for a long while more. Finally, I was laid off when I refused to add a full-time job's worth of computer coding to my writing assignments.

The first time I saw my girlfriend, Nelly was giving a reading at a bookstore in Brooklyn. I thought she was the most beautiful woman I'd ever seen in person; she is petite—just five feet—with a great smile and, I had to admit, a beautiful figure. I was knocked out by what she read. I bought her story collection, *See Through,* and read it twice. I eventually gave her some of my writing and we became really close friends. She was an avid cook, too, and had been a professional baker when she lived in San Francisco. She was warm and gracious and I found her sense of very dark humor hilarious. We both knew entire sections of Denis Johnson's *Jesus' Son* by heart, loved a lot of the same movies, and recommended bands to each other. We stayed friends that way for a couple of years. Our friendship went on for a long while until something changed between us, and I wound up seducing her with food.

At one point, I had a sideline freelance job rating restaurants for *New York* magazine's website. I was given a budget of $75, enough to take one other person with me for two, maybe three, entrées and a couple of desserts. There was not usually enough left over for wine.

I had invited Nelly once before to join me on a review; it was a really mediocre restaurant still inexplicably thriving in the Bedford-Stuyvesant neighborhood of Brooklyn. The meal was terrible, but we had a nice time.

Two weeks later, I had another assignment already past deadline. I asked Nelly and she agreed to go. The day before, I decided to lie. I thought my own cooking, instead of someone else's, might impress her. I e-mailed saying that the gig had been canceled. But would she like to come to my place for homemade ravioli? She said she would and that she'd gladly take the role of sous-chef. I never got around to shouting orders or making her scrub pans. Actually, I did most of the work and just plied her with wine. Whether it was the vintage, the pasta, the very rich, pork-laden sauce—I don't know. But we were a couple from then on.

I got a job as an adjunct professor at Pratt Institute in Brooklyn, teaching creative writing and literature, but it didn't pay enough to live on. I was dependent on Nelly, who didn't seem to mind while I was attempting to find my feet. I got another adjunct gig at the now-defunct Interboro Institute in Manhattan, teaching college kids from dire backgrounds the rudiments of composition. Almost every woman in my classes was a mother, or soon to be one, and many of the men had served time. One of my students, busted for crack, asked me if I could get him his homework while he was in Rikers Island. Another teacher told me that in any given class, someone had a gun in his or her backpack. When I'd stand up in the front of the room, lecturing, I could never put that out of my mind. This job didn't pay enough to live on either. Nelly paid a lot of our bills.

"I'm just waiting for you to figure out what you're going to do so we can get on with the rest of our lives together," she said. We had no idea what to do next because I had no plans, no options. Money was getting scarce. It got frustrating for Nelly, and sometimes she'd just say, "My life is on hold."

We threw dinner parties all the time, though, because we liked the company and I liked the cooking, plus it was cheaper than going out. We'd get ten or twelve people in her dining room around the table, eating my food, getting drunk on wine and whiskey. I'd have Bob Dylan or dub reggae on the stereo. I was ambitious in my expectations of how the food would turn out, that it might be so good it could create a memory in someone else's head that was indelible, forging a bond between us. We could, both of us, all of us, return again and again to the moment when we ate this meal together.

With expectations like that, how could I not fail? I made homemade pasta and a sauce made of artichoke hearts to go with it, and the dish was bland and underseasoned and dry—the sort of thing you eat because you have to, just to be polite. It looked impressive, but the talk just fell off the cliff when people began to eat. There were the cursory compliments, and the topic of conversation changed quickly. Dylan sang and the candles flickered and our shadows were large on the wall. I played with the food on my plate and said maybe six words the rest of the night.

Cookbooks, I decided, made false promises. Beyond and behind the vagaries of instructions like "sauté the squid until tender" lay a body of knowledge that made those instructions workable. I could understand it in musical terms: Any guitarist could hit an E-chord, but it took skills to make an E-chord thunder and shimmer like John Lee Hooker. Neil Young could play a single note for a full minute and make it an arresting solo. Its hypnoticism lay in the nuance.

On an afternoon when the snow fell too hard to go out, I rooted around on the Internet until I arrived on a page selling the Culinary Institute of America's textbook, *The Professional Chef*. It was more than twelve hundred pages, and covered—so it promised—every culinary fundamental. I made a resolution. I would order the book. I would study it and cook from it. I would work my way through it as much as was practical. I would acquire the skills, through sheer repetition and perseverance.

Nelly said, "This looks amazing." We were seated together at her dining room table, just the two of us, her arm around my shoulders, poring over the textbook. Here were the instructions for making stock and dozens of different sauces. Here were the methods for making vegetable cuts, for proper sautéing and braising. It looked like the template of a complete education. But . . . most of the recipes ran heavy on the butter, oil, and cream. Most of them involved meat. Nelly's favorite dinners were vegetable-centric, and she informed me she simply couldn't eat this stuff day after day, nor could I afford to cook it day after day. I did what I could. I made stock—chicken and veal. I tried a few of the salads and vinaigrettes; I made a Spanish dish of shrimp and chicken with chocolate, bread crumbs, and Pernod. I was clumsy and I took a long time. The results were trembly, and perhaps not worth the effort.

Nelly had to give up her place, and she moved into my apartment, which was too small for two people. We tripped over each other, and no matter where we were in its three rooms, we were never more than ten feet apart. Our things were piled up from floor to ceiling. We argued often. We broke up twice, but we loved each other and despite the tensions, we'd reunite within a few hours. It turned into a long winter.

Should we marry? Should we look for another apartment? Should Nelly try for a teaching job far away? Should we move upstate? And the biggest question of all now that Nelly was on the cusp of forty, and me not far behind: Should we have a kid? We jostled and stumbled around these questions that we couldn't answer. What could I say? What sort of answer could I give? I was poor, I had nothing dependable with which to fund a future. I cared immeasurably for Nelly; I cared about learning to cook; I cared about my writing; I was beginning to care very much about scotch and bourbon.

I signed up for a couple of cooking classes around the city: a knife skills class at the Institute of Culinary Education and a sauce-making class at the New School. Each one lasted for just a few hours, and both were great. But they didn't even begin to approach being comprehensive. Still, I left the knife class knowing how to hold a knife properly and how to dice an onion, and the sauce class with a basic understanding of how to make a pan sauce.

I went to the Strand, the used and discount bookstore on Broadway, and bought more cookbooks: Thomas Keller's *The French Laundry Cookbook* and *Bouchon*, Marcus Samuelsson's *Aquavit, Larousse Gastronomique, The Union Square Cafe Cookbook*. I studied the recipes, trying to distill things down to their basics and essentials; beneath all the opulence of a French Laundry dish, what was Thomas Keller really doing? Braising? Okay, then what was he telling me about braising? Nelly gave me a present of *The Babbo Cookbook* by Mario Batali. For my parents' sixtieth birthdays, I made the braised short ribs from *Babbo* and they still reminisce about it years later. Anytime I did well at the stove, it stoked the enthusiasm up a few degrees. Anytime I didn't, it felt like a crisis, like the weather of my twenties was coming back.

Through a friend of a friend, I went to a restaurant in the Bushwick neighborhood of Brooklyn and met with the owner, Paris Smeraldo. The restaurant, a bistro-type place that had gotten a nice write-up in the *New York Times*, was called Northeast Kingdom. Paris offered to let me do a *stage*—an unpaid stint working in the kitchen to learn—and I took him up on it. The chef was a twenty-six-year-old from London, Andy Gilbert, blond, reed thin, and well over six feet tall, and on my first day, no one had told him I'd be coming. After an awkward explanation, he led me back to the kitchen, gave me a knife, a cutting board, and an apron, and had me slice mushrooms. Then onions. Then carrots. The menu's big sellers were macaroni and cheese, a Berkshire pork chop with an herbed cream sauce, and chicken pot pies. Most of it was assembled ahead of dinner service and fired on order. "This is rustic food," Andy said. "You don't need to try and be exact—a rough chop is fine." The kitchen was a tiny box and had three worktables, a convection oven, and two convection burners. Felipe, the sous-chef, was the only other employee in there. Several days a week, after I finished work at Interboro, I'd arrive at 2:00 in the afternoon to turn big vegetables into little vegetables for several hours. I'd watch the first hour of dinner service. When things got busy, I was in the way and I'd get sent out. After a week or so, I was making the oven fries, and, on Saturdays, when I'd get there at 10:00, I'd spend my first hour making crepes.

Both Paris and Andy held cooking school in some measure of derision. Whatever you needed to know, they'd say, could be picked up by doing it. But after a point, there wasn't much more for me to be shown, something Andy recognized. "You know," he said to me as I cut up pieces of chicken thigh for the pot pies, "there are a lot of other restaurants out there where you could learn. I mean, there are places out there that have actual gas stoves."

I wanted to stay. I was feeling good about what I was doing—no one was correcting me when I chopped onions, so I must have been doing it right. And I thought that if I could do some of the service cooking, I'd get a few of the basics down: timing, speed, multitasking. I kept pressing Andy to let me man the oven and two burners for dinner and he kept refusing. But then Andy's wife started bugging him about being at the restaurant six days a week, and he asked if I wanted to try cooking brunch. Yes, I told him. Yes, I did.

The following weekend, I was there at 9:00; brunch began at eleven. I made my crepes, got the potatoes in the oven, cooked bacon, had eggs at the ready. I divided quiche into slices, and assembled the sandwiches for croque madames. And at eleven, the orders came in. This wasn't, theoretically, difficult: I was pretty much just popping things into the oven and frying eggs, but there were a lot of different things in the oven to keep track of. At one point, there were about fifteen different orders being heated, with more and more coming in, and I got lost. I couldn't keep track of the tickets that the servers were submitting, so I pulled things out whenever they looked done, set them down for Felipe to plate, and figured the right order would somehow get to the right person. I couldn't figure out how many eggs I was supposed to be frying; I just started cooking them and assumed they'd be used. There were no complaints. I didn't burn anything. Even if I was lost, my instincts seemed to be somewhat correct, and no one had to wait for food.

Andy had come in late that morning to check up on me. At the end of service, he asked me, "What are you doing on weekends from now on? Do you want to be the brunch cook? We'll pay you for it . . ."

But that was the last I heard about it. I kept bringing it up to Andy, but he kept changing the subject—*We're still trying to figure out some scheduling things,* he'd say, or *We're going to be making some changes and we need to see how they'll shake out.* After a while, I let it drop. But one afternoon, I overheard Andy interviewing a friend of Felipe's, asking about his brunch cooking experience. I finished out a couple more shifts and then told Paris it was time I moved on.

During that summer, Nelly and I were on Cape Cod at my cousin's house for a few days, along with my parents, my aunt, a dozen other cousins and their kids, and a handful of old family friends. One of the family friends, Gail, sat next to me in the shade of a pine tree. Little kids were running all over the lawn playing dodgeball, and I half watched them, drinking a beer, while Gail told me that her nephew had just enrolled in the CIA.

"I'm jealous," I said. "You have no idea what I'd do to go to cooking school."

"Your mother tells me that things have been a little rough lately on the job front."

"I've got nothing," I said. "I'm teaching a class at Pratt in September, and I've got these Interboro classes, but you have no idea how little money I'm earning, and how much Nelly is just hating my guts right now."

"Do you want to be a chef? Is that your dream?"

"I don't know if I can picture myself in a restaurant or owning a restaurant or anything like that. I haven't figured out the fine print with this. But I want to learn to cook. I want to cook for a living. I want to learn really badly."

"Then why don't you go to the CIA?" Gail asked. "I'm serious: no equivocating, no excuses. Why don't you go?"

"It's expensive."

"There are worse things than having some debt. Which will you regret more, debt or not going at all?"

"It's two years out of my life. I'm not twenty years old anymore."

"Again, the same question: Which are you going to regret? You should apply. Really."

Later that night, Nelly and I sat together outside and I told her about the conversation.

"Is that something you really—and I mean *really*—want to do?" Nelly asked.

"Yes. I want to go. I think Gail's right."

"How would we do this? Would you live up there? Would *we* live up there? How would you pay for it?"

"I don't know."

Nelly's tone was calm and matter-of-fact. "The thing is, we've been waiting a while for you to figure everything out. And this feels kind of like you're putting the question off for another two years."

"I feel like this *is* the answer to the question. I don't have all the details, but I want to try and do this."

She took my hand and squeezed it. "Well . . . then let's do some investigating and see what the situation looks like."

LATE THAT FALL, AN envelope arrived from the CIA congratulating me on my acceptance. Nelly and her ex-husband used to own a house together, and with the money she'd made from selling it, she wanted to buy a modest place upstate. We'd keep the apartment and she'd pay cash for a place in Saugerties, where she and I had fantasized about living ever since we'd taken a trip there while visiting her parents in nearby Rhinebeck. Bob Dylan and the Band had recorded the Basement Tapes in Saugerties. The area was beautiful—rural and set right up against the edge of the Catskill Mountains. We'd stay with her parents for a little while. The pieces were falling into place—sort of.

"So basically, the responsibility for our bills and living expenses falls on my shoulders? Will I be fully supporting both of us while you're in school?"

"No—"

"Honey, I just need to ask. How are you going to make money? School is full-time; you have to study hard. How can we make this equal?"

Nelly had been working hard on a draft of her novel. She worked hard teaching, spending hour after hour outside class every week reading and critiquing student fiction. How much more of her time would I be asking her to give up?

"I don't know. I will figure something out."

"Right. And what about those other questions—like, do we get married?"

"I don't know. I don't have all the answers."

Another envelope arrived from school, this one from the financial aid office. The page that detailed the award had figures in two columns: one for Term One, another for Term Two. Combining the funds allotted for the two terms—two years—still left me wholly in the red, and for way more than I really felt comfortable taking on in terms of debt. I threw the paper in the wastebasket in the bedroom, and when Nelly walked into the apartment later on, I told her all the debate, all the worrying, the arguing, everything was moot. I couldn't afford to go.

A week or so later, we were sitting in the living room, reading. Nelly had her feet tucked under my legs, and she laid her book down and looked up at me. "Do you still have the financial aid statement from the CIA? Can I see it?"

"I threw it out. But . . ." I got up and moved toward the bedroom. "I haven't emptied the trash in here for a bit. It's still here." I gave it to her and went back to reading.

"How do you know," she asked after studying it, "that this definitely means it's for two years and not two semesters?"

"It's a two-year program; term one, term two. Year one, year two."

"Will you call them tomorrow and ask?"

I called the next day and asked. After getting my information up on her computer, the woman from financial aid said, "Wow! That is a really generous award."

I felt a little puzzled. "But my question is this: Does term one and two mean semester one and two?"

"Two semesters."

"Really?"

"Well, it wouldn't be very generous if it was for two years."

She and I spoke at some length and then she transferred me to the Admissions Office. When I hung up, I was slated to begin the Associate Program in Culinary Arts at the Culinary Institute of America on June 16.

3

ALL THE ENTHUSIASM, ALL the excitement, all the force of the visions in my head—of me, stove-side, actually cooking—slammed straight into a brick wall.

Six weeks of academic classes (Gastronomy, Culinary Math, Food Safety, and Product Knowledge) coupled with the school's one-month annual hiatus for repairs in July meant nine weeks before I'd get near any food.

The day before classes started, we'd been enduring the last of our orientation, with instructions to refrain from harassing each other and lurid tales of the evils of alcohol, not to mention the ins and outs of fire safety. Then came the words we'd been anticipating: "If you will please go to the lobby outside the auditorium, you will receive your tool kits and textbooks."

It was mayhem—a stampede of just barely postpubescent students in a frenzy to get their mitts on their knives. A trio of faculty members standing behind several folding tables piled up with our toys was overrun and swallowed by the throng. I sat down on a bench to wait it out. A guy sat down next to me. I recognized him from orientation. He was laughing at the commotion. Another guy sat down next to him. "Man," the third guy said. "The kids really want those freaking knives."

Some kids had freed their knives from their tool kit, and I saw the glint of light on steel as they flashed the blades around and squealed and grunted with excitement. The second guy said, "It's like they've just discovered fire or something."

"Yeah, but I have to admit," I added, "I kind of want my stuff too."

"Well, yeah," the second one said. "But please—a little dignity." He introduced himself as Adam Walker. The other guy told us his name was Stephen. Adam was from Texas, Stephen from Georgia.

When the crowd had thinned, Adam, Stephen, and I each went to the tables, gave our names, and were handed a tote bag full of books, a knife roll, and a backpack embroidered with the CIA logo. I didn't look inside anything; I wanted to wait. I wanted to see what sort of tools I'd be making a future with, what books would be guiding me through it. I said good-bye to Adam and Stephen and drove back to Rhinebeck. I sat on the floor in the waning evening light and methodically went through everything.

The backpack was stuffed with packages, and inside the packages were things like spatulas, whisks, a wooden spoon, side towels, measuring spoons, a vegetable peeler, a wine bottle opener, and a melon baller.

I opened the knife kit. A paring knife. A slicing knife. A boning knife. A bread knife. A fillet knife. A long, heavy chef's knife. They were made of solid German steel, beautiful and gleaming. I tested the edge of the chef's knife against a piece of paper, and the blade seemed to float right through it without any resistance at all.

Of the textbooks, I already owned *The Professional Chef* and Harold McGee's *On Food and Cooking,* but they suddenly felt new. Before, when I thumbed through the pages, they felt unyielding and mysterious, but they'd be giving up their secrets now. Months off in the distance, I'd be taking the Garde-Manger class—also known as the hors d'oeuvre class, encompassing the making of composed salads, appetizers, amuse-bouches, basic charcuterie, things like that—and I flipped through the class's textbook. How to smoke a duck. Making my own pancetta. Making sushi. A recipe for sausage en brioche. Empanadas. Tenderloin and horseradish on toast points. Shrimp quesadillas.

I immediately thought about the wedding Nelly and I had gone to the summer before. After the ceremony, servers worked the room with plates of appetizers just like the ones in this book's pages. I situated myself near the door to the kitchen and accosted the servers as they came out with their trays. *I'd be making this stuff, and I'd be learning to make it perfectly, and that perfection*—of technique, of conception—*would someday become second nature.* This was the best cooking school in the country. And I'd be a product of it. Someday.

STEPHEN AND I SAT next to each other in the front row of Culinary Math class. Adam sat a few tables behind us. I rolled my pencil back and forth across the surface of my notebook, made random calculations on my calculator just to see the numbers change, and willed myself to try and pay attention.

If a pound of carrots has a yield of 87 percent, how many ounces will that be? And if that pound of carrots is meant to serve seven people, what will their portion sizes be?

Say you wanted to make this recipe for tacos, which serves ten, for thirty-two people—what would the new portion of red onion be? What amount of cilantro? And if that cilantro has a 68 percent yield, how many bunches of it will you now need to buy?

And if this recipe calls for 1 tablespoon of vinegar, and you are doing 6.2 times the recipe, how many milliliters of oil will you need?

It was basic stuff. It took very little to recall the required math from high school. Plus, we were given worksheets with all the equations and conversions we could possibly need to aid in the calculations. When asked to do an equation, it took me just a few seconds; Stephen was even quicker. I hadn't asked him his age, but I guessed he was around twenty-five or twenty-six. He'd been a business major at Georgia Tech and could probably do these numbers reflexively.

Sometimes I'd look around the room, though, and see that some of the kids sat breathing through their mouths and looking blankly at the board.

The instructor, Michael Nothnagel, loved math. He was tall, thin, with thick glasses and nearly black hair. He had almost certainly been called a nerd more than once in his life, and he was instantly likable, bouncing around the room, drunk on numbers, trying to make his enthusiasm infectious. It didn't take. Around noon, when the class ended, the sun came through the windows and fell on the deep green carpeting. The fluorescent lights buzzed. And most of the room's eyes followed the track of the second hand as it spun around and around toward 12:00.

On other days, we attended the Food Safety class. We learned the rudiments of sanitation and proper temperatures—and exactly what happens to you when you get food poisoning or eat contaminated fish. Most reef fish, for example, weighing more than five pounds, are likely to harbor ciguatoxin, which leads to ciguatera. Ciguatera will keep you sick for years. At the onset you will vomit uncontrollably, and your gastrointestinal system will betray you. Your fingers and toes will tingle. Later, and for a long, long time, your nervous system will reverse the sensations of hot and cold.

We also learned at exactly what temperatures and under what conditions bacteria will multiply. We discovered that all sorts of toxins, viruses, and bacteria lurked on or around our food. Listeria can cause miscarriages and death. E. coli can make you dead. If you stuff a turkey at Thanksgiving, and the temperature of the stuffing does not hit 165 degrees, you are creating a place where salmonella can thrive and be fruitful. At the onset of anaphylactic shock, when a person allergic to nuts accidentally eats, say, a filbert, they will experience light-headedness and swelling of the face, hands, and feet. They will begin wheezing, be stricken with cramps. Their throat will close and their blood pressure will drop. They will lose consciousness and then die. We came to understand, in essence, that food can hurt you.

Gastronomy class was polarizing. It was devoted to the theory and aesthetics of dining, and the reading assignments were sometimes dense tracts full of postmodern jargon and references to Foucault and Lacan. We were introduced to some of the great culinarians: Antonin Carême, the father of haute cuisine; the godlike Auguste Escoffier, who codified the essence and details of French fine dining in his book *Le Guide Culinaire*, upon which the entire curriculum of the CIA is based. A lot of the students were bored out of their minds, unable to get their heads around the idea they were required to learn so much that had absolutely no connection to actual, physical cooking. They'd perk up at the mention of someone contemporary—Keller, Grant Achatz, Ferran Adrià—but an invocation of Fernand Point or Paul Bocuse or Joël Robuchon—people I found fascinating, worthy of awe—left eyes glazed over.

One day in Gastronomy, we were called to the front of the room for each of us to pick up a paper plate with a selection of light and dark chocolates. The first and last chocolates were pitch dark, with a dozen chocolates in between, moving in a color continuum from light to increasingly brown. The instructor asked us to eat the first piece and write down our reaction to it. It tasted disgustingly bitter, inedible, and it took some effort to keep from spitting it into my napkin. I reported as much on my comment sheet. The next piece was cheap milk chocolate; it was cloying and I could almost feel my pancreas twitch. The next had a slightly darker hue and contained less sugar. We moved through the plate, each piece progressively less sweet until we came to the final one. It had an alkaline quality to it and felt metallic on my tongue, but it also had a complexity that I hadn't recognized in any of the others. It turned out that the first and last pieces were the same, and it was to demonstrate how the palate could be manipulated. The progressive bitterness primed the tongue as it went, until what was initially terrible revealed its nuances. I thought the experience was kind of profound and dramatic; a bunch of the kids thought it was bullshit. There was, as far they could tell, no practical application for this knowledge. I suspected that this thinking was also the reason why the library was never crowded.

The other academic class was Product Knowledge, taught by a local farmer and former football coach, Darryl Mosher. Mosher was a big, serious man with a tight crew cut who didn't laugh very much. He was a formidable guy and charged with teaching the students how to identify vegetables and to select the best examples of them. I imagined him as the Vince Lombardi of produce. He was a constant presence at the Rhinebeck farmers' market, and I always envisioned him going through his stock, discarding a too-large zucchini or an overripe tomato, saying, "There's no room for second place at this farm stand." This was a class that everyone agreed was essential. It was also a ton of work. We all knew what broccoli was, obviously, but differentiating between a dozen varieties of apples was challenging. It wasn't always easy telling five kinds of cooking greens apart, or keeping track of twelve or thirteen species of mushrooms.

With every piece of produce, Mosher informed us of how to recognize when one was fresh or perfectly ripe. He offered tastings of just about everything we were shown in class, and because it was summer, there was a lot of produce to study. Everything was to be committed to memory. Apples, berries, cherries, and lemons won't ripen off the vine, but melons, pears, avocados, and bananas will. Tomatoes will ripen but not become more flavorful off the vine, so often, Mosher told us, they are picked while green, gassed with ethylene until red, and shipped to the supermarket where they arrive tasting of nothing. If, at the beginning of the course, you had a hard time identifying the herb savory, or telling the difference between oregano and marjoram, Thai and regular basil, or a selection of various mints, you had better get things straight.

You can tell a piece of broccoli is fresh by looking at the cut at the bottom of the stem; if it isn't cracked or doesn't have the slightest brownish tint to it, if it is pale green and moist, it is pretty fresh. The flowers on top—the green stuff—should be tight and vibrant. It should feel heavy in the hand.

A cantaloupe should have a strong cantaloupe smell. It too should feel heavy, and its "belly button" should be smooth, inverted, and round. The webbing should be raised and distinct, dry, with very little green. A honeydew should feel waxy and tacky, with a little give where it was cut. Tomatoes contain three acids: malic, glutamic, and citric. Dark tomatoes are high in acid; yellow or light tomatoes are lower.

Three days a week, for two hours a shot, we were bombarded with fruits and vegetables. We were to test what we learned by making regular trips to the CIA's storage room—a dark, refrigerated area where all the produce was held before being distributed to the kitchen classrooms. Everything was labeled so you could go through and handle, smell, and squeeze a thousand different herbs and vegetables.

We had two classes for a total of four hours every day. The rest of the time I spent in the library, doing homework and studying. But sometimes, I'd get on the computer and look at the course guides, recipes, and syllabi for the classes I'd be taking down the road. In the Skills Development III folder, I found a document called "Methods," which listed the basic techniques to cooking a piece of fish *en papillote* (in parchment paper), making a dozen different sauces, and pureed soups among a score of others. I found recipes for Green Chili Stew and Bori Bori Soup in the Cuisines of the Americas folder, recipes for potato gnocchi with duck ragu and a hundred different tapas dishes in the Cuisines of the Mediterranean.

I really immersed myself in cookbooks, especially after I'd spend some time rooting around in the folders of upcoming classes. I'd pull a few of my favorites down from the shelves—*Bouchon, Babbo,* Michel Richard's *Happy in the Kitchen, Le Guide Culinaire, The Zuni Cafe Cookbook*—and look at the more elaborate recipes that I once thought I'd fuck up irreparably if I ever tried them. I'd feel bright and optimistic, like the future had open arms, that all these methods and techniques would be within my range, that this was where a demarcation got drawn, one between the legion of home cooks and the professionally trained.

I was outside one afternoon, two weeks after school started, reading Escoffier on a bench. A young, uniformed woman walked straight toward me, holding a Styrofoam container in her hand.

"You've got to try this," she said. She reached out and crammed something into my mouth. I could feel her fingers on my teeth. I ate it, and it was delicious. After I swallowed, I asked: "What was it?"

"Rabbit crepe," she said, wiped her hands on her pants, and walked away.

IT'S A NICE PIECE of synchronicity that farther down the river there's another citadel on a hill: West Point, the United States Military Academy. I came to believe that the CIA had swiped some of the Academy's ethos.

All around the school, I saw signs and bulletins glowering down from spaces in the kitchens, hallways, and administration offices, almost all of them beginning with phrases like "You must" or "You are required to" or "It is prohibited for students to" or "You may not" or "Students cannot."

The CIA dress code informed us that students in kitchen classes must wear "Institute-issued cleaned and pressed chef's checkered pants of proper fit, neither pegged nor cuffed. Pants must be hemmed above the natural heel and below the ankle." It went on: "White undergarments are required for both men and women" and "one plain ring and one watch are the only pieces of jewelry permitted."

Furthermore, men must be "clean-shaven, with sideburns not exceeding the middle of the ear. Beards are not permitted" and "mustaches must be neatly trimmed and may not extend below the corner of the mouth." Failure to adhere to these codes could result in demerits, which dogged your CIA permanent record until death. This sort of stuff extended into the kitchen operations too. I saw a list of regulations for one of the Skills classes, the bedrock basic foundation courses that signaled the real beginnings of everyone's cooking education. It read:

- Plates presented not hot enough or too hot will reflect 1 point deduction from your professionalism grade.
- Each food items [sic] presented _not hot enough_ will be subject to a deduction of 1 point.
- Plates presented with _smudges_ will reflect 1 point deduction from your professionalism grade.

- Plates presented _dirty_ will reflect 2 points deduction from your professionalism grade.
- Plates presented with _poor presentation_ or _not reflecting chef's demo plate_ will reflect 1 point deduction from your professionalism grade.
- Not having a pencil #2 for the scheduled quizzes and tests and/ or a calculator for the costing exam will reflect 2 points deduction from the quiz/test/costing grade.

One day, I watched, horrified, as a student had his sideburns measured with a ruler in the hallway by one of the chefs. He was told to leave the building immediately and not to return until he had shortened them.

"I understand that when you're dealing with a bunch of kids who still have wet dreams, you need to be a hard-ass," I said to Nelly, who was in disbelief after reading all that. "But I'm almost thirty-eight. I'm not here to fuck around. I'm not here to waste time. Enough with the rules and regulations—I'm here of my own volition, I'm not being supported by Mom and Dad, I'm taking it seriously. Just teach me something and I will learn it. I don't need to be threatened."

I'd been eating most of my meals by myself and was doing so for another lunch when Adam Walker materialized at the table and sat down, accompanied by two more students I recognized from one class or another—Culinary Math, I think—and they sat too. One's name was Mike Brookshire, and the other was an utterly silent guy by the name of Gio. It took a minute, but I recognized him: He had been at a table in the B&C dining room one evening. Gio had not spoken a single word. There had been only one other person at the table, some diminutive idiot from Long Island who was running through his tough guy act, telling us, "I'll tell a chef straight to his face, you respect me, I'll respect you. But don't you fucking disrespect me—I'll cut you. Just don't do it. I won't put up with that shit."

During the guy's long rap, Gio had stared at his plate with a weird quarter smile twisting his lips. After the guy finally left, Gio left too. He nodded once by way of good-bye.

Adam remembered my name and introduced us all.

"What's your story?" Brookshire asked.

"I'm from Brooklyn."

"That's it?"

"No. I used to work at Martha Stewart before I came here." I deliberately left the teaching part out—it seemed like it was going to put more distance between me and everyone else; for me, my age was always a shadow, and I didn't want to darken it any further. Plus, whenever I dropped the Martha Stewart thing, it was always a conversation piece. No exception this time: "Holy shit? Are you serious?" Adam said.

"Yeah, I'm serious. It was one of the most miserable stretches of my life. Every day, I prayed for the sweet and final deliverance of death, but it didn't come. Eventually, I just got canned."

"I've got to say," Brookshire said, "you do not look like a Martha Stewart kind of person."

"I was not a Martha Stewart person. Hence the getting canned."

"What did you do there?"

"I was a writer." I had to make the admission, even though I preferred not to. It caused exactly the reaction I hoped to avoid.

"So you're one of the food writer types? Like you're gonna go work for *Gourmet* or something?"

I'd felt invisible a lot of the time, but I still paid attention. I listened to a lot of conversations. My restaurant experience was a lot more limited than almost everyone else's. A lot of these people had been line cooks during high school. I hadn't. And this was a sort of dividing line. Other students took you more seriously if you'd had that experience; it meant you were authentic, the real thing. They seemed to think that it signified a good bedrock for everything we were about to learn. I can't say I totally disagreed.

"I'm sure I'll always write, but—hey, just like you—I'm here to learn to cook."

"The industry needs writers, too." Adam said. "You guys are a necessity when it comes time to write the cookbooks."

"Man, give me a fucking break," I said. "I'm here to cook. I'm not here as a journalist."

"Okay, hey, whoa, easy does it there," Brookshire said. "No need to get prickly."

Adam, Mike, Gio, and I started eating our meals together after that. I found out more about them. Brookshire had moved to New York from California. He'd married pretty young—at twenty-three—and his wife accompanied him to Poughkeepsie, a few minutes off campus. She hated it here and, according to Mike, they did nothing but fight. Whatever rancor stormed inside their home, he brought it to class.

Adam was, thus far, the most ambitious person I'd come across. He knew exactly what he wanted and had plotted out each step to get there. Attending the CIA was something, he said, that he knew he'd do from the time he was eleven. After graduation, he wanted to immerse himself in Asian cuisine, become executive chef at a few restaurants, pass the Certified Master Chef test before he was forty, and then come back to the CIA to teach.

I found out Gio was from Rochester.

These guys were the older students in my classes, and by older I mean they were all twenty-three or twenty-four. None of them had ever done a research paper without using the Internet. I kept skirting the issue of my exact age, but every once in a while, something would slip.

We were talking about music and bands we'd seen. I told them that Jane's Addiction was one of the best live bands I'd ever witnessed. Someone mentioned that he'd wanted to see them on their reunion tour in 2001, but he was too young and his parents wouldn't let him go.

"I saw them on that tour too," I said. "They sucked, so you didn't miss anything. I'm talking about how good they were with their original lineup." I realized at that second that I had started seeing the band's original lineup in 1988, at which point these guys would have been four or five. There was a silence.

"How fucking old are you?" Brookshire asked.

"Pretty old," I answered. Then I changed the subject.

A few others would join us from time to time. Michael Lombardi was usually at the table, an intense guy from Connecticut who never really said what it was he wanted to do, but talked a lot about self-improvement. He seemed to be obsessed with rules. Before a class would officially start, when we were all seated in the classroom, and the second the instructor walked in, Lombardi would begin quieting us down. His clothes were immaculate. His pencils were always sharp.

Carlos sat at our table a lot. He was seventeen, had been taken under Lombardi's wing, and was spastic and kind of obnoxious.

Carlos and I had been seated together at a B&C table for dinner one night. He was complaining about how much drinking and drug use went on in the dorms. He said, "I fucking hate it—all they do is drink. I just don't get it. Drinking is for idiots."

"Hey man, I drink any practical chance I get," I said. "In fact, as soon as I get home, I'm having a really big scotch."

"And I totally respect that," he said without missing a beat. "Look, don't get me wrong—I like to have a good time. But I do it clean."

It was at lunch that I also met Don and Trevor. Don was nineteen, a red-haired kid from Florida, stunningly cocky, with the worst table manners I'd ever seen. When he'd sit with us, I couldn't look at him; he'd eat with his mouth open so wide you could chart the progress of his food with each chew. He'd fallen in with Trevor, eighteen, barely out of high school, head shaved to the scalp and skin smoldering with pimples.

The first day I met Don, he was seated at a table with the others, leaning back in his chair, legs spread wide, gnawing a toothpick. The topic was *Iron Chef America,* a favorite television show of almost everyone you talked to on campus. Don was of a different mind, however. He said to us, "I can't watch *Iron Chef.* Bobby Flay just makes me laugh. If I'm a better chef than you, then I'm not going to waste my time watching you on TV."

None of us knew what to say.

Trevor, at another lunch, told us in passing, and without flinching, that back home in Iowa, he'd been an executive chef. An executive chef is in charge of every aspect of a kitchen. He or she oversees every aspect of a restaurant, approving vendors, paying the bills, maintaining quality control over the food made in the kitchen. He or she outranks everyone. It's typically his or her vision that fuels the menu. An executive chef is a restaurant's driving force.

We listened to him. After he left, we had a single question.

"Executive chef? Did he really just tell us that?" Adam said.

"He must have run that lemonade stand with a really tight grip, for those few hours between history class and curfew," I conjectured.

"What sort of restaurant would he have been at?"

"I don't know," I said. "But I'm just imagining the phone calls: 'Mom? Could you please pick me up? The sous-chefs hid my car keys again.'"

At another lunch, Don told us about the plan he and Trevor were hard at work realizing.

"What we're going to do is, we're in class Monday through Friday, but we're free Friday, Saturday, and Sunday nights. We're looking around to try and find a restaurant space, and we're going to set it up and open just on the weekends. We're going to see if we can do our externship there. Trevor's going be executive chef because he's already done that. He's an awesome line cook. I'm not that good a line cook, but I'm the *bomb* prep cook."

"I can't see you having any trouble at all getting investors for a plan like that," I said.

"Oh, yeah—that's no problem," Don informed me. "Trevor's dad might throw some money in, and I think my grandmother might want to invest."

Our last class before the summer break was on July 2. When we returned at the end of the month, we'd have three more weeks of academics and then begin the meat and fish butchering classes.

Nelly and I spent just a few more days in Rhinebeck. We were set to move into the house she'd bought in a tiny hamlet in Saugerties on the fifth. There wasn't much for us to do until then, as the two stoned, aging hippie restorers worked their way very, very slowly across the hardwood floors. We decided to make dinner for her parents one night, and we went to a Stop & Shop right up the road for ingredients. The produce section spread itself out right inside the door—a few dozen square yards of fruits and vegetables. None of the signs or labels indicated that these came from anywhere nearby.

Not very long ago, I'd still seen the supermarket's stock as almost tyrannical—*This is what we have, tough luck, you'll have to make do. Not up to par? Too fucking bad and, since this is the same stuff that we have shipped in from all the same places, all year-round, how would you even know the difference?* But I had new eyes now. I picked up a cantaloupe and it smelled of nothing; there were light swaths of green all over it. The peppers showed some almost imperceptible wrinkling at the top, near the stems, something I wouldn't have looked for or noticed just a few weeks prior. The cut stems of the broccoli looked okay, but the flowers on the crown were loose and dry. The fennel's fronds were limp and sagging. There wasn't much here that seemed to have ever had a relationship with soil. It was all like a harvested equivalent to a jar of Prego. We left with some herbs and some lettuce, and a compact watermelon that looked nice.

The new house was just a stone's throw from the Hudson. There were train tracks running a small distance away and we loved the sound of the freights rolling by. From the porch, we could see the crests of some of the Catskill Mountains. I found myself not missing Brooklyn.

I spent my mornings painting the walls, moving room to room and listening to Black Flag's discography from start to finish, over and over, singing along, painting at a quicker and quicker pace. In the afternoons, I'd read some of the books I'd borrowed from the library just before school ended: M.F.K. Fisher; a biography of Carême; an account of the case of Bernard Loiseau, who caved to the pressure of maintaining his Michelin stars and killed himself; a history of Chez Panisse in Berkeley.

I always had a strong interest in sources and genealogies. Transfixed by the Rolling Stones as a kid, I discovered Muddy Waters, and after him, I found Robert Johnson and from him worked back to Son House, and then to Charley Patton. From Dylan to Johnny Cash, from Cash to Hank Williams, from Hank Williams to Jimmy Rodgers and Roy Acuff.

When I'd study contemporary cookbooks—*Zuni Cafe, The Elements of Taste, The French Laundry, The Art of Simple Food*—the affect of old-style French cooking was obvious. And on one hand, these were the echoes of the dishes people like Anne Willen wrote about in *Regional French Cooking* or *French Country Cooking*. On the other, some of these recipes stretched back to Bocuse and the Troisgros Brothers, and back through Fernand Point, and to Escoffier before him. I grew fascinated with the breadth of the lineage. Keith Richards plays like he does because he was dyed in the antique blues. To cook well, one should walk the same sort of reverse path. I began religiously poring through classic French cookbooks.

I went out shopping one day at local farm stands and a butcher store up the road. When I got back, I made bacon and eggs with fried tomatoes for lunch. As I ate, I realized everything on my plate had been grown within four miles of our house, and much of it had been gathered that morning. And it tasted that way. I was knocked out by the realization. I was blown away by the food itself. Each bite of the eggs, the tomatoes—these perfect foods—this was the cornerstone of everything I was doing. Each technique we'd learn going forward, each piece of information, was to be put to use in keeping intact the integrity of food just like this.

I had spent a lot of leisure time paging through those high-end cookbooks, often in amazement, sometimes incredulous over how fussy and particular the methodology was. But I understood right then why, when you had ingredients like this—a tomato that wasn't going to get any more perfect—a person would be so ridiculously painstaking. You do not want to dilute perfection. It would be a betrayal.

It was like taking acid; my perceptions widened. On my thirty-eighth birthday, Nelly invited some people we knew in the area and

some friends from the city over. I grilled chicken with a cherry barbecue sauce I'd made. I found my focus turned entirely on the food,
aware of what the chicken was doing at each moment on the grill, the
progress of the color of the skin while it cooked, the feel of the chicken
as it got more and more done. The chicken was free range and local;
I'd brined it for an hour or so before drying it off and putting it over
the heat. I waited a long time before applying the sauce, knowing it
would burn easily otherwise. I began understanding that cooking was
an assemblage of small steps. It was obvious, I guess, but mind-altering
all the same.

Ten days after my birthday, school started up again.

When the kitchens opened for lunch, it was usually futile to try and
get anything from the Asia kitchen. The line was invariably down the
hall, whether it was for the Vietnamese street food on a couple days,
the curry sampler on others, or sushi on different ones. The Mediterranean kitchen was still crowded, but a safer bet. I'd had some really
good gnocchi with duck ragu there, and some surprisingly great thin-
crust pizza, as well as nicely executed suckling pig. The Americas
kitchen was the fallback. It was reliable, frequently pretty damn fine,
and often the least crowded, except on fried chicken day. A few days
after being back, a bunch of us had hit the Americas kitchen and were
taking our plates back to the dining room. There were eight of us at a
table, and most had ordered the duck with raspberry sauce and scalloped potatoes. We began eating. It was dreadful. The duck had been
destroyed with heat, and then destroyed some more. It was desiccated
and leathery, flavorless and tough. I watched as the others ate and
screwed up their faces into expressions of complete distaste.

I took another bite, then sawed at the duck, and started getting
pissed off.

"Whoever did this," I said, "is a jackass."

"Yeah," Adam said. "This is pretty shameful. I can't eat this." He
pushed it away.

"I agree," Lombardi said. "What would happen if you took it back
to the kitchen and told them it sucked? Would they give you another

entrée or something? Isn't that actually the responsible thing to do in this case? Shouldn't they know how bad it is?"

I took one more bite. I started gathering steam. "Fuck that. How could they not know? But seriously—what were they thinking? What were they doing?"

"Fucking it up, obviously," Brookshire said.

"Okay, listen—" I started. I heard Brookshire mutter, *All right, here we go . . .*

"No—listen. Consider a duck—"

Someone said, "Consider that you'll be screwing up the duck in a few weeks, so don't throw stones too hard."

"Bullshit," I said. "Who doesn't love a duck?" People at the table next to us turned to look. "They're cute, they're cool to watch. They're tasty. And—damn—this duck once walked around. It was happy. It enjoyed itself. And look at it now. This creature truly died in vain. A pointless, useless death."

4

THE ACADEMICS WERE DONE. I'd gotten an A– in Gastronomy, an A in Culinary Math, an A in Food Safety, and a B+ in Product Knowledge.

I stood in the hallway outside the dining room, talking to Adam. He had been appointed—no one was quite sure how—interim group leader. This meant he was the liaison between the instructors and the rest of us—about fourteen or fifteen—who'd be in the morning meat class—the first class where we'd get our hands dirty, the first in which we had to be in uniform. Depending on the group and the disposition of the leader, the job could also mean that Adam functioned as a motivator, a counselor, a giver of instructions. This is what Adam wanted. His appointment as group leader was, however, only temporary; there'd be an actual election when the basic skills classes started. Adam was breaking this down for me when he stopped in midsentence and gestured with his chin toward a man in the school's instructor's uniform coming toward us. The man stood over six feet, capped with a head of white hair. His hands, you noticed immediately, were massive. His face was weathered and kind. There was something weary, or sad, at play around his eyes. He looked like a fairy-tale grandfather. As he passed, he nodded and smiled at Adam.

"That's Sebald," Adam said.

Hans Sebald would be teaching our Meat Identification and Fabrication class, a seven-day crash course on the fundamentals of beef, pork, lamb, and chicken. I knew from his school bio that he had been a butcher his entire life and was considered a master.

"What's the story?" I asked. We all asked a lot of questions about the instructors. We wanted some hope, I think, that he or she wouldn't be monstrous.

"Supposed to be a nice guy, but you don't want to cross him. He'll eat you alive if you fuck up."

"Is there a single chef here who doesn't get described in exactly the same way?"

Adam shrugged. "I'm going to send out an e-mail, but be prepared. Watch the required-viewing video online this weekend. Bring your chef's knife, boning knife, and a steel to class on Tuesday. Full uniform." He brightened. "We're going to be deboning a hind shank and tying a roast beef."

I saw the list of others in the group when Adam sent his e-mail. I had hoped that everyone I ate lunch with would be in the class, but that didn't happen. No Brookshire. No Carlos. But Lombardi would be there.

Nelly was out running errands that Sunday when I decided to watch *The Calf Slaughter*. I logged onto the CIA website and went to the online video library. I cued it up, sat back on the sofa with my laptop, and hit Play.

There was Sebald, twenty years younger, brown haired, face unlined. He was wearing a T-shirt, jeans, and green rubber boots, and stroking the head of a calf. It's important, he was saying in a thick accent, that when an animal is slaughtered, it feels no stress, no fear. It degrades the quality of the meat. And, more, the very fact of the animal's existence means that if it dies, it needs to die humanely.

His hands kept playing over and around the calf's ears and neck. The animal's eyes were both plaintive and stupid. Before the slaughter, he went on, the animal had to be somehow "stunned."

"I will now stun the calf," Sebald said. He took a step back, pulled out a Luger, aimed, and put a bullet through the calf's head. The video was in real time, and twenty-five minutes later, he had the calf skinned, gutted, and ready to be butchered.

For the rest of the day, my mind kept returning to the opening of the video, with the calf and then the gun, and Sebald petting the animal. With a lifetime of butchering behind him, when those hands—with so much dying accumulated in his fingers—touched some part of an animal, it must feel a shiver run over its flesh.

I LEFT HOME THE first morning, like I would for the next seven days, at 4:45, and arrived around 5:30. I got breakfast with Adam and another classmate, a kid named Josh, a seventeen-year-old straight out of high school, who had way too much enthusiasm. After we ate, we went up to the fourth floor, found the classroom, and waited for Sebald. It was the end of August. The sun was climbing over the peaks of the Catskills, and I got lost watching its progress.

Sebald walked into class. He seemed even taller than he had in the hallway. His white instructor's jacket looked like a sail. I couldn't get over the size of his hands. He greeted us all and gently explained the rules: no tardiness, no deviation from the uniform; come equipped every day with typed answers to study questions, a calculator, a notebook, and your knives. Failure to do any of these things would result in loss of points. Excessive point loss meant failure for that day. More than two failures meant you failed the class.

He seemed relieved when he was done with this part. Then the class really began. "Unfortunately, for us to eat," he said, "something—something—has to die. And that animal—or plant—deserves our respect. It demands our respect. It demands our attention. Our commitment to not waste it. If nothing else, this is what I want you to learn here."

I was remembering the duck. I was right there with him.

"I have respect for people who choose to be vegetarians, for people who make ethical choices and stand by them. But I also know that death is part of life. And I believe that when an animal's life is taken, it carries a big responsibility on our part to make sure that nothing about that death is a waste, that that death is treated ethically and responsibly.

I'm sure you've all heard how the Native Americans would apologize to the animals they hunted. You should keep that lesson in mind.

"It's also our responsibility to make sure that death comes humanely. I have worked my entire career to make sure that when I participate in the slaughter of an animal, that it feels no fear, and feels no pain."

His brow furrowed. "I know that kosher and halal butchers claim that their methods are the most humane, the most painless. But I've watched it being done. I don't want to get started on that."

There was a very long pause as Sebald stared down at his podium. Then he arranged his papers, took out a roll call book, and said, "Adam, you are the group leader, so you can have the first question: Define the term 'meat.'"

Adam answered correctly, straight out of the *On Food and Cooking* sections we were supposed to read: "The body tissues of animals eaten as food. According to McGee."

When he credited Harold McGee I saw a shimmer of panic run over a few of the others in class. It isn't easy reading, and when I was going through it, I'd predicted that more than a few would bail out after a paragraph or two.

After Adam, he went alphabetically. Stephen got his question right; Dylan did not. Stephen got several points' credit for the correct answer; Dylan was docked several points for his inability to answer.

I was asked: "List the species names of meats used in food service." I got my points for "Bovine, ovine, swine, poultry, and game." The questions went on.

During the lecture we learned basic things—tender meats should be dry cooked, tougher meat from the motion muscles asks for slow, moist heat cooking—and more complex things, like the precise physical makeup of lean muscle tissue (72% water, 20% protein, 7% fat, 1% minerals including iron, calcium, and selenium).

Sebald's German accent—with the same lilts and cadences as Werner Herzog's—was sometimes difficult to understand. The mind tends to turn unfamiliar sounds into sounds you recognize. I'd be taking notes, hearing a normal set of sentences: "The chuck is one of the primal cuts of a side of beef. The round is another primal cut, and its subprimals are the knuckle, eye, top round . . ." etc. And then I could swear he had just said something like: "Night tracking turns nighttime to birds." As classes went on, we'd often look at one another in bewilderment. Naturally, all of us loved the guy.

When several hours had passed that first day, after we had learned the anatomy of a steer carcass, about USDA grading systems and inspection methods, about fat-to-lean ratios, we went to the meat room in the basement to get our hands dirty.

Have you ever smelled a piece of aged beef? That funky, almost rotten-dairy scent that clings to the meat when it's been hung in the cold air to dry? We could smell an intensified version of that the farther down the stairs we went and the nearer the room we got. Even once we'd been inside the room for a while, we'd still notice the scent.

This was a busy area. Meat-free dishes did not hold a place of prevalence on CIA menus, and all the meat used in all the kitchens came out of this room. A lot of it would be processed by students like us, but a lot of it came in from the vendors and was broken down by the teaching assistants, the instructors, or one of the full-time guys hired to keep track of incoming and outgoing material. The really well-cut stuff went to the restaurants the school operated on the campus.

Three large supports were spaced in the center of the room, with a worktable on each side of each support. There was another row of tables along one wall. An instructor's table was placed up front, with a huge meat grinder behind it, and on the far right side of the room was a band saw, Cryovac machines, and a hand-washing sink. A small antechamber beyond that contained an immense walk-in refrigerator and a stunningly cold freezer. Fluorescent bulbs burned an incandescent white overhead.

We chose a workspace upon entering, got ourselves cutting boards, and put on one of the heavy-duty aprons hanging on hooks by the instructor's table. These things weighed about ten pounds and felt bulletproof. Sebald explained why they were a necessity; if your knife slipped while butchering a piece of meat, you did not want to run the risk of stabbing yourself in the stomach, or your groin. "I've seen some pretty nasty accidents . . ." Sebald said.

He pulled out a sharpening stone and showed us how to use it. He showed us when and how to use a boning knife, when to use the standard chef's knife, when to resort to our paring knives. There was a huge bin of beef beside him and when he was done with the demo, we pulled a piece out and took it back to our station. We were to remove the bone.

We wanted long, even cuts—as few as possible—using the tip of the knife. If our cuts were efficient, the membrane holding the meat to the bone could be easily scraped away. Adam, who as group leader was stationed up at the instructor's table, got the bone out pretty quickly. Others did not. Josh was stationed to my left and I watched him for a few moments as he hacked and stabbed at the shank. A young woman named Alyssa who stood off to my right had even less finesse. I'd like to say I was right on with my own cutting, but I wasn't. In my fantasy, the bone popped out with a single stroke of the knife. I clung to this for a few seconds until I had to physically start cutting. I found the shallowest spot on the meat, where the bone was nearest to the surface, went in with my boning knife, and cut in a sharp curve—not even close to straight—without meaning to. I tried again and then again, but the blade went where it wanted. I put the knife down and looked at Adam. He glanced up at me and I shrugged. He came over.

"Oh, dude—" He ran his finger down the cut. "So you got your revenge on this thing, huh? It must have done something pretty awful to deserve this. Here . . ." He took my knife and started a cut. "Like this . . . now, you go ahead."

I picked the knife up and was about to continue. Sebald was suddenly at my elbow. "You're doing this wrong. That's not how I showed you to hold a knife. Where did I say to put your fingers? Yes, there, that's right. Now, long and even, long and even. Go ahead. No, no— that's not right. No, stop, stop. Now we can't serve this meat. If you were the owner of a restaurant, would you serve this? No, you wouldn't. We're wasting money. Again. Try again. Okay, no. Here, give me your knife. I don't want the blade, I want the handle. *Danke.* Like this—" Two or three strokes and the bone sat beside the meat, almost entirely clean. I looked back up front and the bin was empty.

"Is there another one I can do?"

Sebald shook his head. "One per student. On another day, perhaps, you can try again. Clean up here, and I'll be demoing how to tie a roast in a few minutes."

I began to suspect that I was encountering the first of the CIA's educational flaws. I remembered this much from playing guitar as a kid and from taking martial arts lessons over the years: anything you do with your hands needs to be done over and over and over before you can get it into your DNA. One attempt at deboning a piece of beef was just not sufficient. I did a quick cleanup and started following Sebald and Adam around, just so I could see what others were doing, what they did right, and how Sebald was correcting them.

I was quiet for the rest of class and for lunch. I was pissed at my hands for not doing what I had told them to do. The beef I'd cut was destined for use in the student kitchens; later on, we'd see the mistakes and gaffes of meat students when their handiwork came to our classes. Some people would get contemptuous over their work, but I never would. I understood.

Sometimes I drove the scenic route home, which took me past a pair of farms. There were some beautiful steer and sheep with dazzling white coats. I connected the animals grazing on the green slopes along the road home and what I tried to make yield to my knife in class. They deserved better. After I'd see the animals, the drives took on a melancholy tone. At first I thought it was because I was sorry that the animals had died. But then I realized I was sorry because everything had to.

ONE DAY, I DEBONED a leg of lamb, successfully, and was trussing it with butcher's twine. I'd put my knife down on my cutting board with the blade facing me. At one point, I felt a sting in my fingers and realized I'd pulled them along the knife's edge. Blood was seeping down, over my knuckles and dripping on the table.

"Ohhhh, the lamb fights back," Adam said as I went to the hand sink to deal with the wound.

"Nice work . . . if it had to be someone, it might as well be you . . . tell me you didn't bleed onto the meat." Everyone made a comment as I passed.

I washed, got Band-Aids, and patched up my fingers as best I could. They were bleeding a lot, but the wounds were pretty shallow. I put a plastic glove on and went back to finish the lamb. Sebald called to me, though. "Hey, Jonathan—please come back and clean your blood off the wall, *ja*? Thank you."

EVERY DAY, I CAME prepared for the lecture part of class, because we would be asked questions. Even if you knew the answers, inside and out, to every question but one, if you got asked that one question and you flubbed it, you lost your daily class points.

A lot of us—most of us—were benefiting from financial aid, and those points became money. Every deducted point lowered your grade; every lowered grade affected your GPA, and every bit of that effect could see a return when the aid was awarded again the following semester.

Written homework was assigned every day, but it wasn't always collected. If the question part of the class was going badly, if no one seemed to know the answers, Sebald would ask us to turn the homework in. If you didn't have it, you lost serious points.

Both during the academic period and during the onset of the meat class, I spent a lot of time at school and at home, prepping. There wasn't a lot of free time available.

Nelly had taken over completely the running of the house. She paid the bills. Sometimes she'd ask me to contribute, other times she just paid them.

After class, I'd go to the library and use the reference materials to answer the homework questions in exquisite detail—way more than I needed. When I got home, Nelly would often greet me at the door in one of her insane writing outfits—severely faded red yoga pants, clogs, a pink tank top she'd had since she was twelve, hair up high in a disheveled bun—and we'd catch up on the day. Sometimes she'd read to me from her novel—"Is it violent enough?" she'd ask—or describe dogs she encountered on one of her daily walks. We'd eat dinner, I'd study and then retire to the porch to sip scotch and watch the moon rise. Almost everything out of my mouth had to do with school or food. Nelly loved hearing the stories about Sebald and the other students, and we'd pore over cookbooks together planning future dinners, but sometimes she'd have to stop, lean in, put her hands on my knees and, enunciating every syllable, tell me, "We. Really. Really. Really. Have. To. Talk. About. Bills." I was doing the occasional freelance article and bleeding the tiny amount of savings I had, doing my best to extend it. I'd usually deflect any household discussion, begin studying, and then make the first pour. I realized that the two of us only got to interact for about ninety minutes a day.

When the fall semester started and she began commuting down to Sarah Lawrence to teach her writing courses for three days a week, we saw each other even less. As the days passed, the nights got a little chillier.

I ACTUALLY LIKED THE studying, though. In an environment where a person gets to—is encouraged to—fixate entirely on food and its preparation, why would you not want to read and analyze Escoffier's recipes? Or pore over Gray Kunz's *The Elements of Taste*? Or let McGee explain the precise chemistry behind why an onion caramelizes under the influence of slow, steady heat?

At my age the answer is obvious. If I were the age of most of the others, or a different person, it might be a lot more nebulous.

On the way out of meat class one day, I overheard this: "I'm failing everything. I failed Gastronomy. I'm failing meat. I got a D in Product

Knowledge. I need to concentrate on my studies. So as soon as I'm done with this bag, I'm going to quit smoking weed."

And then there was the eighteen-year-old kid who only ate hamburgers. I was sitting with him in the dining hall one day.

"So," I said, "I couldn't help but notice you really like hamburgers."

"Yeah, that's pretty much all I eat."

"Do you want to try some of this?" I pushed a plate at him that had foie gras mousse piped into profiteroles. It had been up for grabs on a buffet table when you walked in the cafeteria door. I was ecstatic when I figured out what it was. I'd eaten as much as I could from the plate. He wrinkled his face.

"No, man. That's cool. I won't like it."

"Really? How often are you gonna get this? Try it." I suddenly felt like my mother.

"No. I just want the burger. I can't wait until they teach us to cook these things."

Sebald taught us to break down chickens. We learned how to get the loin from the ribs of a pig and, further, to separate out the tenderloin. We learned to french a rack of lamb—to trim and expose the bone—so it looked really damned elegant. For some reason, I did well at that. I didn't do as well at other tasks. All along we were to be studying the cuts of meat to be able to identify them on sight. I did find it insane that meat class was held for just seven days; butchering should be a constant for the entire time you were at the school, I thought. How could you possibly get a handle on it in such a short time? I tried to soak up everything that I could.

The ones in class who did the best—like Adam—were those who'd been exposed to this before and were now refining their technique under Sebald's guidance. The rest of us had been tossed into the deep end of the pool, and I was just able to tread water. I might have known the answers to all the questions, but I couldn't perform on demand, at least not the way I wanted. I hoped these were lessons that would be reinforced later.

On the penultimate day of meat class, during lecture and before our trip to the meat room, we were having a ten-minute break. Most of the others ran downstairs to get a cup of coffee from the dining room or smoke a cigarette. Adam, Lombardi, and I were sitting on benches outside of the classroom, killing time.

Sebald came out and sat down on the benches across from us.

"Hey, guys," he said. "I want you to do something. I work with a CSA [community-supported agriculture] farm in New Paltz, and next week, it's time to go to the farm and slaughter the chickens for the members to pick up. I do this several times each year and I always bring a group of students with me. I already have a number of volunteers, but I'd like you to come."

"So we'd be slaughtering chickens?" I asked.

"Ja. There are about one hundred chickens that will be slaughtered. Have you ever done it before?"

"No," said Adam.

"No," said Lombardi.

"Yes," I said. And I told the story.

The night before my twelfth birthday, I overheard snatches of conversation between my mother and father. I heard the words "an hour's drive," "Boston," and "tomorrow night." I puzzled over this for some time until I came to the single, obvious conclusion: Tomorrow night, my father and I would make the trek from our home in New Hampshire to Boston, which was about an hour away. I assumed that we would be seeing the Red Sox at Fenway Park; they were scheduled to play that night and I had been making some noise about wanting to see my first baseball game.

I was on crutches at the time, as a result of a serious sprained ankle. But I was beside myself, a prepubescent package of pure enthusiasm. This would be great.

Of course, it didn't happen. We took a right out of our driveway, which was not the way to go south to Boston. And we kept driving. We drove farther into New Hampshire, for about an hour, to the town of New Boston. We pulled off the town's main road and drove up to a one-story concrete building with a green corrugated-steel roof. A sign in front of the building announced that there was a chicken-slaughtering class being held inside that evening, sponsored by the local 4-H.

Each student in the class was given a chicken and a knife. There were about forty of us, not one over the age of thirteen or fourteen. There were wooden posts running the length of the interior, and each had a Clorox bottle upended and nailed to it. The top and bottom of the bottle had been cut away. We were to put the chickens in and, on command, kill them. We only did one each, but I remember that one being absolutely surreal. I wasn't able to make a causal link between the chicken, my knife, the Clorox bottle, and everything that came afterward.

And that's how I spent my twelfth birthday.

Sebald thought this was hilarious. He laughed really hard. Adam and Lombardi, too. And then Sebald suddenly stopped, stood up, and clapped one of those massive hands on my shoulder. "Perhaps it's time to confront your demons then, *ja?*"

Adam, Lombardi, and I all signed up to go and kill animals the following Friday. Meat class would be over, and we'd be in the thick of fish class—Seafood ID and Fabrication. But this was something necessary. If I really asked myself some tough questions, which I did in the days going forward, I realized that the truism was right: Unless you're a vegan or hard-core vegetarian, if you are going to consume animal flesh, then you should kill an animal. Not just watch the killing and the flow of blood, not be an observer, but touch an animal and end its life.

The next day we took the final. I scored well on the multiple choice and fill in the blanks. I missed a few on the identification test, confusing a quartet of steak cuts that I shouldn't have.

5

A FEW DAYS BEFORE it began, Adam had been apprised of who would be teaching the fish class, and when he told us, the tone of his voice swelled with portent and black clouds.

"We've got Chef Viverito," he said, getting agitated. "The guy doesn't play. He doesn't fuck around. We really, *really* need to be on. We'll be hemorrhaging points."

I felt a wave of tiny, internal palpitations too. I knew about Viverito.

I'd been paying a lot of attention to anecdotes about the chefs. Most of those anecdotes were a bit dull. The stories about the yelling were de rigueur. Everyone yelled. It was simple shock treatment, and you expected a certain level of cruelty. But after analyzing the stories, I began formulating an idea that there were two sorts of screaming, or maybe, more accurately, two different effects the screaming and cruelty could have.

There was the basic motivation and aversion component. You didn't want to be yelled at so you worked hard to avoid it, and when you were yelled at, you wanted it to stop. Elementary cause and effect. These sorts of reprimands rolled right off your back once they were over.

Then there was the sort of yelling and cruelty that made you ashamed, that left you feeling incompetent and gutted. You were being yelled at because you were falling far short of some crucial standard,

not out of laziness per se but because there was—at that moment—
something you lacked. Or maybe even not at that moment, maybe something that was inherently lacking. The yelling, the reprimands, the loud
corrections—it was accusatory, and the deep worry was that you would
not be able to answer the charges, not then and possibly not ever. These
were the sorts of screams that exposed nerves that we spend whole
lifetimes trying to keep under wraps. This yelling was not malicious. It
was mere declaration of fact. But it had the potential to stick with you
for years, or a life. This was the sort of yelling we were all scared of.

I knew about Gerard Viverito, and from everything I'd heard, he
was a commandant of the second camp. Not that he wasn't an expert
in the first camp, though.

Sometimes the two genres overlapped for devastating effect.

There was a story that circulated and had, in fact, been verified.
When he first started teaching at the CIA, Viverito, like every instructor, was assigned Skills I, the most basic of the cooking classes. Every
kitchen has three garbage bins: gray, for trash; yellow, for recyclables;
and blue, for food garbage.

Viverito was a maniac about waste and would not tolerate it. During class, he would periodically inspect the blue bin to make sure nothing was being unnecessarily tossed. One day, he made a discovery:
Someone had jettisoned several fully intact bell peppers and several
whole tomatoes. It's unclear whether he, at this point, called the class
over to watch or simply went ahead with what came next.

While people were concentrating on fabricating their vegetables,
the blue bin got upended in the middle of the kitchen floor. The volume of his voice was reportedly deafening; it was allegedly heard
many, many yards down the hallway. The students were forced to pick
through the detritus and pull out anything that was still usable. Viverito performed an on-the-spot cost analysis and determined that there
was at least $20 worth of perfectly good produce. It was washed off and
put on trays. Everyone had to get on hands and knees and address the
mess on the floor. Then they were given a demo on fabricating peppers
and tomatoes, and a long lesson on how the scraps could be utilized.

This had happened four or five years before I arrived at school, and I had heard the story at least half a dozen times. There were always some variations: people sobbing, the number of curse words screamed at the students, like that.

People were terrified of him. I hadn't even met him, and I was. Once I learned he'd be the fish instructor and I opened my ears to the talk around me, I discovered that no other chef was the subject of as much discussion as Viverito. Other chefs were incredibly popular: Shirley Cheng, the Asia instructor, was elevated to the status of saint; Gerard Coyac was similarly revered, as was another fish instructor, Corky Clark. There were chefs who were despised and derided, talked about in obscene terms. But Viverito was unique.

He inspired strange reactions in students.

At lunch one time after meat class, we were sitting together and another student, much further along in the program, was sitting at the same table, but at a remove. Viverito's name came up and when he heard it, that student looked over at us. "Holy shit!" he said, scrambling out of his chair, putting one foot on the seat and leaning toward us. "That guy is one tough motherfucker, a *tough* motherfucker! That guy is scary. But he is the shit. For real: Viverito is the shit!"

I spoke to a female student who told me this: "One day in class, he was demonstrating how to fillet a halibut and he used my knife. He started cutting, then he stopped and said, 'Whose knife is this?' I told him it was mine and he told me that I had done a great job sharpening it. I felt so good. I was really scared of him. I felt great."

"Do you not get a ton of compliments or something?" I asked.

"You don't understand—that was probably the best day I've had at this school."

Others were of a different bent, but no less passionate on the subject.

"I fucking hate that guy," someone told us at another lunch. "Fucking unbelievable dick. Total asshole."

"How'd you do in his class?" I asked.

"He failed me."

The first fish class was the eighth day, beginning with meat, that I had gotten up not too long after midnight. I'd driven morning after morning from Saugerties with a head full of cement, semidelirious, my heart clutching, and coughing from too much caffeine. I'd drink the coffee outside, on the porch, under a spray of stars, listening to the whistle of the freight trains. I'd move pawns and rooks through the upcoming year, through the program's end point, trying to figure out what I'd do when it was over.

And on this morning, I was laid low with dread.

We were there at 4:30 a.m. to start in on the daily tasks, of which we were provided a list. The fish refrigerator's bins would need to be cleaned each morning and the ice on which the fish rested be changed out. The floors would get messy during this step and need to be squeegeed. There would be orders placed by different kitchens and each requested fish would need to be pulled from the fridge and scaled. Fish that were part of that day's lesson plan would need to be gathered up and placed on trays so that when Viverito arrived, at 6:00, he could get right into pointing out the identifying features of the species and type. Until Viverito showed up, we were to be supervised by Carlos, a short, thick CIA graduate now employed as a teaching assistant.

In the basement of the CIA, the fish kitchen was frigid, the red tile floor was damp, and the room stank of dead seafood.

Carlos spent the next hour barking at us, calling us sloppy and inept, informing us that we would all have points deducted, that our scaling techniques were abysmal, simply abysmal. He was such an asshole that Adam and I exchanged several looks of utter, incredulous disbelief. When someone would ask a question, he was withering with his contempt for our stupidity.

It took about twenty minutes for me to figure out that Carlos was acting. That initial class, I was working the squeegee and I slipped in a puddle. Carlos rocketed over and helped me up and asked if I was okay. He seemed genuinely concerned. Then he went back to being a full-blown prick, making fun of the soaked wet spot running down my calf. When I was mopping up later, he gently told me to stop, explaining that this was the fish room, that the floor was always going to be wet and to take it easy. Then he screamed that I'd put the mop in the wrong place. He kept making marks on his clipboard. Acting or not, a deducted point is a deducted point.

Just wait, Carlos kept saying, until Chef Viverito arrived and saw the mess we were making.

I'd spent the night before and that morning frightened and resigned. I kept watching the clock and the slow crawl of its hands toward six a.m. Viverito was like a Godot that you didn't want to show up. Something disastrous, something that would make you drink, was going to happen.

And then it was 6:00.

Viverito walked in the door looking utterly exhausted and pissed off because of it, but I understood why so many of the female students—and presumably some of the males—had strong reactions. He was a really good-looking guy: dark-haired, young, trim, and walking like the conquering lion of the fish world.

It was the "young" that truly hit me. This guy was not older than I was. I guessed we were the exact same age, or that he might have been a year younger. A sense of dread and a small trickle of shame over my age and my circumstances began to assert themselves.

"My name is Gerard Viverito. We've got a really busy week ahead of us, so I don't want to waste any time. But a couple of things. One, do not—do not—be late to this class. Two, have your homework ready every day. Take notes. For God's sake, take notes. I can't believe how often I'm up here and I look out and I don't see anyone writing anything down. That pisses me off. Three, your knives need to be razor sharp. And when you're carrying a knife through the kitchen, you say 'sharp, behind you' as you go. Even if none of your peers care, I'm going to damn well find out why you didn't let me know."

He went on and explained the grading criteria, the basic day-to-day schedule, a lot of minutiae.

Then he picked up a fish. "Okay. This is an Atlantic cod. It's got three segmented dorsal fins, two segmented anal fins. It's got a chin barb—see, right here—a white lateral line along here, and green leopard spotting along here . . ."

He put the fish back on the tray he'd pulled it from and got another. He went on for about forty-five minutes, explaining the physical characteristics of different fish, and then he showed us how to fillet a whole one. The technique he used was meant for hard-boned fish, like bass, a technique called "the up-and-over," and it was, he said, the hardest technique to learn. Cut from behind the gill plate through the head. Roll the knife, cut back to free the fillet. Slice down the back to the tail. Flex the knife over the spine. Finish by flexing the knife over the ribs. Make sure the fish is "swimming" to the right. Make sure the dorsal fin is toward you. Their eyes stare at you the entire time.

You need to be using your fillet knife and rely on its flexibility and the angle at which you hold it to aid in getting the fillet cleanly from the bones. If you do it wrong, the knife will pop out of the fillet's other side.

All of us found a space around the island of worktables running down the center of the room. It was crowded; we stood shoulder-to-shoulder. We were each given a fish. I got the sea bass. I was close to getting the first fillet off without an issue when I angled the tip of the knife too high. The tip stabbed through the fillet and cut for half an inch downward. Something similar happened with the second fillet. But I pressed the seams of the wounds together and laid the two pieces on top of each other.

Viverito walked by. He had been circling the room, eyes focused on all our hands and cutting boards, like a shark, for the past fifteen minutes. He stopped at my board and looked down. He didn't pick the pieces up to examine them. He just said, "Nice," and walked away, suddenly stopping a few students down to berate them for doing exactly what I had just done. There was a tray on the other side of the room where the fillets were supposed to end up. I took them over immediately, feeling like a cheat and a fraud.

"You know," he announced loudly to the ceiling, "it sounds as if most of you need to take your knives to the stone. How the hell do you expect to cut these things if you couldn't slice a stick of butter with those knives?"

Later: "Anytime any of you want to come in after class and spend a few hours cutting fish, you're more than welcome. And, my God, some of you better take advantage."

After we were done with the up-and-over we moved on to filleting salmon, which required a much more straightforward technique than the up-and-over. You needed to use your fillet knife for the initial cuts, then the solid, inflexible chef's knife to remove the skin.

I started on the salmon and for some reason, started doing the up-and-over. Viverito appeared besides me.

"Oh, hi," he said, with a superlative mockery in his voice. "Just for my own information: Why are you using the up-and-over on this salmon?"

I didn't answer. I actually couldn't think of what to say. After I kept silent for a while longer, he said, "When you remember how to talk and figure the answer out, why don't you let me know. In the meantime, try doing it the way you're supposed to."

After the filleting, we were to remove the skin. When you remove the skin, the knife should be held perfectly flat. Viverito was walking around and then stopped at a vantage point where he could see us all. "Keep your knives flat," he said quietly.

Then, a little louder: "Keep your knives flat."

Another moment passed. He picked up a chef's knife the size of a scimitar raised it up, and started pounding the side of the knife on the steel tabletop. "Keep! Your! Knives! Flat! Keep! Your! Knives! Flat!" he screamed. "Keep! Your! Knives! Flat! Keep! Your! Knives! Flat!"

The sound of steel on steel with that much force is deafening. We were thrown entirely off balance. We stood shocked and staring.

"So please keep those knives flat." He left the room.

WHEN WE WERE DONE fabricating our fish, we cleaned up and moved into an adjacent room for three hours of lectures: further points of identification; the history of cod and the routes of exploration the fish inspired; the pros and cons of farm-raised fish. Each day we'd have a tasting of different varieties of the same species: cod, salmon, clams, and on the last lecture day, we'd taste different caviars.

We all took notes, of course. And I found myself filling page after page after page, in an almost incomprehensible scrawl, trying to keep up with what Viverito was saying. I was in awe; the guy seemed to know everything. He could go off on long, long tangents about the history of fish farming in Hawaii, countless ways of preparing catfish or crab, the disgusting conditions of shrimp beds in Vietnamese rivers.

There was also a daily game of *Jeopardy!* He'd move alphabetically through the roster and we'd pick a question in a given category from the overhead slide projected on the screen behind Viverito's desk. If you got it wrong, he went to the next name. You lost your daily quiz points. There were three slides' worth of this stuff and it could be endless if people kept missing the answers. He'd go on until he proved his point or got bored. He sounded bored pretty frequently. Not with the subject matter. But bored with us as a group and the flubbed answers and the hacked-up fish. His eyes were always red, but if he fixed them on you, you knew you had done something particularly stupid.

The first two days were dense with spoken and silent recriminations. But fragments of the guy's personality began to leak out. One of the class members, Dylan, didn't show up after the first day. Viverito asked where he was.

Alyssa spoke up. "Dylan really wants to be here, but he isn't the most ambitious student. He just . . . he needs to be more motivated."

"So *why* exactly isn't he here?"

Alyssa was a pretty seventeen-year-old, with a soft face. She looked distinctly uncomfortable right now. "It's too early for him. He said he needed to switch into a later class."

His eyes narrowed, and he shook his head side to side almost imperceptibly. He didn't say anything for a minute until he began that day's *Jeopardy!*

Everyone was fucking the answers up—me, Adam, Brookshire, Lombardi, all the kids.

Finally, Viverito just couldn't contain himself. "I have students that are really proud that they've never been into the library. They say it has nothing to do with cooking. My advice to you, and not just to succeed in this class, is this: figure out where that library is. It isn't just the build-ing you went to on your orientation. If one day you think that you haven't really learned anything that day, pick up a cookbook and teach yourself something. Otherwise it's been a waste of twenty-four hours.

"Take a calendar and block off class time. Then block off studying time. Then go to a vineyard and learn how a grape grows, learn how it's picked, learn how it's crushed. How it ferments, how it's bottled. Go on all kinds of mini field trips. And relate them to what you learn. When I went to culinary school, I always said 'God, I wish I knew more about *this*.'

"Go learn so you have a basis of knowledge. We're in the Hudson Valley—we're at a great advantage. It breaks my heart when I hear a student say, 'I'm so bored. This place is boring. There's nothing to do here.' It breaks my heart."

Obviously, I knew exactly where the library was, but I stayed there later that afternoon and going forward. My homework answers were exceptionally detailed and elaborate. I spent even more time studying. It wasn't for Viverito's benefit, however, and not because I was scared of him. The more hours I spent around the guy, I found it harder and harder to stomach the idea of being the person who took the shortcut.

I WATCHED MY BLOOD trickle bright and red under the heavy fluores-cence of the CIA fish room. The gills of a fish—a sea bass, in this case—are heavy, crude syringes, livid with bacteria. There's nothing on them you want introduced under the skin. I'd been scaling the fish; I'd been careless—it was 6:15 and my alarm had gone off at 2:36 a.m.—and the spikes punctured deep into my thumb. I dropped the scaler to the red tile floor, stepped away from the sink, and barked an obscenity. In five minutes my hand would feel like it had been drenched in acid. Minute by minute the pain graded up. Before long, it was exquisite, total. My eyes watered. A little drum of nausea beat in my stomach.

Adam walked up to me, pulled my hand in front of his face, whistled, and said, "Prepare yourself—that's going to hurt like a bitch."

Since the cutting part of the class had started, most of my fillets had been looking like roadkill. I was at that second trying the up-and-over on an undeserving fish.

And then Viverito took a moment from his rounds to stand at my shoulder and ask, "What the hell are you doing?"

I squirmed, just a little bit. What the hell was I doing? I had a cold fish under my fingers, and scales stuck to my forearm. I had a knife in my injured hand. I'd just started cutting away the flesh from the bones. I was also so tired I couldn't recall my middle name. I was angry, because I was so tired. I was full of ire at being made to feel uncomfortable, and, with this man at my elbow, beginning to feel frayed. My mind had gone tabula rasa; there was nothing there. What the hell was I doing? I went for honesty. "I don't know."

He stared me down. He was about six inches from me; I could feel either heat or hostility radiating off him. He kept staring. I noticed that his eyes were seriously bloodshot. I forgot completely about my hand. His lips pursed, and he looked like he might spit bile. His breathing picked up speed. He said, "Yeah—no kidding you don't know."

When this guy cuts a fish, the flesh seems to just swim away from its body. The bones and ribs are bare, and you can hear a chorus of mermaids and sirens singing through the mists. But I was the one cutting, and now he was glowering at me and all I could hear was the sound of everyone else's knives. I shot a look around; I had never seen my peers as focused on anything as they were right then on their fish.

He began speaking a mantra: "Fish to the right. Fish to the right. Fish to the right. Fish to the right." Every syllable was a drill right into whatever confidence I owned before class started. "Where's your right hand?" he asked. I had no idea. My head buzzed with static. I moved a hand. He pushed it away. "No, not that right hand. Your other right hand. Come on. Oh, for God's sake, come on. I said, 'to the right.'"

I felt different emotive sparks start to flicker all through my head. I wanted to turn and grind the fish in his face. I wanted to drop under the table and crawl away. I wanted to fall to my knees, kiss his hand, and beg him to leave me alone. I wanted to cut the freaking fish correctly. I wanted to sleep. I wanted to remember where my right hand was. All these things in turn, in reverse, simultaneous.

I started flopping the fish around. At some point, I must have gotten it right, because he walked away. My hearing came back. I heard him yell at someone: "If I ever see you pick up a fish by its tail again, I swear I'll stab you." And then to someone else: "This is a really easy technique if you know what you're doing. Which you obviously don't."

My hand had reverted to a high alarm of pain.

I began thinking more about acting. I know everyone has a role to play. His was to be the Idi Amin of this chilly, fishy Uganda-in-a-basement. He wore scales instead of medals. My role was to be cowed and terrified, and to grope around my guts for some kind of grace under pressure. Strike the last one. I got the first two down, though. I knew he wasn't like this outside of the room. Probably. But for me and everyone else: what I was in the classroom is what I'm like outside it, only distilled. Ever done anything you're ashamed of? Something rotten you surprised yourself with? You wonder how you could have sunk to doing it. It's not so dissimilar to the feeling of seeing your masks dismantled and getting a good glimpse of the sun-deprived skin underneath.

I had a neighbor in New Hampshire, an older guy, whose lawn I used to mow when I was a kid. Once, he said this to me: "Jonathan, never try to teach a pig to sing. It frustrates you and annoys the pig."

I was wondering if there was any point being in this class, any point being in school. Exposure to knowledge, to technique, did not mean you were going to pick it up, be able to put it to any use. There might be no point in trying to teach me to sing. But I still stayed after class was over, in the library, looking up the answers to the study questions and writing them down in minute detail. It was hard to write; my hand was killing me.

The next day, we took a break during lecture and everyone left the room except me, Alyssa, and Viverito. She asked him: "What do you do when you aren't teaching?"

He looked irritated, then, all of a sudden, he didn't. "I don't know. . . I try and teach myself something every day. I work in my garden. If I have nothing to do, I'll spin a globe and stop it with my finger, and if I don't know anything about the culture and what they eat where my finger's pointing, I'll look it up. Sometimes, I go and see music."

People started coming back into the room. "What sort of music do you like?" Alyssa asked.

"I used to follow the Grateful Dead around, but, obviously, I can't do that anymore. But I went and saw RatDog a few nights ago."

RatDog: Bob Weir's solo project. I couldn't help myself. "You saw RatDog? Were they good? Do they do original stuff, or is it all Dead material?"

"All Dead stuff. And Dylan. You a Dead fan?"

"Yeah. I never followed them around, but I'm pretty fanatical. I always loved the Dead, and they were great when I saw them. But I came of age listening mostly to punk stuff."

"Really? I grew up in DC, and I went to a lot of punk shows. I used to listen to the Bad Brains, Black Flag. . . ."

"So did I . . . I still do."

"I saw the Rollins Band, Fugazi—"

"Me too . . ."

"Jane's Addiction in a tiny club. Back in the late '80s. They were amazing."

"I saw them in a tiny club also. And they *were* amazing."

He looked at me for a second.

"Yeah—I'm old," I blurted out. He kept looking, then shook his head, as if he was trying not to laugh.

"Okay," he said to everyone. "Let's get back to shellfish depuration."

And there he was at my shoulder again, just as a fillet came free from the side of a haddock. I put the knife down. He picked the fillet up. Then he picked the bones of the haddock up and ran his finger over the big scraps of meat I'd left clinging.

"Poor thing," he muttered as he put the fillet back down. He made a scratch on his clipboard.

During lecture, Viverito stopped what he was doing and asked us, "Who's going on Chef Sebald's chicken slaughter this afternoon?"

About five of us raised our hands.

"You should all be going," he said. "I don't need to tell you that chicken doesn't originate wrapped in plastic. If you're going to eat it, which I assume most of you do, you need to see what it's really like to take those chickens down.

"Man, I have to tell you—chickens are dirty, filthy, disgusting animals. Those of you who are going will find out. But you'll definitely learn something. And Chef Sebald—he might look like an old man, but when you see that guy maneuvering half a steer carcass, you know he's no joke."

AFTER CLASS, WE ATE lunch and scattered for an hour or so. We were to be in the parking lot at 1:00, at which point we'd meet Sebald and carpool into New Paltz.

I had changed out of my uniform into the grimiest, most ripped jeans I owned and a T-shirt I'd used all summer to paint in. I'd brought an extra, just in case I got sprayed with blood. I'd spent a long time the night before sharpening my boning knife on my water stone.

I sat on a bench at the edge of the parking lot with about fifteen minutes to kill. I saw my friend Brian walking up to me. I hadn't seen or spoken to him since the end of academics. He was wearing jeans, distressed sneakers, and his white chef's coat.

"What's up with the coat?" I asked. "That's going to get ruined."

"I just realized I'd forgotten my T-shirt."

"Are you naked under the coat?"

"Yeah. I've got no choice."

I gave him my extra T-shirt. He offered to launder it before he returned it, but I thought of the shirt being covered with chicken viscera and told him it was a gift.

Adam and Lombardi appeared.

Brian was explaining that while we had started this block of classes with Sebald and meat, he was in a group of students that had started with fish, then switched to meat, and that Viverito had been his instructor. "That guy's the shit," Brian said. He was full of admiration.

Adam got right to the heart of the matter: "What was the final like?"

"Oh, shit man—" Brian came back from his reverie. "It was pretty hard. You had to ID something like twenty or thirty fish and there was a hundred-question written part of the test. Also, do you guys have to write essays?"

I'd forgotten: Yes, we did have to write essays to be turned in the last day. "Well," Brian continued, "he is not an easy grader. I worked my ass off on that thing, and I did just okay."

Everyone looked at me; they knew where I'd come from. "Well, look—" I said. "You don't know, I might not do so well . . . he might hate the way I write . . . ahh, screw it, I know this is where the GPA's going to get resuscitated."

"Did you guys know he's set to take the CMC test?" Brian was referring to the Certified Master Chef Exam. Only fifty-nine people had ever passed the test; a handful of them worked at the CIA. President Ryan was one of them. Most of us knew about it from reading Michael Ruhlman's book *The Soul of a Chef,* which followed the fortunes of seven chefs aiming to achieve the CMC title. The test lasted a week and most people failed; a lot more than fifty-nine have tried. The command of techniques you needed, the grasp of tradition, of pairing flavors and textures, of plating, the breadth of knowledge required— it was staggering to contemplate. But pondering the phenomenon of Viverito . . . of course he was going to take the test. Of course he'd pass. None of us had ever tasted a thing he'd cooked, but you just knew.

"That guy will pass," Adam said. "No question—he'll get the title."

I was surprised to find myself suddenly feeling terrible. This guy— an actual peer—was capable of demonstrating a real mastery of something, demonstrating an excellence you could measure. I was partly jealous of his accomplishments, partly envious of his mind. And partly, what I felt was mournful. I had spent a lot of years in a drift. How strange to be pushed into direct contact with someone who had no idea about wasted time. Or to be among people who weren't old enough to have wasted any.

THE RIDE TO THE farm took about half an hour, through the center of New Paltz, up along a steady slope to where the Shawangunk Ridge pitches itself straight against the sky. During the whole trip, gray banks of clouds hid the sun, spat down some rain, and retreated. The mountains are a dark blue and green; looking at them at that moment, they were so beautiful you understood why people will fight so hard to stay alive.

The farm's dirt driveway cut through green fields, and a few yards down from the road a sign read WELCOME CIA STUDENTS AND BROOK FARM FRIENDS. For most of the ride, the four of us in the car had talked food, Thomas Keller and the cult of celebrity, run down other students we didn't care for, and generally avoided the topic of killing. With the farmhouse in sight the conversation swerved down a darker bend; we made jokes that weren't all that funny and laughed too hard at them. We parked the car, gathered the knives, and took heavy steps to the backyard.

The yard would have been big and open, normally, but this afternoon it was crowded with vehicles and equipment. As we walked toward a set of tables to put our things down, we passed a mobile chicken coop, presumably filled with the work at hand. A dozen or so feet beyond that was a fifty-five-gallon drum full of bubbling water on top of a propane burner, and next to it a cylindrical tube with finger-sized rubber pieces extruding off the interior sides and on the bottom. Nearby were a few tubs filled with water. And throwing their shadows onto the tables were six traffic cones upended and nailed to a cross-beam. I remembered the Clorox bottles from my twelfth birthday; I had a good idea what the traffic cones were for. Beneath the cones, someone had dug a trench about six inches deep. On this assembly line, no one part of the process was more than a few feet from another.

The farm was run by a husband and wife team. They were a good-looking couple, at the upper end of their fifties, or early into their sixties. A lot of years of hard work had helped sculpt their faces. They looked a bit young to have been on the countercultural vanguard, but seemed more a product of the early '70s; they'd probably done a post-Woodstock retreat back to the land; if they hadn't spent time on a commune, I would have been surprised. If you've ever seen Robert Kramer's genius film, *Milestones,* this was a pair from the cast three decades on. They radiated warmth.

Both of them shook our hands and thanked us in advance for our help. On one of the tables were bread and butter; suddenly buckets of freshly picked corn appeared. The wife and the husband dumped the corn in the bubbling water. Given what was set to happen, the idea of food and eating seemed lunatic. But no one else appeared to hold that point of view; the bread disappeared. People took corn as fast as they could. The wife was suddenly in front of me holding out a pile of it. "Go ahead," she said. "It was picked and shucked just a few minutes ago." What do you say in the face of this kind of hospitality? The corn was something to exult over—someday I hope I'll have some that good again.

Here were all these people gathered together, eating, but there was nothing celebratory to the moment. The ambience was muted, stilled, with the tenor of a commemoration. A stereo in my head grabbed on to the line from Bukka White's antique blues song "Fixin' to Die Blues": "Just as sure as we live, sure we're born to die." Over and over in my skull, as I tried to suck stuck corn from between two teeth. The wife said a few words about how the chickens had lived well, been treated well, and she read a poem she'd written from the bird's point of view, absolving the killing because it was natural to die, and saying how the chicken's short life had been a good one.

And then it was four in the afternoon, and the light was thick. Things began dying. By the coop there were two wooden cages. The husband took a few of us to the coop, crawled inside, and handed out chickens two at a time. Six chickens were put into each cage. The cages were carried back to the crossbeams; we reached in and each picked up a chicken by its feet and held it upside down—if held that way long enough, chickens go into a trance; they'll fight you, though, when you first try to turn them feet up. Once they were sedated, we drew them headfirst through one of the cones. Sebald spoke his softly accented instructions: Hold the head with your thumb under the chicken's beak. Put the bottom end of the knife blade against the bird's throat. Draw the blade across, applying firm, even pressure. The head should pop right off. All of us stood thronged together, knives in hand, waiting. The first bird went into the cone.

It was really coming onto fall now. I'd noticed a few of the leaves beginning to tint with color. My parents were getting a little bit older. We'd all see another winter, but only so many. We have a finite number of times to watch a full moon wax, to see it turn the topography around you a dusky silver.

The chickens had been brought to the farm as newly hatched spheres of down and had grown ineluctably toward this point in time. The farmers' daughter, a girl of maybe fourteen or fifteen, had appeared. She wore ratty jeans and a green T-shirt. She still had her adolescence all over her; someday, when that awkwardness dropped away, she'd be very beautiful. She was keeping to herself, sitting off at a distance. The first chicken went into the cone. The daughter just broke. She streamed tears but wouldn't look away. She sat with her arms crossed, weeping with more intensity. She'd helped raise them. She'd witness the entirety of their transition.

That first bird: a young woman from school was the first to kill, and it didn't go as well as it could have. The knife seemed to stick; the bird freaked out; she responded in kind but got the knife through the neck. She had blood running down her cheeks and held the head in her hand. She was blameless; it's hard for your hands to know what to do. In the cluster of students around her, I saw one of the teaching assistants from school, her eyes also shining with tears.

Most of us were shifting uncomfortably from foot to foot. I held my knife with a tight grip. Other students were reaching into the cages and pulling out the chickens. I watched people lifting the birds up, watched their wings flap frantically, heard them squawking, saw them being killed.

I love my parents and I want to live forever. I love my girlfriend. And I felt a wild surge of resentment move like electricity through me, angry that everything has to end. People I'd known or admired or were influenced by, pets I'd kept, family I'd loved. Jerry Garcia was dead. William Burroughs was dead. My dogs, Nigel and Cedric, were both dead. My grandmother, gone twenty-two years and still walking into my dreams, was dead. My uncle, too.

My turn came. I could feel the bird's pulse under my thumb. I positioned the knife as instructed and drew it hard across the chicken's throat. And then I was holding its head in my hand, blood on my arms and shirt, watching the body convulse. My foot slipped and slid into the trench. My work boot was glistening with blood.

The body was dunked into the same hot water that had cooked the corn. When the feathers began pulling away, it was removed from the water and put into the cylinder. The cylinder whipped the bird around and the rubber extrusions pulled away the feathers. Any feathers left were plucked by hand at a nearby table. Then we gutted the chickens, the viscera still hot. The carcass was then washed and put into a tub. We went through this for hours, until past dusk, stopping when the hundredth chicken was finished. About two hours before the end, I got stung on my neck by a bee. Sebald made me stop, put ice on it, and sit for a few minutes. "Karma, huh?" he'd said.

In the early evening, I'd watched three other students playing around. In front of the daughter, who sat without saying anything to anyone, eyes red and wet, these three made bloody handprints on one another's shirts and took pictures. They held up a living chicken with one hand, knife in the other, with a stupid rictus of a smile splitting their faces, and took pictures. I noticed my friends and some others staring at them in disbelief. After a few minutes, I couldn't look at them anymore.

At the end of the night, the husband and wife asked us to gather in a circle and tell them what we'd learned. One by one, we each mouthed the same platitudes about respect for food, being closer to the food source, and like that. But what I actually learned I still only feel.

For the first few minutes, the car ride back was hushed. Then we started talking about food, the cult of celebrity, running down other students we didn't care for.

The next night, Nelly and I roasted a chicken. When I carved it, I got every last scrap off the bones.

I SPENT THAT WEEKEND writing my essay for Viverito in a fever of righteousness after having killed the chickens. I also had something to prove.

My essay was titled "Farm-Raised vs. Wild: Why We're Doomed." Viverito had spent a lot of time sniping at American culture and distancing himself from it. "There's no television in my house. We have a set, but that's solely for watching movies. Yeah, I know *Top Chef* is a lot of fun, but for God's sake—read a book."

Or: "I don't eat mammals. Maybe—*maybe*—I would not be opposed to eating animals that were raised naturally, cows allowed to be pasture raised rather than feed-lot raised. Chickens allowed to roam around the fields rather than being raised without beaks in little henhouses. But I'm not going to put that shit into my body otherwise."

One day he was incredulous: "I was shopping the other day and I kept getting nearly run down by all these people on those Rascals puttering up and down the aisles. I was just freaking amazed. Get your ass out the chair and get your heart rate going, you near-diabetic, obese mother . . ." He trailed off, not finishing the word, glowing with indignation.

I did eat mammals. I watched TV. I've never ridden a Rascal. But I understood. Part of me thought that you can't spend years listening to Fugazi, Black Flag, or the Dead and not harbor—or least empathize with—those anti-mass-cultural impulses. Part of me also thought that these positions were the logical outcome of thinking morally and ethically and not being a sociopath. I found myself mentally yelling "Amen" to a lot of his pronouncements.

I wrote: "In a blog entitled Liquid Life, the blogger described her reaction to her first taste of wild salmon: 'Alas, my celebratory mood was interrupted when I took the first bite. It tasted . . . fishy. And it was really . . . chewy.' She went on to note, 'I knew that there was no way I was going to eat the rest of this muscle-y fit fat-free wild-caught salmon. I just couldn't. I am going back to my farm-raised salmon.'

"Well, who can blame her?" I continued writing. "And beyond questions of blame, who can even be surprised by a reaction like that? For all the lip service paid to notions of experiencing the most we can out of life, living every day to its fullest, and all those other Oprah-like platitudes, it's in the realm of the quotidian where we, as a culture, seem to like our experiences least. Many people are willing to commit some act of hyper-insanity like sky diving or sheer rock climbing, but appreciating a new piece of food is a Herculean undertaking. Of course, it doesn't stop at food; you could look at the arts—film, music, visual art—and see over and over the same unwillingness to submit to a new experience. That which reinforces old sensations (with increasing diminishing returns) gets rewarded, but anything on the cusp of the new is usually damned to obscurity (at least until the artist dies), or, at best, to a cult following. Steven Spielberg could buy and sell me a thousand times over; for every movie John Cassavetes made, he had to mortgage his house to fund it."

My mind was a fugue of outrage. I kept writing: "Tangential stuff? Sure, because I'm supposed to be fixating on the notion of farm-raised fish vs. wild, but it really isn't such a stretch to see the preference of the Liquid Life blogger as symptomatic of an American intellectual laziness. Of course, laziness implies that there's a goal to reach, or something to be done or accomplished that is being ignored. We've lost sight of any goals. We're on the way to being rendered incapable of even recognizing goals. At a nexus of profit, habit, convenience, and torpor, we've achieved a great failure. And for an example of the essence of this failure we don't need to look much farther than the end of the fork."

I went on. And on. And on. And then wound down: "Farmed fish and factory-farmed produce and meat aren't going anywhere. Of course they have their uses; if you can save lives and prevent malnutrition, then a life-giving but inferior product will certainly do in a pinch.

Plus, they earn untold sums of money. But neither are the problems they engender going anywhere. And just as red meat was once villain-ized, then redeemed in favor of the demonization of carbohydrates, so America's current infatuation with 'being green' and eating organic will probably wane when a new trend is established—or as soon as it becomes inconvenient. Only a relatively small minority work to make a positive impact anyway. Everyone else continues thickening their precious bodily fluids with high-fructose corn syrup."

I was done with the essay. I called Nelly up to read parts of it to her. I spent hours afterward on the front porch studying the characteristics of all of the fish we'd seen in class; I looked over every note I took; I had a two-inch-thick pile of index cards with key terms on one side and the definitions on the other. I went to bed at 9:00 and got up five and a half hours later.

Soon after I got to school, we assembled in the fish room to take the identification part of the final. We were all standing shoulder-to-shoulder as Viverito held out the fish toward us. I guess we all have our blind spots. I had had a hard time spotting immediate differences between rainbow trout and brook trout. Viverito showed us an example of each, and I couldn't make the distinction.

Adam was immediately to my left. He was a lot taller than I was, and he held his test paper at my eye level. My eye saw that Adam did not have trouble making the distinction. I weighed the ethics for a moment; I didn't mean to see, but I did. If I didn't do well in the class—and I was convinced, given the condition of almost every fillet I cut, that I wouldn't—it could mean some finance pain down the line. I didn't mean to see it, but I did. I filled in the blanks. The test went on, and I didn't miss any others. When it was over, Viverito asked that the tests be passed to him. This did not feel good.

I just couldn't do it. I erased both of the trout answers and handed the test in. Adam watched me doing it. "Those were the right answers you had," he said to me.

"Well, actually, they were your right answers. You were holding your test right in front of my face, but I couldn't bring myself . . ."

"I'm kind of impressed."

"Yeah, whatever."

We went into the lecture room and took the written part of the test. I knew every answer but one. I was the first person finished. I turned in the test and my essay and left the room. It was 9:00 a.m.

A few minutes later Adam was finished and we wound up walking the campus and talking—about Obama's candidacy, about race in the America, about our parents, about the school experience so far. Lunchtime conversations were usually either about other students, class, or a litany of dick and fart jokes. This was the first time I'd really *talked* with another peer at the CIA. Adam was smart and perceptive. The guy would be going places.

At one point, Adam asked me, "Did you like the fish class?"

I said, "Well, I told you, I used to teach. So I've been on the other side of the desk. I've gotta say, that is one of the best educators I've ever encountered. Hands down. It isn't that you're going to remember every single thing he said or be an expert at cutting up fish after seven days. But come on, didn't you find yourself studying really hard?"

"Shit, yeah."

"Okay, that's the mark—that guy made you and me want to be like him. Not *be* him, but be *like* him—know as much you can, to be really good. We wanted to measure up. That's being a really good teacher."

At 10:45, we walked back to the fish room to see if there was any progress on the tests; Viverito had promised to start grading as soon as they were handed in. One of the others, a guy named John Howze, was seated on a bench outside the room. When Adam and I walked over to him, John looked at me, chagrined, and said, "You are a total asshole."

"For what? What did I do?"

"He picked up your essay as soon as you left the room and read it. He was laughing out loud. I think you've ruined it for the rest of us."

Two more people came out, and the room was empty except for Viverito. The three of us walked in and Viverito held my paper out to me. He'd written "Excellent" across the top.

"What was the paper about?" Adam asked.

"It was a total denunciation of American culture," I said.

Viverito said, "Hey, man—I love preaching to the choir."

On the Saturday after the last fish class, Nelly and I were in the supermarket and I felt an urge to grill beef for dinner. I stalked the meat aisle, looking for hanger steaks. I found one. It was not all natural, it was not organic, it was not grass fed, it was not local. I put it in the cart. Nelly and I did the rest of our shopping. We slogged through the checkout, paid our money, went home, had cocktails. At 6:00, I fired up the grill and cooked our meat. Nelly made salad. At 6:30, we ate. Nelly had a small portion of meat, and I ate the balance.

After dinner, I was playing with the cat, Cash Money. Cash Money is an obligate carnivore; he requires meat. I do not. He liked playing with the plastic rings from the top of Gatorade bottles, and I stood in the kitchen tossing a ring and watching him attack it. This went on for a while. I poured a scotch and went to the porch to sip it. Through the window, I watched the cat keep on attacking the ring. Dinner didn't taste right anymore. I don't know what the connection was, between the cat and dinner; I just knew that one existed.

I had in my mind an image of a steer, and I pictured that steer hobbled and ruined. I pictured a perfect piece of meat, beautifully marbled, exquisitely cut. I pictured a syringe full of hormone, another full of antibiotic, another full of weird chemistry. I pictured all of them being injected into the meat, then cooking it, then eating it. I envisioned chewing, I saw the additives blending with saliva, I saw myself swallowing.

I felt a definite disgust whenever I saw an ad for some triple burger at a fast-food joint, or an all-you-can-eat buffet at the mall down the road in Kingston, but I'd bought, cooked, and eaten that hanger steak.

Nelly, as if by prompt, said to me the next day that she felt it would be worth it to spend the extra money on clean meat, if we were going to eat it at all.

We made a pact.

6

On the first day of Skills class, we marched into the kitchen like a bunch of invading Pattons. We were ridiculously early. We were ridiculously excited. This was the start of the real thing: real vegetable cuts, real sauces, real stocks, real heat under real pans with real food.

Everyone had cut vegetables before, and made sauces, and cooked things, but not all of us had done so under the guidance of a genuine, classically trained chef.

We'd all read enough, or seen enough television, or just been sufficiently indoctrinated by the CIA to understand that classical, traditional techniques—which meant French methodology—would be the mainstays of our arsenals for the rest of our cooking careers. Know this stuff and you could build off it without limit. After all, was there really anything in Saint Keller's Bible that wasn't practiced by Escoffier, too?

Skills I would run for three weeks and be followed, logically enough, by Skills II, a seamless slide from one right into the other. Both would be taught by the same instructor, Chef Bobby Perillo, a new guy. Perillo's biography had been posted on the CIA website. A CIA grad from the class of 1986, he had been a sous-chef at Balthazar, restaurateur Keith McNally's famous Manhattan bistro. He'd been the opening chef at McNally's Schiller's Liquor Bar, had worked as a tournant—a sort of kitchen jack-of-all-trades—at Charlie Palmer's Aureole. Most recently he'd been an instructor at the French Culinary Institute in New York

City, a school that was widely derided at the CIA—like every other cooking school—mainly because it wasn't the CIA. Maybe he hadn't trained under Bocuse, but it was still an impressive résumé.

Adam had met with him and told us Perillo seemed "cool."

The group of us who'd been together in meat and fish had been split up again. Brookshire was in the new group, Lombardi was there. Seventeen-year-old Carlos, presumably still doing it clean, was with us. There were some other people I'd seen around who walked into Skills, and many I'd never seen before.

When we entered the kitchen, a stack of cubbyholes for our stuff sat on the left and opposite that, a pair of sinks, a worktable, and two immense steam kettles. Two banks of four ranges and ovens extended from one wall out into the main space, two ranges and ovens on each side, and two more of each running along the back wall. There was a dry storage closet and shelves stacked with pots and pans and a dish sink with all sorts of utensils—kitchen spoons, spatulas, spiders— hanging above it. The room smelled like mop water and was dimly lit with fluorescent lights that were on their way to being spent.

We'd wanted to get into this place for two and a half months.

Perillo was there when we came in, standing by a small podium opposite the ranges. He had a look that many—though not all—the chefs seemed to have, a sort of weathered appearance that signified a lot of time spent in the heat on one's feet, of years of line cooking, enduring a bloodstream boiling with adrenaline. He sort of bobbed and weaved as he stood, like a boxer whose feet had been nailed to the floor. He kept his hand cupped near his groin. He had short, dark hair with streaks of gray, and he was smiling widely. He did seem cool.

He recapped his bio for us and explained that he and his wife had just moved up from the city and lived in Woodstock, and they hadn't quite gotten used to it yet. He told us that this was the first class he'd be teaching at the CIA.

"I'm probably as nervous and excited as you are," he said. "I remember walking into my first Skills class. And now I'm teaching it. This is a significant moment for all of us." I began to like the guy.

We'd all been assigned workstations, but most of us had been unable to decipher the chart Perillo had made. We went ahead and assigned ourselves. Perillo didn't care. "Just stay wherever you are for the rest of Skills I."

I had taken the spot directly across from the chef's demo station, which afforded me the front row for everything Perillo would be showing us. I was determined I'd soak up every damn word, every movement of his fingers. I was partnered up with Gio, who nodded hello as he joined me.

Perillo told us to get ourselves set up and we went right to it. We got the cutting boards from a shelf in the back and pulled metal bains-marie from the closet to hold our utensils. We each grabbed a plastic tray and lined it with paper towels for our knives. We unpacked our knives—chef's knife, paring knife, boning knife, fillet knife—and our utensils—vegetable peelers, wooden spoons, plastic heat-proof spatulas, tongs. Then he told us to gather vegetables from the worktable near the door: two onions, two shallots, two garlic cloves, two potatoes, and two plum tomatoes. We'd also need a small pot to boil water, and a bowl for an ice bath. We put water in the pots and turned the stove on.

The blue ring of gas that burned fiercely underneath the pot will always be indelible in my memory. It seemed incredibly momentous— the first cooking school flame.

While the water heated, Perillo demonstrated how to cut onions. One onion was to be sliced in one-eighth-inch slices, the other diced in one-eighth-inch dice. He cut the ends off each onion, then cut them in half. He peeled away the skins. To slice the onion, he simply cut it across the grain. But his hands flew and the onion seemed to just fall apart into perfectly equal slices. To dice an onion, he turned the root end of one half away from himself and made several horizontal slices, stopping just short of cutting all the way through. Then he started making cuts perpendicular to the slices, each with an eighth of an inch between them. Next he cut perpendicular to those, each evenly spaced, and the onion dissolved into perfect dice. He held up the butt end of the onion and told us to save it for stock. He took out his paring knife and performed the same operation on the shallots and the garlic clove. His motions were effortless and the results flawless. So effortless, that matching him seemed entirely possible, even probable.

Peel the potatoes, he instructed, and square off the round edges. He made the peel disappear and, within a few seconds, had a rectangle of potato. He told us to cut one potato lengthwise into quarter-inch slices, then cut the slices into quarter-inch strips. In turn, each strip was to be cut, at quarter-inch intervals, into cubes. He demonstrated and wound up with perfect quarter-inch diced potatoes. The second potato was cut into eighth-inch slices and then into eighth-inch julienne.

Finally, he took the tomatoes and incised an X into the bottom of each one. All of our pots of water were boiling at this point. Perillo dropped two into the pot nearest him, let the tomatoes swim for a moment, then removed them with a slotted spoon and plunged them into an ice bath. After a few seconds he took one out and the skin just peeled away. He cut the tomato into quarters and, with a paring knife, sliced away the seeds and pulp. Next, he cut the tomato quarters—he called them "petals"—into quarter-inch strips and made dice out of them. That, he announced, was how you made tomato concassé.

He informed us we would have seventy-five minutes to repeat his performance. We would put the results on a tray in small piles. We would also save our scraps so he could see how much we'd wasted. He instructed us to bring everything up for evaluation once we were done.

I figured seventy-five minutes was about sixty more than we needed. Simple cuts, repeated. That was it.

Adam *did* require just fifteen minutes. Yet another Michael—Michael Crosby—required only a few minutes more. A second Adam, Adam Aubrey, finished at about the same time. There was a second tier of people who took a bit longer but came in way under the mark: Brookshire, Lombardi, and someone new named Yoon, from Korea.

That left a dozen of us hacking apart the vegetables, watching the clock's hands jump forward in bounds.

Slicing the onions was no problem for me. I had addressed myself to a lot of onions at that restaurant in Brooklyn. The dicing, however, was new. The restaurant where I'd worked was proudly rustic, and this attitude extended to its vegetables. Exactitude was not a priority. After I made those first few horizontal cuts and started in on the perpendiculars, the fucking onion was collapsing under my fingers. Within a minute, it looked as if I'd tossed it into a wood chipper. A good deal of my enthusiasm was evaporating away, that peaked excitement that had been stoked so high when I walked in. I had never thought of myself as fragile before, but the DMZ between a sensation of skulking in the kitchen and maneuvering confidently through it was turning out to be pretty narrow.

Gio was working really slowly, but his cuts were right on. I watched what he did for a moment, got a new onion, and then tried to emulate him. Things worked out a little better this time.

My shallots were a mess. So was my garlic. The tomatoes looked okay—a bit uneven—but the potatoes were absolutely mystifying to me. No matter what I did, no matter how I held my knife, I could not get the slices to come out evenly; they were wedged, or one end was too thin and the other too thick. The julienne looked like wooden toothpicks soaked in water for too long. The dice reminded me of some weird-shaped die my friends and I had when we played Dungeons and Dragons as little kids.

Adam was moving through the room, stopping at different work-stations, offering advice. He got strange—even extreme—reactions. I couldn't hear what was said between Adam and whomever he was talking to, but I watched the looks on their faces as he tried to help. The expressions were bitter, pissed off, and their body language announced he should get the hell away from them. Adam looked increasingly hurt, then defensive. He made his way over to me as I was gathering up my scraps. I wanted him to tell me that they weren't as bad as I thought, but he couldn't.

"Really?" he asked as he poked through the potato dice. "Really?"

I said nothing, just kept gathering the scraps.

He continued. "You know, next time, you should try this . . ." and he went to pick up my knife.

"You know what, man? Not now." I was really irritated. I was every bit as hostile as my classmates. Obviously, I wasn't mad at him. Not really. If I didn't want to be angry at my performance in the future, I should learn how to not repeat whatever mistakes I was making. "Wait, wait, wait—I apologize. I'm sorry. Show me what you were about to do."

"Look at the way you're standing," he said. "It's at a weird angle to the table. When you go to cut, even if you're holding your knife completely straight—which it looks like you weren't—you're at a bad angle relative to the food. Hold your knife like this—and now stand like this . . ."

A line was beginning to form at Perillo's desk. The clock said there were just a few minutes left. I thanked Adam and got in line.

As I waited, I could hear Perillo ripping everyone's efforts apart. He was saying, "No, no, no . . . does this look even close to a quarter inch? . . . Uh-uh . . . you're going to really need to do some practice outside of class . . . hey, you know they offer tutorials in the Student Learning Center on basic cutting techniques? . . . no, no, nope."

I got exactly the same comments as the others. And I think my face bore the same contours of hostile disappointment, but I was having a hard time figuring out where to place it.

As we were cleaning up, a man from Administration came in. He announced that it was time to elect a group leader. While Adam had been performing the job for the past few weeks, the man said, we would—right now, this very second—have the opportunity to make a choice. The group leader should be less like one of us, the man said, and a little more like a sous-chef for the class.

I had no desire whatsoever to have the job, nor, I realized, would anyone have voted for me if I did. Adam had a lot of kitchen experience. He knew what he was doing. He was willing to take on all the extra responsibility. That was good enough for me. I made up my mind right then to stump for Adam if he needed it.

"Adam, do you want to run again for group leader?" the man asked.

Adam said he did.

"Who else would like to be a candidate?"

No one said a word. I could see a couple of my classmates consider-
ing it. I could almost see the gears working in Adam Aubrey's head.
Young, deadly serious, a native of Illinois—you just looked at him,
listened to the way he barked out "Yes, Chef!" to whatever Perillo said
to him, and could tell he would very much like the power.

Crosby looked like he, too, was giving the idea some thought. A
bunch of the others, three or four of them whom I didn't know yet,
looked at Crosby like they were urging him to raise a hand, but he didn't.

I looked over at Lombardi. He seemed to be the most likely candidate to run against Adam, but he'd be starting as a resident assistant in
the dorms soon. Plus, I guessed that Adam would have taken it person-
ally if Lombardi did run.

So Adam ran unopposed. He made a short speech about wanting to
be a good group leader and asked if we could have a meeting to discuss
what sort of leader he should be. This seemed to puzzle a lot of the
students. You got info from the chef and passed it on. What's the issue?
And if there was an authority figure already in class—the chef—was
there a need for another one? They actually started to look more
resentful than when Adam was trying to dole out advice.

At 6:10 Perillo let us out for dinner. Six ten pretty much meant dinner was over. There were twenty servings of each entrée available in
each of four classroom kitchens, with about five different entrées on
offer. Hundreds of students were vying for those hundred plates, and
when a kitchen opened at 6:00, the good stuff was gone by 6:05. By
6:10, it was down to the dregs. Tonight, there was some steamed flounder available in the Asia kitchen, some johnnycakes with mushrooms
in Americas. The Mediterranean kitchen was completely cleaned out. I
got the johnnycakes, which gave greater nuance to the word "bland."

But what weren't bland were the desserts, and the desserts were the
downfall of many CIA students. Baking and Pastry students sent the
desserts they made on large, multitiered carts, which were unloaded
onto long tables. During meals, you were allowed to help yourselves to
as many desserts as you wanted. These were not light desserts: tirami-
sus, custards, dark and white chocolate mousses, pies, and tortes. If I

had had a decent meal, I would usually pick one dessert and eat just part of it. It wasn't difficult getting someone else to eat the leftovers. Others would take two or three desserts at a shot and eat them all. People started getting bigger. Uniforms that had once fit nicely got tight, and in the hallways, as the students walked, you could hear the frictive, whooshing sound of fabric on fabric as swollen thighs rubbed together.

Some people actually lost weight. I did. Since I was tasting a lot of food all day, I didn't feel much like eating large portions of anything later on. By the end of the second semester, I'd find myself eleven pounds lighter.

As we ate, talk turned to the election we'd just had.

"Well, that was democracy at its finest," Brookshire said. "We got blindsided with that one."

Adam said nothing. He toyed with the flounder.

"Why didn't you run, then? You had the opportunity," I said.

"I don't have time. I'm busy."

"Adam's busy too. You don't win if you don't run."

"It doesn't matter now," Aubrey said, emphatic as always. "What's important is that we get behind Adam. It's important for us to be united."

"Well . . ." I was trying to phrase this carefully. "We're not dealing with matters of national security. We're cutting vegetables." Adam looked a little hurt. "Sorry, Adam, I don't mean to denigrate the office. But, you know, for all of us: a sense of perspective, huh? I think it's probably a good idea to have someone who can add a little fuel to the fire. But what's important is, I don't know, maybe that we learn something. The rest'll take care of itself."

"Well, I already know how to do a julienne. I already know how to dice an onion." Aubrey was being a bit dismissive and it irritated me. Maybe it was related to that tray of vegetables I'd just had evaluated.

"You do? Wow. Wow! Well, let me go to the dessert table and get you a cookie. You deserve it. It must suck to be stuck with us."

Lombardi broke in. "Okay, anyway—Perillo: thumbs-up or thumbs-down?"

We agreed it was too early to say. We finished eating after a few more silent minutes. On our way back to class, Adam pulled me aside.

"I know that being group leader isn't like being Obama or anything. I just have a lot of experience. I want to share the wealth. I want to teach by example. If someone's making really terrible vegetable cuts, I want to show them how it's done."

"Okay. I'll be really honest here. I'm thirty-eight years old. I'm at this school with no real experience. I've got a lot of years behind me that I'm not getting back. And I'm pretty insecure here. I'm imagining that everyone else without the benefit of your experience is in the same boat. You need to tread lightly. If you want to teach by example, that means not making a show of teaching. Get what I'm saying?"

"Yeah, that makes total sense."

I'm not sure he understood what I was getting at.

Each day, Perillo showed us something new. On the second day, he demonstrated how to make meat broth.

You cut up some mirepoix (two parts onion, one part celery, one part carrot); you make a *sachet d'épices* from a few crushed peppercorns, a clove of garlic, some parsley stems, thyme, and a bay leaf, all tied up in cheesecloth; add a pound and a half of beef, cover with a quart of water; and simmer the whole thing until the meat is fork tender.

He showed us the basics for making stock: pounds of mirepoix; many pounds of chicken parts or veal bones (which could be roasted or not to make dark or light stocks, respectively); a few large sachets; hours of simmering, constant skimming.

We made stock every day, right at the beginning of class. After dinner, right before lecture, we'd strain it, put it in gallon bags, seal them, and soak them in an ice bath. Sometimes we'd use the stock for the next day. Other times it got sent to the restaurant kitchens.

He showed us how to make onion soup, using veal stock we'd made the night before, topped with slices of baguette that had been smeared with a Gruyère and butter mixture, and toasted. Because I had made it, and because it was the first fully composed dish I'd done at school, it tasted like the greatest soup I'd ever had. I think it was, in fact, the greatest soup I'd ever had.

We learned to make consommé, clarifying broth or stock with a raft—a mix of eggs, ground meat, tomatoes, and onions. As the liquid heats up, the raft coagulates and floats to the top, looking like gray meatloaf. As the liquid simmers, the raft pulls all sorts of debris from the stock, and results in a soup of crystalline clarity.

It was like sorcery, and Perillo was the magus.

We learned to make roux. Homemade mayonnaise. Potato and leek soup, lentil soup with panfried croutons, fish chowder. I found myself becoming obsessed with sauces. I loved those things: They made everything—a panfried pork chop, a piece of roasted meat, a steamed vegetable—taste infinitely better. We went through each of the "mother sauces," those traditional French sauces that serve as the basis for an infinite number of variations in classic French cooking: velouté, espagnole, tomato, béchamel, hollandaise.

I was inordinately knocked out when I compared Escoffier's recipe for hollandaise to that of the CIA's: They were almost identical. A reduction of vinegar, wine, and peppercorns. Add egg yolks. Put the bowl with the yolks over a pot of just simmering water and whisk them into thick ribbons. Bit by bit, add clarified, or melted, butter, whisking after each addition. Finish with lemon juice.

We were taught what to do if the sauce broke—if the butter and yolks separated—and then deliberately let a hollandaise go so we could resuscitate it.

My attempts at all these things were largely successful. That was thrilling. When Perillo evaluated my work, I was mostly told to add a little more salt, or to make the consistency of a sauce a little lighter, or thicker. Minute things, things that didn't indicate failure or incompetence.

I'd watch myself, making these motions over a bowl of hollandaise, or a pot of sauce espagnole, and see a chain of phantoms making identical motions, stretching back from this moment, now, under the shitty fluorescent light, through kitchens all over the country, all through Europe, back through a couple hundred years and feel the strange thrill of being a citizen of tradition.

But before we'd do any of this stuff, we'd spend time at the onset of every class cutting vegetables. They might include a few variations—batonnets, oblique cuts, lozenge cuts, tournéed potatoes—but always included the slicing and dicing of tomatoes, onions, shallots, garlic, potatoes, and, as of the second day, a bunch of parsley that needed to be chiffonaded into ultrafine green slivers.

Perillo would cut most of us down. He had a model he kept at his desk of vegetable cuts cast in plastic—dice in a variety of sizes, obliques, juliennes, and so on—and he'd hold our cuts up against it. He didn't even need to say much that way. We could see quite plainly how we were screwing it up.

"You need to be exact. That's all there is to it. There's no faking this. You either do it or you don't. You either can or you can't."

I *was* getting better. My cuts were getting straighter, generally, but at some point my knife would always strike out in directions of its own, and I'd be left with something halt and uneven. It would be that much more upsetting in light of any success I'd enjoyed at the end of the previous day's class.

On my way home one night, I stopped at Walmart, a store I'd always vowed that I'd do everything in my power to avoid. But I needed something. I bought two twenty-five-pound bags of potatoes. I spent hour on hour the next two weeks cutting them at home. I analyzed the exact angle at which I stood, judged the angle I held my knife. The counter became chalky with dried starch, our garbage pail heavy with diced potato.

We loved Perillo in the kitchen, when he wasn't judging our cuts. His demos were impressive, and he was patient when we were cooking.

He didn't seem as enthused when he lectured.

Each lecture was based on slides shown on an overhead projector. One might read: "Béchamel: A Grand sauce of milk thickened with *white roux.* The amount of roux required to thicken a *béchamel* varies according to what it will be used for. A light consistency may be used for soups, a medium consistency for sauces and a heavy consistency for a binder."

Perillo would stand up front, doing that strange bob-and-weave, and address us:

"So, let's talk about béchamel sauce . . . it's a grand sauce . . . it's thickened with roux. But you'll want to use different amounts of roux depending on what you're going to use the béchamel for . . . you'll want maybe a light consistency for soups, medium for a sauce, and maybe heavy if you're doing a binder."

He'd go on doing very slight variations on the slides. But once he was done reading to us, we were free to leave. The end of the nights were always fun; we'd leave the lecture room and head back to the kitchen to gather our stuff. Perillo would always be in there talking and joking around, and he and I occasionally bonded over missing New York City, our favorite bars there, bands we'd seen at CBGB's, city things like that. One night, late into Skills I, he mentioned that he'd enrolled in the CIA right out of high school. He graduated from the CIA in 1986, which meant he'd probably graduated from high school in 1984, making him just about four years my senior.

Perillo lived a few miles farther up the road from me and we took the same route home. One day he walked up to me as I was chopping onions and said, "Jonathan—do you drive a little Nissan pickup with a Dead sticker on the back?"

I did. I also drove like an old man, always at or under the speed limit, hands at ten and two on the steering wheel.

"Yeah, I do," I said. "Why? Have you been stuck behind me on Route 9?"

"No, no, no." He paused. "Well, yeah, maybe a bunch of times."

One night I drove home and passed the scene of a really terrible accident right outside of Rhinebeck. It was one of those tableaus that stick in your mind for years afterward, and I felt sick seeing it.

The next afternoon I walked into the kitchen and Perillo said,

"Thank God. I saw you leave school last night and I left about a minute after you. Then I got to Rhinebeck."

"Did you see that accident?" I said.

"Yeah, and I thought it might have been you. I looked for your phone number on the roster and couldn't find it. I almost called the police. I kept thinking, 'Do I hold class if Jonathan got killed?'"

ONE NIGHT, ADAM BEGAN finding out what responsibility tasted like. Just after Perillo finished his close reading of the overhead slides, Adam asked everyone to stay for a group meeting. Perillo left the room.

Once we were alone, Justin, a young guy fresh from the navy, where he had cooked on a battleship, asked, "Why are we having this meeting?"

Adam responded, "I just wanted to talk for a few minutes about how we're doing as a group and maybe get some ideas of how we can get better. We're finishing our cleanup later than we should every night. I think we can figure out how to be more efficient."

I thought we were doing fine. The same people did the dishes every night, not because no one else would but because the same three people kept kicking out anyone who tried to join in. "You're too slow," they'd say. So everyone else stopped trying. But what the hell—if Adam was group leader and we elected him, then we could sit for five minutes while he exercised his office.

Justin thought differently. "Is this mandatory?"

Adam said, "I can't make it mandatory. But I'd really appreciate it if people would stay for five minutes so we could talk."

"Oh, okay," Justin said. "If it isn't mandatory, then fuck this." He got up, gathered his stuff, and walked out the door. About five people looked at one another, got their things together, and followed him out.

Eleven of us remained. Adam shook his head, started to speak, then shook it again.

"Hey, we're here," I said. "Fuck 'em. Let's talk."

It would only get worse.

———

ON THE LAST DAY of Skills I we took our knife skills practical. Each day, Perillo had decreased the amount of time we were allowed until, on the final day, we had twenty minutes. I finished in sixteen. I brought the tray up and he took a look.

"Okay . . . not bad . . . the potatoes are nice and even . . . except for this one . . . and this one . . . the tomatoes are perfect. And look at this parsley chiffonade—very nice. Definitely nicer than this garlic, though . . . shallots are good . . . onions are nice . . . slicing looks a little off, maybe. But you did a good job. Who would have thought?"

"I would have." That was uncharacteristic of me.

He paused for a while. "Yeah, me too."

Skills II began a few days later. I was sharing a station with Lombardi just to the left of Perillo's demo area.

Skills II is a continuum of Skills I. You learn to take the veal stock and espagnole you made in Skills I and turn it into demi-glace. You learn to turn the demi-glace into more complex sauces—sauces Robert, Diane, poivrade, bordelaise, charcutière, all of which involve mixing the demi-glace with wine reductions and shallots. The Diane is finished with cream, the Robert with mustard, the charcutiere with julienned cornichons.

We learned about cooking all sorts of vegetables, about blanching, steaming, sautéing, or roasting beets, zucchini, green beans, and so on.

Rice and potato cooking came next. We were quizzed relentlessly on the different ratios of water to rice depending on the type of rice you used: 1.5:1 for long-grain white; 3:1 for long-grain brown. We learned to make polenta, not by stirring constantly as the polenta sat on a burner, but by putting it in the oven and having to stir only occasionally. I was dubious, but it turned out to have a deeper, richer flavor than any other polenta I'd had. I started making it at home all the time.

We made fresh pasta, something I'd been taught to do by an older Italian friend of my parents when I was twelve. But Perillo showed us a couple extra steps—two different periods of air drying after rolling the dough out and then after cutting it—that made a distinct difference in texture. I always made my fettucine pretty thick; Perillo showed us how thinner is better.

That day, Brookshire was working right across from me and Lombardi.

He always looked supremely confident, yet he'd get some pointed critiques on pretty much everything. He'd still look supremely confident after getting flayed. When he'd get in the weeds, he'd get defensive. On our first time out making pasta, his was dry and flaky and looked like pastry crust. I pointed out that maybe he should start over and use more eggs.

"No, the ratio is fine. I think I got some bad flour."

"You mean the flour from the big bin where we all got it?"

"Yeah, I must have gotten a bad cup."

"Maybe you should get some better flour and then start over?"

"Nahh, this'll be coming together any second."

Perillo tried the ravioli and fettucine I brought him for evaluation.

"Jonathan, you have a real touch for pasta." A bunch of the others looked over when they heard him say that, for which I was glad.

After the first week of Skills II, Perillo introduced a new wrinkle into things: We began to make complete meals. One menu might be braised short ribs, polenta, and glazed root vegetables. We'd get a short rib each, a measure of demi-glace and one of stock, and access to the herbs and dry ingredients we'd need. The rib got seared and then put into the stock and demi-glace with reduced wine, tomato paste, a bay leaf, and thyme. The polenta was roasted as the rib cooked. We'd cut and cook the root vegetables—rutabaga, parsnips, white turnips— shock them in cold water and hold them until the last minute, when we'd glaze them with butter in a sauté pan. The kitchen almost always smelled fantastic.

Perillo would walk through the kitchen and, every day, announce, "If you take a shortcut now, you'll be taking them for the rest of your career." He never singled anyone out, but you'd do a replay of the steps you'd just taken, look at what you were doing right then, and what you were about to do, and decide if he was talking to you or not.

The meal needed to be finished at a certain time. They weren't being served to anyone but ourselves, but it put some effective pressure on us to get it done. You were assigned a specific minute. You had to be standing at Perillo's table at that minute, your plate hot and arranged as he'd demonstrated, no earlier, no later or you got docked points.

People were constantly late. Liz, an attractive Californian with a gentle face and great skin, whom I liked because she laughed at every moronic joke I made, always seemed to come in a minute after she needed to. She'd rush up to Perillo's desk, sweating, hair and toque askew, and slam the plate down in front of him, looking up at the clock.

There was a guy in class whom we referred to as Ox. He was tall, stocky, and perpetually confused. We'd be making mashed potatoes and, following some inner dictate, he'd supplement the recipe, sprinkling in spoonfuls of nutmeg or cayenne. He could sear the living shit out of a beef medallion and still have it completely raw inside. The interiors of his chicken were a beautiful shade of sunrise pink. He was at least five minutes late, every day.

And always—always—at ten minutes past his deadline, Perillo would begin to shout, "Carlos, let's go. You're ten minutes late. Eleven minutes. You're bleeding points here. Please, Carlos. Show me mercy. Come on, give me something. Anything. Show me what's on your plate right now."

Carlos would ignore him and bring his plate to Perillo when he thought it was ready. No earlier.

I DISCOVERED SOMETHING about myself that made a few things at school difficult.

Perillo would walk the length of the classroom while we cooked, telling us to "Taste, taste, taste. Build flavors. Season early. Taste what you're doing and make the adjustments. Taste, taste, taste."

I'd always had my preferences for food. I prefer to not eat raw bell peppers. I like onions better when they're cooked. I prefer white rice to brown.

There are some things I react a little more forcefully to.

During the summer break at school, Nelly and I had some friends over. They brought with them several cheeses that stank alternately of vomit and putrescence. The more corpselike the scent, the greater their enjoyment. Nelly, who doesn't eat as much of the substance as she'd like, mainly because of my disgust, was delighted. The taste of the stuff, which I do distinctly remember trying as a kid, is a too-intense flood of dairy. Way more creamy than I can really handle. And, of course, with accents of rot. I had to stand well away from the plate they were all gathered around.

Cheese—unless it's cooked with something—and fish—oily mackerel, bluefish, and salmon especially—induce a low-grade, opaque nausea. That's really a drag: Those are two foodstuffs you run into with circadian frequency in cooking school.

I've tried to do away with the aversions. I read food writer Jeffrey Steingarten's book *The Man Who Ate Everything,* which claims that it takes about ten encounters with a food you can't stand to change your stance. At least for little kids. I figured I'd try as an adult and see what happened.

My third dinner at school, in the B&C dining room, I was confronted with a plate of broiled salmon. I drew the tines of my fork through the fillet's flaking outer layers of pink flesh and cut off a chunk. I would start nipping this aversion right here and now. I ate it. It tasted terrible. I got through six more bites before I admitted defeat.

A few nights later, I did battle with a plate of gravlax, later still more salmon, then sea bass, and tuna. At no point did any of them taste good to me.

And now Perillo had us cooking this stuff. One day, we were given a fillet of salmon to poach in a court bouillon (water, wine, vinegar, bay leaf, carrot, onion, garlic, celery) and serve with a sauce béarnaise.

I made the bouillon and set it to simmer. Then I started the béarnaise: beat egg yolks with a vinegar–shallot–cracked peppercorn–tarragon reduction; ladle in clarified butter; beat the hell out of it with your whisk; hold it over hot water until you're ready. When the bouillon was set, I tasted it. It was pretty much all you can expect from water, vinegar, wine, and so on. I tasted the béarnaise. A little rich, a bit thick. I thinned it with a few drops of water. Then I tasted it again. I added some more salt.

The bouillon was now at about 175 degrees. I figured the heat would drop ten or so degrees when I added the fish, which would still be in bounds for proper poaching temperature. I laid the fillet in, gently, and let it poach. Killing time, I stirred the béarnaise. I waited ten minutes, watching the salmon fillet float dumbly around the liquid. The color began to fade and turn from red to pink. At some point near the eleven-minute mark, it looked just done. I removed the salmon from its bath and blotted it dry. I poked it with my finger; it seemed to have the requisite amount of give. Then I put it on a warm plate, sauced it with the béarnaise, grabbed a couple of utensils, and carried the whole thing over to Perillo.

"Hey," he said, tipping the plate back and forth. "Nice consistency with the sauce." He cut the fillet open. It had the same appearance as the salmon that had defeated me at those dinners. He tasted it, chewed, and looked at me. "Okay, take a bite."

I hesitated.

"Do you need a fork? Here." He handed me a fork.

"No, I have one." Another couple of silent beats went by.

"Well, the clock's ticking—let's go."

I reached over, cut a piece off, and put it in my mouth. I wrinkled my face.

"Well," he said. "What do you think?"

"Oh, man," I answered. "It tastes like . . ." *Shit? Yes, it does. But no, you better keep it clean.* "It tastes like mud." He looked distressed. He leaned in with his fork and speared another bite.

"No, no, no," he said, chewing. "It's not that bad. Okay, you need a little more tarragon in the béarnaise, but it's not the end of the world.

Don't beat yourself up. The salmon's done really nicely. It's not mud—
you did a nice job."

I thanked him and walked back to my station. I paid close attention
to the color of the fish. I started poking it again and again with my
fingers, just to remember the texture of it for next time.

WE HAD OUR SKILLS II final on the last day of class. There would be a
written component after dinner, but during class we'd cook. We'd
gotten our menu assignment: beef medallions—sautéed—to be served
with a sauce chasseur, along with deep-fried onion rings, potato gratin, and broccolini. I had to present my plate at 5:41.

There were things that could be done in advance. At 4:45, I heated
up a gallon of water, salted it heavily when it came to a boil, blanched
the broccolini, and shocked it in ice water to keep it green. I rolled it
between paper towels and set it off to the side. Later, a few moments
before presentation, I'd heat it up with a little butter and a splash of
water, season it, and put it on the plate.

For this test, each minute you were off, you lost five points. I had
not been off for the two weeks we'd had our appointed times. I'd
watched others continually come up two minutes, three minutes,
even, with Carlos and Ox, fifteen minutes late.

By 5:00, my gratin had been in the oven for a while. We'd run short
of the right type of pan to use, so the one I was forced to employ was
too small. The gratin kept bubbling up and over the sides. I could hear
the liquid sizzling when it hit the bottom of the oven and smell the
burning as it cooked away.

I had been working with Lombardi for three weeks, and I liked him
quite a bit as a partner. After an initial feeling-each-other-out period,
we watched each other's back: turned things down when the burner
was too high; got supplies, equipment, and ingredients for each other;
and stayed out of each other's way when our minute came to pass. This
day, he was set to go about twenty-five minutes before me.

I tied butcher's string around my medallions to give them some

shape and seasoned them with salt and pepper. I cut up the onions for
the onion rings. I chopped some parsley last minute for my partner's
garnish. I wiped my station down. It was about 5:10.

Sauce chasseur was one of the first things we made when Skills II
started. It's usually used for chicken, but tonight it would be plated
with the beef. You sauté some mushrooms until they begin to caramel-
ize, throw in some shallots, and wait for them to turn translucent. You
take some cognac and white wine, deglaze the pan so all the brown
bits come up, and let the liquid reduce by half. You add demi-glace.
Cook it for a little bit, strain, and wait until you're just ready to use it. If
you've read the recipe instructions correctly, you'd know that some
seeded, diced tomatoes get added and briefly simmered, and the whole
thing is finished by adding a little butter and stirring until it dissolves.

At 5:25, the oil for the onion rings was way too hot. I turned it
down, floured them, then put them into the batter. I'd let them sit for a
few until it was time to fry them. I'd taken the gratin out of the oven,
where it had been drooling over the edges of the pan, about fifteen
minutes earlier. I fired up a pan to sauté the medallions, which I'd let
rest after they were done for about seven or eight minutes.

I tasted my sauce. It was a little sharp, but I'd add the butter right
before serving, so that sharpness would be blunted. I dribbled a little
clarified butter into a sauté pan, waited a moment, and threw the
medallions on. I'd had the heat way too high. I pulled the pan off the
heat and told myself to put it back on in a moment. Time was beginning to erode much more quickly than I'd anticipated. It was almost
5:30. The onions needed to be fried. I'd forgotten about the broccolini.
I fired up another pan to heat it. The kitchen clock was right in my line
of sight, and the seconds were liquid and slippery. After a minute or
two, the onions went in the oil. When I turned the heat down, I'd accidentally turned it off. They bobbed for a moment with a few timid
bubbles popping away at the rings' edges. I cranked the heat up and
put the medallions back on the burner. A skin was forming on the
sauce. I was also missing something, and I couldn't remember what. It
was 5:35.

I stopped myself for a second, watching the medallions sear. I tried to bring to mind what it was I knew I needed moments ago. I had no idea. The heat on the onions was back to what I wanted, but the rings I'd thrown in a minute ago were no good—just by looking at them, you could tell they were oil soaked and terrible. The oven was on, the flattops were going full tilt, most of the burners were on; it was pretty hot. I felt two trickles of sweat run between my shoulder blades and I very much wanted a drink of water. I got the old onions out of the oil and tossed some new ones in; they began to brown right away, and I suspected maybe they wouldn't be entirely done when I had to serve them in five minutes. But then again, five minutes—even as fast as they were evaporating right now—was a pretty long time.

I flipped the medallions, and they looked great: a nice, dark brown sear. I put the broccolini in the appointed pan, dribbled some water over them, and tossed in a generous pat of butter. The butter melted, started to emulsify with the water, and I pushed and pulled the pan so the vegetable would jump and flip and coat itself with the glaze. I seasoned it quickly and put it aside. One task down. It was 5:36.

Some pools of red juice showed on top of the medallions and they came out of the pan to rest. I would have preferred they rest for ten minutes, but it wasn't going to happen. The oil in the pan was almost smoking, and I poured it out in the compost bin positioned right behind my station. I deglazed the pan with a healthy shot of wine, ladled in some sauce chasseur, checked the onions—another minute, maybe two—and realized what it was I'd forgotten. I grabbed a plate and threw it in the oven to warm up. There. As simple as that: problem alleviated. The sauce was bubbling nicely; the pan came off the stove. 5:38 and counting. I pulled the onions out, shook the basket, tossed the rings into a bowl and pelted them with a handful of salt. The clock said I had about ninety seconds. The plate came out of the oven, a ladleful of sauce went on it, with the two medallions set on top. The gratin— I'd spaced on that one; out of sight, out of . . . So I cut a wedge with my paring knife and shoveled it alongside the medallions. The broccolini got plated. I bit into an onion ring—maybe it could have gone another minute, but it was a minute I just did not have.

What I did have was about thirty seconds. There was some sauce on the edge of the plate and I wiped it off with a clean paper towel. Then, strangely, I put the towel to my lips and tasted.

Shit, I thought. *Dammit.*

It hadn't been the warm plate I'd forgotten about. The sauce was sharp on my tongue, very acidic. I'd completely forgotten to swirl some butter in to finish it. I'd done some pretty good cooking that afternoon, and it was about to go to ash because I'd forgotten one simple step—one of the most basic steps in finishing a sauce like this— and the doneness of the broccolini, the perfect medium rareness of the beef, the beauty of the gratin was all going to be overshadowed by the lack of a tablespoon of butter.

I figured it would take me ninety seconds to get some butter into the sauce still steaming in the pan, wipe the old sauce off, and replate. That would be ten points off my grade. How many points do you get docked for missing butter?

I carried the plate over to Perillo. I'd take the risk.

I was the second-to-last person to be evaluated. Sixteen people had gone before me. I stepped up and the evaluation began. I was already angry at myself and feeling seriously defensive.

"Nice meat—just the right color," he said after cutting into one of the medallions. He ate a forkful of gratin. "Okay, the potatoes are cooked just right." The fork went to the plate. "I might have taken the broccolini out thirty seconds earlier. It doesn't have the bite it needs. The onion rings—maybe a little longer in the oil next time. It's not the end of the world, just a tiny bit underdone." Finally, he ate a tiny morsel of the beef. "Consistency of the sauce is good, beef is tender. Okay, nice job. Really nice job. Just watch that broccolini in the future." He scrawled something down on his grade sheet.

I stood for a second and almost told him, "Hey, man—come on. Bust me on that sauce. It's really sour. Come on." But I went back to my station instead. I tried the sauce on the plate again. And it did suck. I heated up the sauce in the pan, swirled some butter in, mopped most of the old sauce off my plate and ladled on the new. I started eating my dinner. And then I figured it out. Perillo had eaten sixteen bites of meat, sixteen bites of gratin and broccolini, and sixteen onion rings. His palate had to have been sapped. He'd only mentioned textures during the critique. He probably couldn't have really tasted everything.

The gargantuan (in myriad ways) Fernand Point, whose book *Ma Gastronomie* was at home on my bookshelf, wrote, "Success is the sum of a lot of little things done correctly." I had roasted a chicken at home the previous weekend and forgot to take out the wishbone. That means I wasted meat when I carved, the wishbone getting in the way of my knife, forcing me to leave a big chunk of breast meat behind. The next day, I was making chicken stock in my kitchen, was preoccupied with all sorts of things I needed to do, and forgot to rinse the bones. When I served some homemade pasta to some friends that evening, I neglected to top it with the garnish of fresh basil I'd chiffonaded. I just simply forgot. I realized that I forgot things a lot.

If you take a shortcut now, you'll be taking them for your whole career.

My timing had been on, my reflexes good, my prep work had gone smoothly, but it was hard to keep it from being overshadowed in my mind by the lack of a tablespoon of butter. At least, I told myself, you figured out what you'd screwed up. Chances were pretty good I wouldn't do it again.

When Perillo's written final was over, we went back to the kitchen to pull bags of stock from the ice bath and put them away for the next Skills group on Tuesday. Brookshire and Adam were on their cell phones and I overheard them making plans to meet up with some other students in New Paltz. There was a SUNY satellite in New Paltz, and all the bars were there. It was something akin to the East Village of the Hudson Valley, except with a greater concentration of fake IDs. Liz said she'd go. Aubrey, too. A few others agreed to tag along.

As I secured my knives, I heard Brookshire call my name. "Dixon—we're going drinking in New Paltz. Why don't you come? You can be the chaperone."

"I don't know, Mike. I think my vomiting days might be behind me."

"You can be the designated driver."

I saw Adam standing behind Brookshire and he made a motion with his head, as if to say, "Come on, come with us."

"Designated driver?" I answered. "Wow, that sounds like the best time I'll ever have."

But I pondered for a second. I'd really been starved for conversation. I'd only seen some Brooklyn friends a couple of times since we'd moved up here. I'd often feel loneliness exert itself, like a mild headache.

Nelly was waiting, but I didn't think she'd mind. She'd occasionally expressed concern that I had no friends in the area to speak of. I had an hour's drive home already—longer from New Paltz—but I had a three-day weekend in front of me. I could also crash with Adam or Mike if I really needed to. I had just gotten a check from a freelance article I'd written, so there was some cash in the bank. It had been a while since I'd sat drinking Irish whiskey in a bar with loud music playing.

"I'm going to take a pass, but I appreciate the offer." I think I saw a very slight flicker of relief on a few of their faces. "I'll see you guys on Tuesday."

I got in the truck with a low note of something forlorn droning in the back of my skull. I just couldn't stand to feel a gap deepen and widen, sitting in dim light, watching them flirt and pick up women, getting increasingly careless behind the alcohol, getting drunk the way you only can when you're that young. I wasn't in the mood to try and relive it, and I didn't want to be a drag on their good time. I put the Dead on and drove home to my girlfriend. We had a drink together, watched an episode of *Criminal Minds* we'd recorded, and went to sleep by 11:30.

7

"Coyac's a rock star," one instructor told me. "Even among us other chefs, Coyac's a rock star."

Gerard Coyac's résumé listed the titles saucier, poissonnier, rôtisseur, and executive chef for a dozen or so restaurants in New York City, the Hudson Valley, and Connecticut. He had been the chef for the commodore of the French navy and for the New York Stock Exchange Club.

Even before I knew who he was, I'd noticed him. White haired and red faced, eyes popping, wiry, and short, he moved straight backed down the hallways, head snapping to the left, to the right, a walking synonym for intensity.

He was, people said, a repository of tradition, a caretaker and tender of the methods and science of the gilded classics. Coyac was the CIA's principal of the old school.

Skills III under Coyac felt like a true sink-or-swim proposition. The class devoted more time to the basic techniques we covered in Skills II—sautéing red meats, sautéing white meats, stewing, poaching, roasting—and one class to vegetarian cooking. The fruits of our labor would, for the first time, be eaten by other students, and Coyac was said to run his Skills III kitchen with no less seriousness than he'd run his professional kitchens.

My growing predilection for French cuisine would get a serious bolster in his class. But Coyac famously brought a lot of volume to his

teaching and, in essence, I didn't want to get yelled at. Viverito's reprimands were bruising enough, but the guy still—you could simply
sense it—pulled back at some point. Coyac allegedly did no such thing.

A few years prior, I'd had my arm tattooed and it hurt. In the middle
of it, I grew shaky in the stomach, and the world whooshed in and out
of my vision like I was looking through fog. The tattoo came out nicely
and was worth the unpleasantness. I willed myself to recall this lesson—
but the tattoo took two hours. This class would last three weeks.

On a Tuesday afternoon at 1:30, my new Skills III group clustered
outside of Coyac's kitchen, waiting for the morning group to finish up.
Adam was there, as were Lombardi, Carlos, Brookshire, and a few
from Skills II with whom I hadn't done much interacting: Ox, Yoon—
fresh from the Korean army, and Sean—whom I had decidedly mixed
feelings about. Sean seemed to rack up a serious debit of absences, sicknesses, and tardies and still talk his way out of them. He didn't play
well with others. He was greedy with communal ingredients. There
were a lot of new faces, but one was familiar. Tara was in our group—
the loon from my first lunch on campus, a complex of twitches and
insanity. She was standing away from the rest of us, arms crossed, lips
pursed, looking very much at home in the alternate universe she occupied on her own.

These were to be the members of my group until graduation. Sta-
tistically, some of us would drop out, others would experience some
delays, but this was the core.

Coyac walked past, gave us a glance, and swept into the kitchen.
The morning group began to straggle out, and we made our way in. A
couple of people were dispatched to the storeroom to pick up the day's
food supply and the rest of us milled around. The room was narrow.
There were five workstations, a bank of stoves, two sinks, and a large
reach-in refrigerator. And the omnipresent fluorescent light—which
made everyone's skin look sallow, and as if we were about to have mug
shots taken—followed us everywhere.

The food arrived, and Coyac made an announcement. A life in
France rendered his accent hermetic. Our group was silent and still.

No one had any idea what he'd just said. So he said it again, looking incredulous, but this time gestured at the food. We swooped in and began putting it away, heaving bags of whole, raw chickens, long loins of beef, and packages of root vegetables and potatoes into appropriate homes. He said something else, during which I caught the words "ingredients" and "station," but I didn't know what to do with this knowledge. He'd posted a chart on the wall, we noticed, and it broke us down into teams of three or four, assigned us a station, and indicated which menu our team would be preparing. I found myself at station number 2, standing with Sean, Carlos, and a new guy, another ex-army Korean student, named Joe. Joe had not spent much time in the States, and most of his English vocabulary consisted of obscenities.

In Skills II, each of us had roasted a single chicken, prepared two servings of potatoes and vegetables, made just a cup or so of sauce. Now we'd be doing ten to fifteen servings each class. This was daunting, but not because of the quantity—roasting many chickens is not much more difficult than roasting one, and the only foreseeable difficulty in making mashed potatoes for fifteen instead of two was that peeling took longer. The problem was in trying to organize the activities of four people so that things flowed in a unity of effort rather than resulting in unruly clashes and collisions.

At 2:00, according to our syllabus, Coyac would lecture for about forty-five minutes. At around 3:00, we'd begin cooking. Things needed to be ready around 5:30, and the doors opened to the public at 6:00. Just before the lecture, Sean, Carlos, Joe, and I stood around our steel worktable. We'd gotten cutting boards for ourselves, bains-marie for our equipment, and some plastic containers for our trash.

"So who does what?" Sean asked the other three of us. "How do we do this? Do we each take a turn at everything? Does one person tackle one thing?"

Carlos said, "Nothing here is difficult. Peel some potatoes. Break down some broccoli. Peel some carrots. We've got two hours. There are four of us. This is nothing."

"Fucking easy," Joe said.

"Yeah, it is easy," I said. "But let's all of us truss up the birds and peel the potatoes. That's the pain in the ass stuff."

Coyac called us over for lecture and went through, step by step, the process for prepping and cooking the chicken. His accent lost its murk the more he spoke. The oven, he informed us, must be preheated to 500 degrees. The ten chickens were to be trussed, then placed in an oiled pan. The chickens would then be roasted in the farthest reaches in the back of the oven for twenty minutes, and basted periodically. Mirepoix—celery, carrots, onions—would be placed in the pan and, when the juices gathered and spilled from the cavity when a chicken was tipped, and those juices ran clear and were not streaked with red, the chickens were to be removed from the oven, placed on a sheet tray, and kept near the stove until needed.

After the lecture, we started. Coyac had told us to get the chickens in immediately, so I hurried. There are a thousand ways to truss a chicken, but my way was not Coyac's way. "No, no, no, no, no, no, no," he intoned. He cut a length of string from the spool on our workstation, picked up my knife, and cut my truss away. He made deft motions with his hands and the bird was hog-tied. He began muttering as he worked: "Dammit . . . shit, shit . . ." and so on. "There," he said to me, "that is how you truss a *poulet*. Did you remove the wishbone?"

"Uhhh . . . ummm . . ."

"Oui or non? Oui or non? Oui or non! Hurry up!"

"No, I didn't remove the wishbone."

"*Dammit!*" He slashed at his handiwork with my knife. "So not for you following directions? This is great. Fantastic. Why I get out of my bed I don't know." He had the wishbone out. "Why I bother I don't know. Did you season the cavity? It doesn't look like you seasoned. Watch me season. What is this shit?" His face glowed crimson, his eyes bulged to the point of popping.

I watched. He cut another length of string and trussed the bird, picked it up, and tossed it into one of the pans. It thumped and bounced.

"Come on, come on, let's go, let's go!!" He shook his hands at me. I grabbed the next bird and started cutting away the wishbone. I left too much flesh attached and it snapped as I was pulling it loose.

"Dammit." He hung his head, shook it, and walked away to the next table. My teammates had stood watching the whole exchange. They each grabbed a chicken and began removing the wishbone.

I mentioned to my team while we were working that I really liked making sauces, and the three of them were in immediate agreement that the pan gravy would be my project. When the birds were done, I'd have to boil off the liquid in the pan, and remove the bulk of the fat. I'd continue cooking the mirepoix until it caramelized, then *singer*— sprinkle flour over the whole mess to make a quick roux. I'd add chicken stock. I'd bring it all to a boil, strain it, and simmer until it was done. I'd also attract Coyac's attention. I'd been watching him as we prepped the chickens and nothing escaped his notice. It was actually somewhat incredible. He could have his head down, attentive like a surgeon, focusing on someone's work and making comments, and as someone else moved to drop shallots into a hot pan, he'd snap his head up and yell that the pan was too hot before they were even near it. You had the feeling that you could never take—never even ponder the idea of taking—a shortcut because of some sixth or seventh sense he had, a culinary ESP with which he could anticipate what you'd do minutes before you did it.

I'd tipped one of the chickens so the juices gathered and spilled from the cavity. They were mostly clear, but with rivulets of red. Five minutes later, I tipped again and the juices were entirely clear. Out came the chickens and over came Coyac.

"Okay, *allons,* let's go, come on . . ."

I knew I was supposed to be making the gravy, but I wasn't certain that the next few seconds in his mind were the same as in mine, so I hesitated.

"*Let's go!*" he yelled, bumped me aside, and pulled the pan that had held the chickens to the top of the stove's burners. He cranked the heat up and stood back. I pulled my scraper from the bain-marie, shook off the water, and tended to the mirepoix. Coyac didn't move.

"Leave them alone," he said. "You're not helping them out any. Okay. Now, pour off the fat. Okay, good—no, not so much, leave some in the pan. That's too much. More. More. Good. Stop. Where's your flour? What the . . . get the damn flour! Fast, fast! Come on, move it, dammit! Sprinkle it over the pan. No, no, no, no, sprinkle it—you're dusting it. A little energy here, come on. Okay, go on—it's not going to stir itself. Let's go! Now! Do you see—it's like making a brown roux, just like it, keep it cooking . . . a little more . . . watch the color now, see it: from blond, from blond, from blond to brown. Do you smell it? Remember that smell, go ahead get your nose in there, remember the smell, remember the color . . . now, a ladleful of stock . . . whisk it, whisk it . . . why waste that much energy? Whisk it like this . . . good, more stock, more, more, whisk it . . . beautiful, beautiful . . . season it . . . come on, don't be so damn timid . . ."

I strained the gravy into a saucepan and let it simmer. Coyac took a tasting spoon and dipped it in. He brought it to his mouth. Then he slammed his hand on my back; my lungs fluttered and my clavicle squeaked. "Very good," he said and walked away.

We addressed ourselves to vegetables, a job that could have been done by one person, but none of us wanted to look idle. We broke the broccoli down, peeled off the outer skin, blanched it in boiling salted water, shocked it in ice water, and set it aside to drain. We peeled carrots, cooked them in stock and sugar, removed them upon tenderness, and reduced the liquid to a glaze. We peeled and boiled the potatoes, pureed them with butter—tons of it—in a food mill, and set them to rest in a double boiler.

It was curious how the CIA dealt with vegetables. They did not hold pride of place on any one of the school's menus. With something like broccoli, or with green beans, they were cooked to the CIA's estimation of doneness, which, depending on the chef, often meant hovering on the near side of mush. And these vegetables were not permitted to stand on their own; they were invariably chaperoned to the plate with thick butter sauces. Or, if you had spinach or kale or collards, they were cooked beyond recognition in the company of a pork product—bacon, ham, tasso. The protein was the star of every dish, and protein was usually a supporting actor as well.

At 5:45, Coyac was back to show us how to plate the meal. The potatoes went into a plastic pastry bag to be squeezed onto the plate. One half of a chicken, cut into two pieces, was nestled against the potatoes. Gravy was poured around the perimeter, and three ounces—specified by Coyac—of each type of vegetable went on the opposite side of the chicken. Coyac's example plate was full of symmetry and height. My plate, Sean's plate, Carlos's plate—each looked smeared and lumpen. Joe's looked really good. At 6:00, Coyac yelled that the kitchen was open, and the first few students walked in. At 6:15, each station had gone through all of its food. We'd been instructed to hold back a few of our chickens for our dinners. We made up our own plates—I went nuts with the gravy, because I couldn't stop looking at it as I ladled it over my food; I'd made it and it had been given the slap of approval—and went into the adjacent dining room to eat.

Coyac's step-by-step direction through the making of the gravy stuck with me. I thought about it on the drive home, and the next morning when I got up to do homework. I'd heard the dictum "cook with all of your senses" a few dozen times, and I'd encountered Fernand Point's aphorism "Success is the sum of a lot of small things done correctly" just as often. Watching the color of the roux so closely, drilling the scent of the roux into my memory—it all coalesced.

For years, I never cared for Neil Young's *Tonight's the Night* very much. It had a drugged, drunken haze in its favor, but it had always sounded out of tune and clumsy to me until one day—one bleak, snowy afternoon alone in Brooklyn—I felt compelled to put it on and it struck me that it was one of the best things ever committed to tape. It was agonized and emotionally white-hot, and it was some of the realest stuff I'd ever heard. But I had not been ready to really *hear* it before that afternoon.

I really *heard* those dictums and aphorisms now, and I assimilated Coyac's step-by-step instruction into it in a way that I was incapable of before that specific hour of class. This was somewhat exhilarating, because it was a lesson that wouldn't leave me, and the thrill of discovery and understanding is unlike anything else.

When a piece of beef or pork or chicken is done cooking it has a specific feel to it when pressed with your finger. When a chicken breast is sautéing, and it's done, there's a nearly undetectable but distinct scent and very subtle sound. There is a color a green bean will take on when it is at the perfect doneness.

On Sunday afternoon at 5:00, I turned on *Iron Chef America* to watch Kent and Kevin Rathbun, chefs from Georgia and Texas, respectively, go at it with Bobby Flay. The secret ingredient was elk. I knew two things about elk—that it was a lean meat, and that I'd never tried it. I imagined it must be something akin to venison, which I had tried, but still wouldn't know what to do with it, if asked.

The Rathbun brothers made elk carpaccio with a cilantro glaze and dried peaches; elk and fennel meatballs with cabbage carbonara; chili-seared elk strip loin with blue cheese grits and beer barbecue sauce; and a few more dishes, each paired with a wine. What got to me—and I was a tiny bit upset, even as I was knocked out while I watched—was how far beyond my own thinking these guys operated. I was making progress in the kitchen, but I still wasn't an advanced culinary thinker. These were not dishes concocted by Ferran Adrià or Heston Blumenthal—Futurist food, science fiction food; instead, they were relatively traditional: meatballs, grits, beer barbecue sauce. But there were a lot of flavors being balanced, a lot of deceptively simple complexity on the plates.

Nelly and I had some kale in the refrigerator that I imagined we'd sauté with some garlic and olive oil. We also had chicken breasts, which could be sautéed too, and served with a pan sauce of reduced wine, stock, and butter. We had a selection of starches: rice, a handful of organic fingerlings, an assortment of dried pastas. Almost six months in school, with shelves full of a few dozen cookbooks, and my thinking was still conservative: visions of plates filled with a protein, a starch, and a vegetable.

The next day at school, we were eating dinner together. It had been poaching day, and I'd given away my portion of salmon and hollandaise and hit up another kitchen for my supper. When I arrived back at the table, everyone had just started talking about *Iron Chef* from the previous night.

Adam said, "I've eaten at Kent Rathbun's place—Abacus—and it was pretty good. Actually, really good. But I don't know—it seemed like a safe menu. Carpaccio? Yeah, okay, fine, whatever. Not real ambitious. Meatballs?"

"Bobby Flay must have sucked harder than usual, because that food didn't look so exciting," someone said. "I could do blue-cheese grits. And fuck Bobby Flay, by the way."

"The food on that show is almost always mediocre," Brookshire said. I was already annoyed at him because when I'd been making hollandaise earlier, he'd appeared at my shoulder (Coyac was engaged elsewhere) to remark, "I've never really seen hollandaise sauce quite like that. You're a definite trailblazer, playing with the classics that way."

I opened my mouth. "Yes, all right, everyone at the table has a bigger dick than Bobby Flay or the Rathbun brothers or myself, since I thought it was pretty damn fascinating. But if everyone's such an Escoffier in bloom, why the fuck are you here and not out there running a kitchen? I wish I could have come up with that menu— either Flay's menu or the other guys'—but I can't so, you know, I'm here."

"I think I'm sensing career-changer insecurity," Brookshire said. "And older-guy crankiness."

"Yeah, yeah, yeah—I am old. In fact, if I'd been a more sexually precocious fourteen-year-old, I could be everyone's dad. But you know that old cliché about wisdom and experience? It's a cliché for a reason. I fucking wish I were your age and doing this. I wouldn't have the massive ego. You should deflate that massive ego. It's a real hindrance, trust me."

Adam was measured. "Jonathan—no one's saying any of those guys aren't good cooks. But you have to realize that maybe some of us could have come up with those dishes. You know what I mean?"

"Yeah, so shut the fuck up, Grandpa," someone said.

I DON'T THINK ANYONE realized how easy Coyac had gone on us the first few days. We'd been ready on time the initial day because the menu was so basic, but as class went on, we'd opened late for service three or four times in a row, and Coyac's temper was beginning to fray.

On frying day he swooped in like a Valkyrie.

Frying was a little trickier than roasting or poaching or sautéing—each of those corresponding dishes could be done a little bit ahead, and the roasted beef or chicken, the salmon or sole, the chicken breast with fines herbes sauce could be reheated when it came time to plate. The fried dishes needed to be done almost to order; the panfried pork cutlets our team was cooking had to be started just a couple of minutes before service began and cooked steadily until they were gone. They needed to be breaded just before cooking, and the oil would need to be changed out at least twice. It wasn't an insurmountable schedule, but it did require some timing. Plus, we needed to make a sauce to go with some green beans, and cook spaetzle.

The spaetzle, Coyac said, needed finesse. The batter needed to be just right. It needed to go into the boiling water in the proper quantity so we could make enough of it to serve and serve it on time, but not so much that the water lost its boil and made the spaetzle soggy. After it was drained, the spaetzle would be sautéed in butter until browned perfectly. Seasoning was essential. When he walked us through it, the instructions sounded more like warnings.

Carlos and Joe were working on the vegetables and the pork. Joe pounded the cutlets thin, and Carlos trimmed the beans. I got the sauce going—vinegar, shallots, and wine reduced and then added to a measure of sauce espagnoles, seasoned, and finished with a good chunk of butter. Sean gathered up what we'd need for the spaetzle and when he'd gotten everything, I joined him.

Coyac was at our side before we even started mixing. "You guys work like pigs," he said. "Look at this," he said as he gestured at our table. There was flour all over the place, green bean tips scattered across the table surface, piles of crumpled plastic that Joe had used for the pork, rogue pieces of shallot, and an empty container of wine vinegar on my cutting board. "I don't care if it's all your mess"—he pointed to Sean—"or none of your mess, but you do not let your station get like this." He looked at me. "What's the matter with you? How can you work like this? Do you live like this at home?"

He moved to Joe. "Why is this pork still out? Put it away. Put it away. Now! Come on, let's go. Where's the spaetzle batter? You haven't done it yet? Oh, for God's sake. For God's sake. Come *on*! Why is that sauce at a boil? You know what 'simmer' means? What does it mean? Tell me." I opened my mouth and then closed it. "Okay, we can look it up after you turn the heat down. What? Do you need an invitation? Turn it down! It's probably burned already." He walked away, then turned back. "Before you do one more thing, clean that table. Wash your cutting boards, wipe that table down. Change your bains-marie. There's no way you're going to be ready for service. I can't believe this."

I felt a flush of heat in my face. All of us kept our heads down and did what we were told. Later, Sean and I stood over the spatezle batter.

"It's too thin," I said. "I think we need to thicken it up."

"No, it's too thick. I was about to thin it out."

Coyac yelled from behind us, "The spaetzle is fine!" Then he screamed. *"Cook! Cook! Cook!"* We did.

Two tables over from us, Ox and a guy mysteriously named Twitch were teamed with Lombardi. Ox and Twitch were both nice guys but prone to making a lot of mistakes. A lot of mistakes. Since the first class I'd been watching Lombardi, pained to the core of his love for order and efficiency, throw his hands up and look like he might be on the verge of weeping. Ox and Twitch were handling the spaetzle and had just finished boiling and draining it when Coyac appeared at their table. Coyac wore a look of complete incomprehension on his face. He stood getting redder, lips open, hands tensing into fists at his sides.

"Oooooohhhhhhhhhhhhhhhhhhhhhhh," he began.

Ox and Twitch turned toward him.

"Ohhhhhhhhhhhhhhhhhhhhhhhhhhhhh," Coyac continued. Then he erupted.

"Shit! Shit! This is shit! What is this *shit!*" He reached into their bowl and took out a large handful. He shook it in their faces. "What is this? Were you going to try and serve this? This is useless! Useless! This is the worst spaetzle I have ever seen in my life. In my life! This is just . . . just . . . just *shit.*" He tossed the spaetzle onto the floor and stamped his foot in it, grinding under his shoe. He pivoted and walked away toward the other side of the room. Then, he stopped. He stood immobile for a moment, turned, and walked back toward Ox and Twitch. He looked down at the pile and stamped it again, ground it, kicked it. He turned and strode out of the room.

I started to laugh, then laughed some more, and kept going. I couldn't stop. Just about everyone joined in.

Except Tara. She stood in a posture of indignation, close to outrage, hands on her hips, turning her head to look at all of us. "That was *not* right," she said. "*Not right.* That is not the way to teach anything."

A couple of classes later, on election night, our team was doing chicken fricassee, and for some reason, I was in charge of it. I saw Coyac approaching me, and I felt uneasy, but at the same time excited; I figured some more scales might fall from my eyes, even if he was about to make me feel like an idiot. I had a large rondeau—a heavy pan with tall sides used for braises and stews—over low heat on the stove and a pot of velouté—chicken stock and roux—that I'd made simmering behind it. I had leeks ready to go. The recipe called for white pepper, which I found flat-out disgusting—the eczema of spices—and had planned on adding just enough so I could tell Coyac that I had used it. A jar of the stuff was on my cutting board. And I had chicken pieces seasoned and ready to go. Coyac watched me add butter, tilting his chin up as I went to indicate that I should add more. He watched the rate at which it melted and told me to turn the heat down. I placed the chicken in the rondeau and it sizzled. He bumped me away and pulled the pan off the heat.

"No color on this. The chicken should have no color. Everything should be pale. The leeks should be translucent. You had the pan too hot. You need patience for this. Patience. It will get to where you want it. If you rush it, you'll ruin it. Easy. Relax." Together, we cooked the chicken lightly in the butter. He took over for a few seconds, picking the chicken up with tongs to gauge its progress and my eyes moved back and forth from the pan to his face, watching everything. In a few minutes, we removed the chicken and I added the leeks.

"You want these to sweat," he said. "Not sauté. Just let them rest in the heat. Let them give up their liquid. Do you smell that? Can you smell the difference between the leeks sweating and if you were sautéing them?" I could. "Okay, let's add the velouté. Good, good, now get the chicken back in there. No—gently. Use the tongs, but don't break the skin. You need to hurry. Quicker." He picked up pieces of chicken from my platter and laid them into the liquid, which came up over his fingertips as he worked. That liquid had been simmering a second ago; it was hot. He didn't miss a beat, just wiped his hands on a towel.

"And now," he said, turning to grab the vessel of white pepper, "it is time for seasoning." He began with just a pinch, but then added more and more, and finally, in a fit of enthusiasm, upended the entire vessel into my mix. He looked enraptured in a Proustian sort of way, eyes distant, a quarter smile on his face, transported, perhaps, decades back, feeling the heat and smelling the smells of the kitchens of France where he'd learned what would become the rest of his life.

As the fricassee cooked, the white pepper scent reminded me of the chickens from the CSA farm after they'd been slaughtered, plunged into hot water to loosen the dirty, encrusted feathers, and eviscerated.

"Hey, Chef," I asked as he was about to walk away. "That white pepper—do you genuinely like it?"

He did a double take. He looked me up and down, distraught and incredulous, as if, when he was looking the other way, I'd sneakily pissed on his leg. "Yes," he pronounced with gravitas. "Yes. It is good stuff."

Later, Coyac stood over the fricassee, stirring it. He tasted. He turned. "The conziss dancy is not right at all. But the flavor is good."

This was a pretty cryptic assertion. I had no idea what a dancy was, or what sort of modifier conziss was. But the chicken apparently had good flavor.

He returned after a few minutes. "What did I just tell you about the conziss dancy?"

"That it was no good."

"So fix it." I had no idea how. I looked at the fricassee; the sauce looked a little thin. I decided to take the chicken out and reduce the sauce. That should fix the . . .

Conziss dancy. *Consistency.*

At dinner, I ate the fricassee without much interest because the taste of the white pepper irritated me. But I kept at it.

What could I say? The fricassee was made the way tradition prescribed. The goal of the CIA is to instill a sense of that tradition, not to foment rebellion or dissent. What Escoffier did in his hotel kitchen is the classical culinary golden mean. It is a papal bull of cooking methodology, not to be deviated from without fierce soul-searching and debate.

So, I told myself, *when your food is seasoned against your will by a man with roots way the hell deeper than anyone else around here in traditional French cuisine . . . go ahead and taste it. This is what tradition says it is supposed to be like. Now you know. And now that you know, if you want to do something different, you have a history to react against.*

The penultimate night, Coyac had a brief, private conference with each of us.

"You need to speed up," he said to me. "You're thinking too much.

You're pondering, pondering, pondering everything you do, but you're not *doing* it. This is your Achilles' heel. If you work hard, if you truly apply yourself, you will be a very, very good cook. I can see it. You'll be great. You need the speed. You need to hurry, hurry, hurry. But when you hurry, you cannot be sloppy or clumsy. You'll get there if you work. But you need to work hard."

Tara came out, shaking her head. She wouldn't sit near us or tell us what had gone on in the other room. She stared at the floor.

When Dan came out, he told us, "Coyac said I move too fast." Dan nodded in thought, smiling.

"Hell," he said happily. "I'll take that."

"Not sure he meant it the way you're taking it, big guy," I said.

"Shut up, Grandpa."

Adam came out. He sat down, stretched his feet out, cracked his knuckles, and said, "He had nothing to say to me. Daddy's getting an A."

"Oh, fuck you," Tara said, quietly, to the floor.

8

OVER THE WEEKEND, I worked on a notebook I'd bought at Barnes &
Noble. It was small, flexible, and sturdy, and I intended to make it into
a reference for myself. I wrote down the methods and proportions for
all the basic sauces we'd learned—tomato, hollandaise, velouté, espagnole, béchamel—and a selection of sauces that derived from them. I
wrote down the water-to-rice ratios of seven different varieties. I did
the same for grains. I copied out Thomas Keller's instructions for a
sauce gribiche, Escoffier's version, and James Peterson's version from
a fantastic book I d gotten in a used bookstore, *Glorious French Food*.
Things like that. In the back, I began copying out recipes that I'd tried
and liked enough so that I wanted to repeat them: *arepas*, sautéed leeks
and chestnuts, marinades I used for grilling meats. I'd add to it as my
time at school went on, and when I went on my externship.

The externship was beginning to be a thorn. Not-so-subtle pressure
trickled down from Administration to get a site for the externship—
a four-and-a-half-month stint in a restaurant somewhere in the country or world—secured. We'd be seriously penalized if we didn't. You
received a grade for your externship, and if you didn't have everything
set on time, you could lose up to ten points from that grade. I hadn't
made any real moves toward finding one yet. I was cowed.

In the deepest, most private reaches of my fantasy life, I wanted to
go to Per Se. As my fascination with French cooking grew, so did my

fascination with Thomas Keller's world. I had heard his name ad infinitum since the moment I stepped on campus, but I began understanding
him differently than I had before. The French Laundry and Per Se were
synonymous with beauty and imagination, elegance and refinement.
And after delving more and more into Escoffier, Point, and Bocuse, the
degree to which Keller was dyed with that tradition became illumi-
nated for me, and I saw him and the people who carried out his vision
as the closest anyone could spiritually come in a modern context to
working at, say, the Ritz with Escoffier himself. And the stacked
motions of perfection, one perfect component melded with another and
another and another, were even more appealing after time with Coyac.

But maybe the very fact that I couldn't bring myself to tell anyone
other than Nelly about where I wanted to go, that I kept it locked away
like a shame or trauma, said a lot about my chances.

Whenever I diced an onion, I still had large pieces splitting off from
the sides and ends. I suspected this wouldn't fly at Per Se, or any place
like it. I was—in every sense of the word—still a student. But I had a
thread of logic that went like this: If I were picked up and tossed into
the deep end, it might be a shock, it might bring with it a period of
suffering and distress, but in the end, I would wind up swimming. It
was even possible that the experience might catalyze something previ-
ously veiled. I might turn out to be really good.

People at school would inquire, "Where are you going to try and
get your externship?"

The most I'd give away was, "Somewhere in New York City."

From a database on the school's computer system, I got all the contact information for Per Se, then helmed by Chef Jonathan Benno. I
started looking at other New York City restaurants and made a star-
tling discovery: There weren't very many that were registered with,
and approved by, the CIA. Maybe around twenty or so. All of Danny
Meyer's places were listed—Gramercy Tavern, Eleven Madison Park,
Tabla, the Modern, and so on—as were David Bouley's restaurant and
Jean-Georges Vongerichten's spots. Odette Fada's San Domenico was
there. Daniel Boulud's restaurants were all listed too.

I spent a few minutes looking over Boulud's listings. It said outright that students could expect to work about ninety hours a week, with one day off.

I considered that prospect. That would be an amazing education—total immersion, breathing haute cuisine for every waking hour. But three things occurred to me. I thought about Nelly first. She was my anchor, my partner. She was always supportive, even when I could tell my school schedule was driving her nuts. I was completely in love with her. She would probably have some issues if I disappeared for four and a half months. I wanted our relationship to survive, and I didn't want to be apart from her for that long. Two, I would be thirty-nine years old pretty soon. Physically—and this was difficult to admit to myself—it would be hard to pull off ninety hours a week, eighteen weeks in a row.

And three—the hardest to acknowledge—I knew that with scant kitchen experience, with only a handful of months of school to lay claim to, I was simply not good enough yet to survive in that environment. A lot of my peers had experience, and their education at the CIA was one of refining. They knew a lot of the basics and could advance immediately to concentrate on learning the more nuanced details. They already knew what a consommé was and how to make one. They could focus on the minutiae of how to perfect the consommé. The rest of us were trying to learn all of it from scratch, to acquire the rock-bottom basics.

We started Cuisines of the Americas with Chef Paul Sartory on a Monday in early November and would be cooking our way through a series of regional menus—New England, the Midwest, the South and Louisiana, Florida and the Caribbean, the Southwest and Pacific Coast, Mexico, and South America—spending two days on each. The menus seemed somewhat arbitrary; eggplant Parmesan came on the midwestern day, for example, along with braised short ribs. But more than that, the syllabus was incredibly ambitious.

"How are you supposed to learn Mexican cooking in two days?" Nelly asked, next to me on the sofa, paging through the syllabus.

"What kind of grasp can you get in that amount of time? South American cooking in two days? Southern cooking in two days?"

I didn't know. And in the next block, we'd spend a few weeks trying to learn to cook Chinese, Japanese, Thai, Vietnamese, Indian, and Korean food. Three weeks—that seemed even more ridiculous.

I read through our recipe manual. I had never cooked a mirliton squash or made crawfish étouffée like I'd be doing on days five and six of the class, and I'd never made a Mexican pork stew with red chile sauce like I'd be doing on days eleven and twelve. But I'd made stews before, and I'd braised meats. The unfamiliar elements were the flavors—the chiles and spices, crawfish, black roux. Every culture the world over roasts and grills, braises and stews, sautés and pan roasts.

"You can't learn that stuff in two days," I told Nelly. "But each class—it's like practicing scales."

That was the best analogy I could come up with. If you're a musician, you learn your scales. A scale becomes a chord and a chord becomes a progression; the progression becomes a song, and a song can become a symphony.

Sartory was a handsome guy of about fifty-five or so, a model of restraint, and entirely unflappable. He did not get angry. When things went wrong, he did not waste time yelling; he simply figured out a way to fix the problem. He'd nail you, gradewise, for whatever fuckup you engineered, but he would not shout. And as far as fixing problems went, Sartory had a lot of opportunities with our group.

We were at the six-month point. We'd not had a break. We spent more than eight hours a day together under pressurized circumstances. We always worked in teams, but the teams were always divided alphabetically. Whenever I showed up to class, I knew I'd have either Carlos or Sean as a partner, and often both. Joe was earlier in the alphabet and often got paired with Brookshire. I thought Carlos was scattered and moved recklessly through the tasks at hand. I found Sean was lazy. And it started to get more irritating the more comfortable I got in the school's kitchens. As for me, I can imagine what they thought. I'd been a teacher for several years, after all, and I was often hit with the spirit during class. I started not discussing things with them, instead I talked at them. "Okay, so we're supposed to make the stewed pork with the chili sauce. Sean, I'm thinking you might want to handle the pork. Carlos, I bet you'd do well with the vegetable prep. Since I seem to gravitate toward sauces, it's probably best if I tackle that. Okay? Let's go." I was becoming a bit of a jerk.

Carlos would usually just go ahead and do it. Sean was a little more passive-aggressive. He started showing up late and doing whatever he felt like. More than a couple times, Sean and I wound up prepping the same components of a dish. We'd each arrive at the stove with a pan full of mirepoix, or each peeled a pound of shrimp without the other being aware.

The exchanges between all of us in class got more curt and louder.

During the Skills classes, ingredients were truly communal. If you needed a pound of onions and only had half a pound, everyone would give up some of theirs so you could get yourself right. If you were short on thyme or Chablis, and someone else had it, they'd give what they could and adjust their recipes accordingly. These impulses were eroding away.

A lot of hoarding started, even if the person doing the hoarding didn't need all the extra ingredients. Or pans. There were eighteen of us and a finite number of cooking vessels. We would take what we thought we *might* need and hide it in the reach-in refrigerators underneath our stations.

Unless they were in your momentary clique. Little alliances formed at the beginning of a class, but they would often not last until the end. One afternoon, Brookshire and I might have been fast friends since 2:00 p.m. But the second he'd show up at my side and say something like, "Oh, well, I guess that's one way to cube your beef," I'd start to resent him. And if he needed a particular sauté pan that I had in my possession, he'd go on needing it.

Once, we'd been supportive of each other. No matter how inedible someone's dish may have been, you still told them it was great, just by way of encouragement. Now their dish was dissected behind their back with purposeless cruelty, the line between the food and the person smudged in a wash of sarcasm and spite: "I can barely be bothered to throw this out. Only Tara would fuck up seasoning this bad."

There was always Tara. Asking a thousand unnecessary questions, growing in volume with each class, perpetually confused and acting out from the fog of her bewilderment. She'd storm up to you and hiss, "You need to get your stuff out of the convection oven *right now*. Chef told me to put my meat in there. You've had it in for twenty minutes and I wanted to let it go but now I need it. Get it out of there. Right *now*." Sartory had, in fact, told her to use the regular oven, which she had not yet preheated. Upon being informed of this, she'd walk away, saying nothing, and glower at you for the rest of class.

We were also getting sloppy. Food was frequently burnt, or underdone, or raw in the center, or just destroyed.

On the first midwestern day, when Carlos and I were preparing eggplant Parmesan, I sliced and salted the eggplant, letting it drain its bitterness away. I set up a breading station with a tray of flour, a bowl of beaten egg, and a pan of bread crumbs. Carlos assembled a tomato sauce. Carlos was starting to bread the eggplant in slow motion. I went ahead and prepped other things. I returned and he'd made no headway. Slowly, methodically, meticulously rolling the eggplant in the flour. Dipping it into the egg. Pressing it in the bread crumbs.

"Carlos, I swear—you are slower than a fucking crippled mule." I started grabbing eggplant and breading it. He stopped what he was doing and stared at me. I raised my voice. "Hey, can you maybe get the oil heated up so we can fry these?" Carlos went away and heated the oil. When I was done breading, I just came out and ordered Carlos to start frying them and walked away to do other things.

I was slicing fresh mozzarella when Adam walked up to me and grabbed my arm. "Hey—you better go check on your eggplant; Carlos is burning the shit out of it." I rushed over, and at least half the pieces he'd cooked were unusable. The oil in one of the two pans was discolored and filled with burnt-to-black crumbs. Time was becoming an issue; we'd need to serve this stuff in about forty minutes. "Check on the sauce," I said, and bumped him out of my way. I kept frying in one pan, heated up new oil in the other. When I finished, Carlos and I assembled the individual dishes of eggplant Parmesan—and one big dish, meant for our group dinner—to go into the oven. We put them in at almost 500 degrees.

Most oven racks have a curve on the edges to prevent tipping when you pull them from the heat. Ours did not. As I pulled, a tray of ten individual eggplants in small casserole dishes, and one giant panful, tipped at an impossible angle and slid. I leaped backward out of the way, and the mess spilled and shattered on the tiles.

I bellowed obscenities; Carlos yelled, "What did you just do? What did you just do!" The kitchen was at a standstill. Sartory was at my back. He put his hands on my shoulders and shook.

"Hey," he said. "Hey, hey, hey—listen to me: it's just food. Did you get burned? No? Okay, let's solve this. How much did you lose? Okay, that's okay. It was an accident. Shit happens. We've got ten servings left? Then that's what we have to offer. You guys finish up a little earlier is all. Tomorrow, you make it again, and use a different oven. So let's get this cleaned up, and we'll go from there. Accidents happen, accidents happen." I don't know if we got marked down or not, but I loved Sartory right then. He got down on his knees with the two of us and helped clean up.

THAT WEEKEND, NELLY AND I went to the local supermarket. There was a parking space right by the front door and as we were pulling into it, someone else immediately to our right was getting out of his car. It was Viverito. He was heading into the store as Nelly and I got out.

"Who are you looking at?" she asked.

"See that guy? That's Viverito." Nelly turned to see.

"Oh!" she said loudly. "He's handsome." I ducked out of sight. As we walked in, she said, "Are you going to say hello?"

"Nah, the guy's off-duty. I'll leave him alone."

"Oh, come on, Jonathan Dixon. That's ridiculous. You should say hi." When we walked in, he was standing over a crate of broccoli right inside the door. He looked strange to me in jeans and hiking boots. He glanced up and I saw a flash of recognition.

"Chef Viverito, how are you?" I held my hand out. "Don't know if you remember, but I was in your fish class."

"Jonathan, right? Yeah, I remember." He looked at Nelly. I wasn't sure how to introduce him, but he saved me the trouble. "Hi, I'm Gerard." They shook. He turned to me. "How are your classes? You must be getting close to your externship, right?"

Nelly said good-bye and wandered off.

"Yeah, I'm close, but I'm really not certain where to go."

"You haven't applied yet?" He looked surprised. "You better get going, man."

"I'm at a loss. It has to be in New York City, but . . . I don't know, I don't know if I'm skilled enough for Per Se, which is"—I couldn't believe I was admitting this—"where I really want to go. I just don't have a ton of experience yet."

"Well, Jonathan Benno is pretty damn amazing. But, yeah, that'd be a pretty high-pressure place. Where else have you thought of?"

I mentioned another place.

"Now *that* will be high pressure. If you're prepared for a lot of abuse, then, hey—go to it. But, you know, I got to a certain point where I just thought to myself, 'Man, I'm *tired* of working for screamers. I don't want that anymore.' Guys our age"—and here he gave me a pointed look—"are maybe not as eager to put up with that. That's stuff you suffer through when you're a kid."

"I looked at Daniel Boulud's places but, get this—the description on the database says you'd be working ninety hours a week."

He looked outraged. "What?? Ninety hours a week? Are you kidding me?"

"If I were fifteen years younger and not in a relationship, I'd consider it."

"Ninety hours? No way. That's insane." He started walking away. He stopped. "Do you need a recommendation?"

"Yeah, that would be . . . great."

"Come by the fish room Tuesday morning. Bring your list of potential sites."

I made up a list that night: Gramercy Tavern, Tabla, the Modern,
Per Se, San Domenico. I'd start with those. The next day, I was early
for class and ran into Perillo in the hallway. I was glad to see him. We
talked for a few minutes and the subject of the externship came up.
Since he was from the city, I showed him my list. Perillo read it silently.
"Huh," he said, handing it back. "Per Se? I don't know, Jonathan . . ."
He trailed off and I felt a little foolish.

"I think you might need . . ." he continued.

"Yeah, I know—more experience."

Perillo nodded. "San Domenico—that's a good one. Odette Fada is
great. But, you know—you're more mature than your classmates."

"'Mature'? That's a great euphemism, Chef. Thank you."

"No, I mean it literally, in this case—you're older, you're more
mature. I don't think at this point you want to go anyplace where
you're going to get screamed at."

"What about Tabla?"

He shrugged.

"Gramercy Tavern?"

"Michael Anthony is amazing. Just amazing. You'd learn a ton. But,
if you had asked me without the benefit of having this list, where *you*
should go, I would have told you the Modern. It's classical; it's contemporary; Gabriel Kreuther is brilliant. It's a calm kitchen. You should be
there. It's *exactly* where you should be."

On Tuesday, I returned to the fish room. Viverito was hunched over
his computer. I knocked.

"Here's my list," I said.

He read it. After a few moments, he said, "You know where you
should go? The Modern. I think that'd be a great place for you. What
do you think?"

"You're the second person within twenty-four hours who's told me
that. I say okay."

"I'll do one recommendation for Kreuther, and then another with a generic 'To whom it may concern.'"

I began, for the first time, to feel excited about the externship.

SARTORY MIXED THE ROSTER up a little bit one night, possibly in an attempt to save us from one another, and I was working with Brookshire on a dish of black beans and sautéed snapper. We burned our beans because we weren't paying attention. We doctored them with half a pound of butter to make them semiedible. When it came time to cook the snapper, someone had accidentally turned our oven off. We were supposed to have started the snapper in a pan on the burners and finish it in the oven. So in the middle of service, none of our fish was cooking, and the line waiting for it grew and grew.

Another team's guava-glazed ribs had been cooked to dust, and some of the students eating them had complained. I'd tried the curried goat and it was tooth-meltingly spicy—a miscalculation of measurement on someone's part.

Sartory stood by his desk looking grim and a little sad. He'd put out the fires where he could but, in all, we'd had a pretty poor showing. He let us sink under the weight of our own carelessness.

Brookshire and I finally got the late orders of the snapper out. No one spoke; all you could hear was the small clatter of pans on the burners, ovens opening and closing, meat on the grill. Then, above it all, I heard Tara start to yell.

"Shut up! Shut up! I don't want to hear anything from you! *Anything!* You have no right to tell me *shit!* You do not have the right!"

I stepped around the corner and Tara was wet eyed and red in the face. She stood screaming at Adam, who was making gestures to calm her down. Sartory looked over and then made himself busy with his computer. Tara strode right out of the room, and Adam went back to his station. I could see her knife kit on the table next to Adam's and I realized they must have been partners.

Adam called a group meeting that night. I was there. Gio was there.

Brookshire, too. A couple of others. But most everyone else declined to show up.

Adam canceled the meeting and he and I walked together to the parking lot.

"Well, Captain Bligh," I said, "looks like you had a mutiny."

He was much more upset than I thought. "I keep trying! I don't know what people want from me. I'm really, really making the effort to be a good leader."

"I understand that. But Thanksgiving is a few days away. We've got the Asia cooking class, then Christmas, and then it's pretty much time for externship. I think you have a bunch of people who are just a little burned out and they just want to get through it. I know I'm feeling burned out. All you can do—all you really should do—is just try to make sure people communicate if they need help. But otherwise . . . most of these cats are just delirious with ego and hormones anyway, and unless you're a faculty member, I'm not sure they're going to recognize you as an authority figure."

"I have more experience. That's all I'm trying to do: pass it on."

"Yes, and I have no problem with that. I'll take whatever guidance I can get. Not everyone is like that, though. Just keep that in mind."

I LOOKED AT THE syllabus one afternoon and saw that two days later, Sean and I were partnered up to make roasted ducks in a port-raspberry sauce. When I read this, I stood upright. I remembered being apoplectic when I'd eaten this duck months ago, gnawing at the dried and nasty flesh, declaiming that the duck had died in vain.

On duck day, I arrived early. The night before, I'd made a meticulous list of all the necessary ingredients for the duck, the port-wine sauce, scalloped potatoes, roasted carrots, and broccoli. I gathered every ingredient and all the pans I thought I'd need. I cranked up the convection oven to 475. I got out the duck stock that two students had made the night before.

Sean was late—forty minutes late. I was pissed, but as far as I was concerned, my only true partner was the spirit of the departed duck.

"Hi," he said. I didn't answer. He shuffled. Then cleared his throat. "Okay, then. I'll start on the duck. Do you want to get the potatoes peeled?"

I leaped in front of him. "No. No. No. I'm doing the duck. No one else is touching it. I'm sorry. I know that sounded bad. But this is personal."

He just stared at me, utterly perplexed. From behind him, Lombardi said, "It's probably better not to get between Jonathan and those ducks."

"All right . . . how about I start the sauce, then?"

"No," I said right away. "The sauce is part of the duck."

There was a lengthy silence.

"Right. Yeah. Okay. Ummm . . . why don't I start peeling and cutting up the carrots? Those aren't part of the duck, correct?"

"That's true," I conceded.

"And the potatoes? Is it okay if I touch those?"

"Yes. Yes, that would be acceptable." He walked away. I addressed myself to the ducks. I arranged them on racks in two giant roasting pans. I patted the skin and the cavity dry. I ran my fingers over the chilled skin. I laid my palm on one of them. I started massaging the bird.

A voice to my left asked, "What are you doing, Grandpa?" It was Dan. I felt a sudden sort of disgrace, like I'd been caught leaving the bathroom without washing my hands or something. "Uhhh . . . ," I started to say. "Well, I guess I'm massaging the bird." I took my hand away.

"Of course you are. Hey, why don't you come back to Earth? Come rejoin us." He walked off. I felt too embarrassed to continue massaging. I seasoned the birds instead. When the oven reached the right temperature, I opened the doors and put the birds in. I watched for a few seconds through the door glass. Then I went ahead with preparations for the sauce.

The sauce started out as two gallons of stock. It would need to be reduced to a couple of quarts. I got it boiling away. I kept veering between the oven and the pot, back and forth, constantly monitoring. I'd watched Sean fabricate the carrots and get the potatoes put together and under the heat. I saw him at the stove with a small pan and some raspberries, which were part of the sauce.

"What are you doing?" I asked as casually as I could.

"Chef Sartory told me to make a gastrique and add it to the sauce." He was boiling the raspberries in vinegar and sugar and reducing it all down to a syrupy consistency. This was messing with my goal of being the sole caretaker of the birds. But he was operating under orders. And I recognized I was getting a little out of hand with all this. I nodded and walked back to the ovens.

An hour after the birds were in, they had browned pretty nicely; the convection ovens cook things quickly. I called Sartory over and asked what he thought. He prodded and pressed the skin. I followed suit. He squeezed the meat on the leg. So did I. "Take 'em out of there," he said. And I did. The ducks began to rest.

I focused completely on the sauce, which wasn't reducing the way I wanted. I got the biggest rondeau in the kitchen and dumped the stock into it, with all its aromatics and now the gastrique, and turned the heat to high.

And after a little bit, that was done, too. I remembered reading in *The French Laundry Cookbook* how Thomas Keller instructed the staff to strain everything through a chinois fifteen or so times. If that was what was done at the French Laundry, then I'd do it here. The duck deserved no less. Each time I strained the sauce, the amount of sediment in the bottom of the chinois was lessening. On the sixth none was there. I swirled in butter. I picked up a spoon and tasted it. It was exquisite. I could have done shots of the stuff. Rich, with a hint of sour from the gastrique, and the flavor of raspberries throughout.

We carved the ducks, which had now rested for thirty minutes. The skin was crisp. My hand feeling weighty with trepidation, I pulled a large scrap of meat off the bones. I put it in my mouth. It was moist and tender. The potatoes and carrots came out. We plated the meals and served them. We sold out of the duck within about twelve minutes.

9

CHEF DAVID SMYTHE WAS running a couple minutes late, but it was an early Christmas in the hallway outside his Cusines of Asia kitchen. A hand truck sat weighted with ingredients for that day's cooking. Adam and Brookshire, Dan and Sean were buzzing around it like humming-birds, darting their hands in, pulling out packages of lily buds and dried mushrooms, four or five bottles of different soy sauces, a bag of Chinese long beans, a trio of various rice wines that looked like the real thing, covered with bright calligraphy and import stamps, not packaged under the familiar Kikkoman aegis.

It felt like a particularly good time of year to be a culinary student. Christmas was three weeks off, followed by a two-and-a-half-week break. In the interim, we'd be studying the fundamentals of Asian cuisine, with a few days each spent in China, Korea, Japan, Vietnam, Thailand, and India. The schedule had an edge of impossibility to it; every one of those countries had a long, complex, and well-developed cuisine—way more long and intricate than France or Italy or America—and the idea that two days here and two days there would be anything more than a dilettante's layover was absurd. But—and I'd used the analogy just recently with Nelly when we were talking about my three days with Sartory and the cooking of Mexico—this was learning a few chords from our scales, and it was up to us to figure out how to make rudimentary, then more advanced, music from it later on.

We each had different reasons why we were more excited for this class than we'd been for any other, except maybe Skills, when we first felt a stove's heat on our faces. Adam, for one, was obsessed with the happy meeting of French or American food with Asian food, though he refused to call it fusion because the word had connotations of badly imagined food pairings, like taco pizza or something. He idolized Jean-Georges Vongerichten (who was living out Adam's dream), had spent time in Thailand, Japan, and Vietnam, and saw these three weeks as an opportunity to let some seeds that had already been planted start germinating.

I myself suffered from a lot of misapprehensions about Asian cooking that I wanted to diffuse. I couldn't figure out why every one of my stir-fries tasted fundamentally the same, or why the wok I used at home didn't transform ingredients so they tasted like dishes in Chinese restaurants. I understood that adding lime leaves and coconut milk to a dish made it taste vaguely of Thailand, but very little beyond that. Once in a great while, I'd open one of the two Asian cookbooks I owned and make an attempt. But not often; I didn't have many of those ingredients on my shelf. To make the dish, I'd have to trek to Chinatown or Jackson Heights in Queens, drop a small pile of money, and then bring them back home, where the volume of new and unfamiliar ingredients felt intimidating. I'd learned enough so far at school to look back and know why: You didn't just toss ingredients together. You had to finesse them, build with them. You didn't mix flour and stock together, crank the heat under it until it got thick, and call it gravy. There were a lot of intricacies involved. I wanted to see those intricacies performed by expert hands. Plus, I loved korma. Any type of korma. No matter how bad, how greasy. When I paged through my recipe packet, I saw the dish on the menu during the Indian portion of the class and got really excited.

A few of the people in the group were still so young and unexposed to much beyond the small towns in Georgia and Texas and Florida where they'd grown up that this was truly an exotic new world, one that had nothing to do with the moo goo gai pans and lo meins on the standard green-and-red-printed take-out menus from strip mall restaurants.

And as for the three Asian students in the class—Sitti, Joe, and Yoon—I suspect they were cracking their knuckles and waiting to kick everyone's asses. Since Sitti was from Thailand, I resolved in advance to stick close by him, if possible, when Thai day arrived. He'd recently won a cooking competition in Manhattan for some of the Thai dishes he'd cooked at home. He never mentioned his win to any of us, but we'd heard about it through the rumor mill.

Outside the classroom kitchen, at a little past 1:45, Adam finally stood up from examining the contents of the bins on the cart and announced, "This is going to be a good way to end the year."

We were milling around, clapping one another on the shoulders in mute, male affection. We weren't clapping Tara on the shoulders. But the tensions that had been building in prior classes among all of us— the tensions of long days under pressure, the irritations with people's bad kitchen habits, their sloppinesses or shortcuts, reiterated day after day—none of them were there this afternoon.

I was in an especially good mood. Over the weekend I'd watched *It's a Wonderful Life,* and every time I watched it, I spent a few days afterward in love with life and humankind. I loved Christmas. It made me sentimental and sappy. I had also watched *Gimme Shelter* in honor of the anniversary of Altamont and had been singing Rolling Stones songs to myself ever since.

Smythe arrived, well over six feet tall and slender, and we followed him into the kitchen.

"Okay," he said, moving down a long bank of six worktables stretched end to end, walking back and forth and around, "your assignments are taped to the fridge. Find your assignment, find your partner, find some cutting boards, find some bains-marie. Get yourselves set up. Lecture in five minutes."

The worktables took up most of the room. Behind the tables, opposite from the door, was a squadron of huge, industrial-sized woks sitting over gas jets. A tandoor oven stood just beyond the woks. At the opposite end of the worktables sat a deep fryer and a steamer. We took it all in for a moment, then fell out to discover what we were doing and who we were doing it with. Brookshire and I were partners, and our assignment that day was to make a dish called "Aromatic Lamb Shoulder with Mushrooms."

Brookshire and I got ourselves set up side by side and were about to go digging for ingredients when Smythe started his lecture. He did a tour first—a quick demo on how to turn the woks on, where dry ingredients went, which refrigerator we'd use, all the minutiae. We were all shoulder-to-shoulder in a half circle around him. Then he said, "I know this is insane. I know that there is no way—not a chance in hell—to become literate in Chinese cooking in just a few days. Or Korean cooking. You guys"—he indicated Joe and Yoon, who were both Korean—"you guys have spent your whole lives becoming literate in Korean cooking and I bet there's still more you could learn." Joe and Yoon nodded. "But I propose this to you. Braising is braising the whole world over. Sautéing is sautéing by any other name. You cook green beans to the same point of perfection in China as you do in Provence. The flavors might be new, they might be unfamiliar, but not for long. I'm your guide here. I'll show you what you need to know."

Smythe continued. "You are not to use recipe sheets in this class. You can write down a few basic things on index cards—ingredients, some notations about method and technique, but you need to have this stuff internalized. If you follow a recipe blindly, you're never going to really get that recipe into your blood. You need to memorize it, envision it, see it in your head. Then you're going to be cooking. But not if you're doing cook-by-numbers. If you get flubbed up, if you lose where you are with your recipe, you can come up and look at the book up front. But keep in mind, I start removing points from your daily grade for each second you're standing there trying to figure out what you should already know.

"If you find yourself short of an ingredient, you have until two fifteen each day to put it on the supplemental order. After that, you're shit out of luck. And your grade will suffer for it. You need to be prepared and organized.

"I've heard from Chefs Coyac and Sartory that this is a particularly strong group. That there's a lot of talent here. I want to see it come out. I *need* to see it come out because we have so much to do and so, so little time."

He looked at his watch. I looked at mine. It was 2:15. Dinner was at six.

Smythe said, "Let's discuss China." He began with geography, breaking China apart into provinces, discussing which foods were indigenous to which province, foreign influences, the economics of each region. As he spoke, every word was echoed by the small cacophony of our pens scratching in our notebooks. He went on to talk about different dynasties, then about soy sauce, delineating each of the several types, the differences in character not only between those types, but between brands of the same type. He took the same tack with rice wines. Bean pastes. Different tofus, and how they're made, from the harvesting of the soybean through to the finished curd. It was 3:00 now. The intensity of the pen scratching was letting up. But Smythe wasn't. He was on to topography now, and how differing climates affected cuisine. From there to climate change, to the evolution of industry in China, to communism and Chairman Mao and some of his favorite dishes. Smythe took us to the influx of Chinese immigrants to California in the nineteenth century, of how what we know in America as Chinese food came to be and proliferate. It was 3:45. Pens and notebooks had been laid down some time ago.

"Well . . ." He trailed off. "I guess that's probably enough for now. Wow, I've talked for a while." I thought I saw a very faint trace of a grin flit across his mouth. "We have a little less time than we'd probably like, but hey . . . get cooking."

Almost everyone—Adam, Tara, Brookshire, Sean, and I—looked pissed off. On the first day, with this cooking so few of us had ever been immersed in, having to serve a steady stream of students in a few hours, we could have really used any extra minutes lost to his lecture; most of the chefs I'd had barely went on for forty-five minutes. We careened around the room, bumping into each other, not so gently nudging each other out of the way, groping through the dry storage and spice racks for ingredients, grabbing up vessels to hold them. Over at the pile of things from the cart, little violences were playing out. Yoon and Adam were after the same bag of scallions, the same cache of carrots and ginger. The bags were being pulled apart, the contents falling, the volume of voices edging up.

I was checking out one of the woks, and Smythe appeared next to me, reaching for a tool that hung on a hook on the wall. I thought about the twists, turns, loops, and free associating he'd just done for more than one hundred minutes. I don't know why I said it, but I remarked to him, "So I guess you're kind of the John Coltrane of lecturing chefs."

Smythe looked at me, expressionless, and said, "I prefer to think of myself as the Pharaoh Sanders of lecturing chefs." He plucked the tool from the wall and walked on.

By 5:00, the room was mayhem. Haste does make waste, and a lot of it: The surfaces of the worktables were covered with vegetable scraps, meat trimmings, spilled ground spices, and small puddles of soy sauce. The attempts at high-speed cooking we were all making saw us getting careless. Brookshire and I had split the labor so that he would sear the lamb, simmer it, and measure out the dry ingredients. I'd handle the vegetables. I quartered a couple pounds of mushrooms, with spastic hands that tried to move faster than they were able, and, when I went to sweep them into a bowl, I swept half of them onto the floor. No one noticed but Brookshire. He said softly, "Just pick them up." I moved on to mincing ginger—it was in ugly chunks when I was done, not close to a mince—and garlic, which didn't fare much better. I rough chopped cilantro and made stalks of celery into tiny cubes. The clock kept jumping forward toward six, and none of us could move fast enough.

Adam and Tara were hissing into each other's faces; across the room, near the spice rack, Dan and Yoon were bitter over who was going to use the last of the dried chiles. Around the room, other partners weren't talking to each other. Smythe was at his computer, sipping tea. We had a poor handle on the prep work, had only barely started cooking, and still had to set up all the equipment: get the soup warmer hot, get the deep fryer on, set out dishes, remove the tops of the two worktables closest to the door (they doubled as steam tables to keep the food warm during service). At six, there was a line at the door. Students kept poking their heads in to check our progress. Smythe was still at his computer, watching us, looking up at the clock, and shaking his head. Brookshire was setting our lamb into trays, spilling sauce all over. Other pans full of moo shu vegetables, braised cabbage, and dumplings arrived. The rice wasn't done yet. At 6:20, we started serving. Two people put rice on plates. Others of us stood with spoons over the lamb or vegetables or dumplings and ladled them out according to what was ordered. We took a long time doing this, too. The students who'd waited—and more than a few had walked away— looked angry and put-out. When the last ones got their food and left, we all stood still for a moment and looked at the mess.

"Twenty minutes late," Smythe remarked. "That's pretty bad. I've seen groups smaller than this one get the job done on time. And look at this place. I mean . . ." He trailed off and gestured. Around where the rice was, there were more grains on the table than in the pan. It looked as if it had snowed.

"Go eat. Be back in half an hour."

We filled our plates, then went to the cafeteria, where we all sat in silence, eating the food we'd made. It tasted pretty good, but we were all so shell-shocked from the rush and fumbling that no one seemed to enjoy it. I just wanted to go home for the night.

We got back into the kitchen and spent an hour and a half cleaning up. When we were finished, it was around 8:45. Smythe said, "This can't happen tomorrow. I know it was the first day, but you were all running around like little kids, pushing and grabbing and whining. Figure out how you guys are going to cooperate. Figure out how you're going to communicate better. What you did tonight wasn't A-, B-, or C-level work. It was D-level, F-level.

"And I have a little more I want to say about China."

Out in the parking lot, I turned the key in the ignition, and nothing happened. The lights had come on when I opened the door, so I knew it wasn't the battery. I turned the key again and pumped the gas and eventually a sputter morphed into a cough, then into a hack, and the engine turned over.

The moments I'd shared with Jimmy Stewart over the weekend, those two hours that injected me with so much goodwill, had taken a hit during class and evaporated completely when the truck hiccuped. I had to stop and admit to myself that actually, I was playing opossum with reality.

For the last week, Christmas carols had been on the radio—I'd really crank the volume when "Good King Wenceslas" came on—and people had already decorated their houses with lights and little statues of Santa and reindeer. If the truck not starting was anything other than just the cold, I'd need to get it looked at and I'd need to get it fixed. And this was an impossible thing, because I had no money whatsoever in the bank. I had exiled that fact from my mind through sheer will, but it was furloughed now.

The next day, Smythe's lecture took up only one hour. He discussed tea: green, white, and black; the caffeine levels of each one; how they were, in Indonesia and parts of India, picked by trained monkeys; how to brew the tea, on and on. It was like the day before: frantic note taking in the attempt to capture each piece of information, giving way to selectively recording only pieces of information, giving way to giving up. It was a torrent of information that jumped from context to context. But there was no denying that Smythe was a serious intellect.

Adam agreed with me when I commented on it later during prep time.

"But," I added, "I guess we're just being given *all* of that intellect."

We were a little better behaved that second night, but we still snapped at one another, got outlandishly angry that someone had maybe taken a little more ginger than required, still dropped things, and wasted things out of carelessness. We opened at 6:10 that night, cooking the exact same menu as the night before. We ate dinner and then cleaned up almost silently again.

When I got back to Saugerties, I found that Smythe had sent us all an e-mail. The subject line was "The Group Falls Down." It read:

Just a note that I have spent the last half hour closing the kitchen.

The stocks and items cooling in the back sink were still in there as I was closing the room. Their temperatures had not been monitored.

The sink was not clean, vegetables under the ice.

Steamer and steamer drip pan not clear of rice residue.

Dishes still in the warmer.

Catch pan under broiler not clean.

Reach-in doors and reach-in floors not clean.

No closing forms filled out (there are 2).

Why did I stay to clean up the mess?

Because my training is such that I could not leave the next shift with the mess, and my concern for the people I feed is such that I could not allow the food service facility I operate to fall into such shabby and careless condition.

I will point out that there are 2 stewards (team #6) each day. I am not sure why their training is not working. For example (another example): Why would they not point out the problems with so much bare-handed raw food contact all day? Isn't that the job?

Officers in the brigade have a responsibility to assure the safety of the operation.

That did not happen today. It was: careless, sloppy, unprofessional.

Team #6 does not earn a passing grade on this day for the above reasons.

No joke! You better take this much more seriously.

ADAM CALLED A GROUP meeting before class. He wanted to discuss the past two days and try to fix the problem. We all sat at tables in the empty cafeteria. The drink machine hummed and clicked in the background, and we could hear Sartory's class setting up for the day.

"Why were we able to get through Coyac's class—*Coyac*—and not fuck up like we're fucking up now? How did we get through Sartory's class, being as bad as we are in Smythe's class? What's the problem?"

"You want to know what the problem is?" Tara said, indignant. "We have no time. He talks, and talks, and talks, and talks, and we have no time to cook."

"I think Adam's aware," I said. "Obviously he is. He has no time either. I think what he's getting at is why we're such horrible slobs. And we shouldn't be fighting with each other. I know we all think we're a pain in each other's ass, but we still need to work together every night. And besides, it's Christmas. Peace in the kitchen, goodwill toward men."

"Yeah, exactly," Adam started, but Tara cut him off.

"I don't think you're a pain in the ass, Jonathan. I just think you're incredibly lazy."

"Excuse me?"

"I don't think I've ever seen you wash a dish. And it always seems to me that you have your partner doing the hard stuff while you sit back and watch."

Brookshire spoke up. "No. First off, I wouldn't take that if that were the case. Second, Jonathan pulls his own weight. And why would you say that here in front of everyone? If you were so concerned about it, why try and embarrass him right now? And me, too? Do you think I couldn't handle the situation if it were true?"

Carlos yelled out, "Can we stop talking about how lazy Jonathan is and talk about why we suck?"

Tara said, "I think the two are connected. Mike—have you ever seen Jonathan wash a dish?"

Brookshire thought for a second. "Actually, Jonathan, I haven't ever seen you do a dish."

In one sense they were right. I rarely did dishes. But the reason is, there were always three people at the dish sink. One person who scrubbed and passed it off to his or her right, where the next person rinsed it, and then passed it to a third, who dunked it in sanitizing solution and then put it away. Because of the volume of dishes, people invariably did a half-assed job. The dishes were always greasy and flecked with pieces of food. Every pan in every kitchen was afflicted with that same sheen of grease. When I was in Perillo's Skills class, I had done dishes, but I'd done them meticulously because the grease disgusted me. So it took me longer. I remember Dan, who was rinsing, getting angrier and angrier about my pace, and Carlos, getting impatient too. Finally, they kicked me out and took over. It happened the next time I did dishes too, and then one more time before I decided I'd dedicate myself to sweeping and mopping the floors and scrubbing down the worktable surfaces.

Gio said, "Who cares if he does dishes or not? Everyone here contributes. And when he was my partner, he was great."

I still hadn't said anything.

Adam tried to get things back into order. "Jonathan isn't the cause of the problem. And if he didn't work, as group leader, I'd make it my business to say something. And I haven't needed to."

Tara said, "I think we really need to talk about this group leader thing. I did not elect to put you in charge. You are not my chef." I heard something that sounded like assent from a couple of people.

I stood up. Class was in forty-five minutes. I was tired of this; every single one of these meetings went exactly the same way. "I'm going to the bathroom for about forty-five minutes," I announced. Adam looked at me, anger and what seemed to me like betrayal veiling his face. I stopped at his shoulder and leaned in toward his ear. "This is bullshit," I said. "You and I can talk later."

We didn't, really. When I showed up for the beginning of class, Adam quietly asked me, "You okay?"

"Fine," I said. "You?"

"I guess."

"I think you should start practicing for your final," Smythe said. He'd laid out trays full of ingredients: fish sauces, black bean sauce, bean paste, different soy sauces, different sesame oils, tamarind, rice wines. "Start tasting, start memorizing. On your final, I'll be asking you to identify everything on this table by taste."

We moved dutifully around the table, filling small plastic cups with things from the trays and tasting them. It was interesting; you could recognize experiencing the essence of, say, the black bean paste in a finished dish, understanding how it helped make something delicious—even if it was overpowering on its own. The fish sauces were almost nauseating. Everyone—myself, Sitti, Adam, Joe—all made a face of distaste. I guessed when it came to an entrée, this stuff was like salt: You didn't want to taste it, you just needed it in there.

It was the fifth day, the Korean menu. Joe and Yoon moved through class with supreme confidence. It occurred to me, as Brookshire and I were preparing Ginseng Chicken, that I had eaten Korean food once in my life, when I lived in Woodside, Queens, right after moving to New York City. My grandfather was in town and one of his business associates took us out to dinner at a Korean barbecue restaurant right by my apartment. We all had barbecued pork and beef for dinner, lacquered with soy and sugar. How could it not be delicious? But otherwise, I had no experience with this food at all.

As Brookshire and I did prep, washing fresh ginseng, soaking jujubes, mincing shallots, Joe and Yoon called out to each other in Korean, looking around at all of us and laughing. I felt like they were mocking us, and me in particular. After the meeting, which I refused to think much about, my paranoia was slightly piqued.

They were, I decided, in actuality, probably remembering some nightspot in Seoul they'd been to.

Brookshire and I finished a minute or so ahead of schedule. The chicken had braised in water, garlic, dates, and the ginseng. After the meat was cooked, we seasoned the broth, and brushed a glaze of soy sauce, rice vinegar, and sesame oil over the bird. When an order was called, we'd be putting the chicken in a bowl and serving it with broth.

"Hey," I asked Brookshire. "Did you taste this?"

"No. Did you?"

"No. We should probably do that." We tasted the dish. Then we paused.

"It tastes good," Brookshire said.

"Yeah," I agreed. "But is this how it's supposed to be?"

"How wrong could we go?"

"Probably not very wrong. But still—is this how it tastes in the mother country?"

"Ask Smythe."

"Okay. I will." I called over to Smythe and asked if he could come taste the dish. He got up from his computer and came over.

"It looks good," he said. He turned and went back to his desk. Brookshire and I looked at each other.

"Hey, Joe," I called out. "Can you taste this for us?"

Joe came over and tasted the chicken. "It's good," he said.

"Does it taste authentic?"

"Authentic." He repeated the word a couple of times. "Shit if I know. It's chicken. It's been poached. I like it; it's fucking good."

On day seven, Smythe was at my shoulder watching me make miso soup. I was doing the ichiban dashi—the primary broth for the soup. I had a sheet of kombu, or kelp, in front of me.

"No, don't rip it," he said, putting his hands on mine to keep them from ripping the seaweed. "It makes it gooey if you don't cut it with scissors or a knife, and that's no good. Call me when you're about to mix everything."

I put kombu and dried bonito flakes into a pan with cold water. I heated it up, and, just before it boiled, pulled it from the heat. I strained it, and started mixing miso paste in. I was just about to add scallions and cubes of tofu. I called out, "Chef Smythe, I'm set."

He didn't look up. "You're doing fine."

It occurred to me that I hadn't really witnessed him tasting anything—of mine or anybody's.

I'D NEVER BEEN A big fan of really spicy food, because after a dose of heat, it seemed you stopped tasting anything but the tingle and burn on the tongue. Almost everything we did in the Asia kitchen bore a heavy measure of hot pepper. My midsection was in an uproar, but I wasn't able to figure out what was on account of peppers and what was on account of money.

Brookshire and I made roasted spareribs on day nine, and I had the extra assignment of doing vegetable crepes. It was Vietnam night. I toasted a cup of mung beans in a skillet and soaked them for an hour. I got coconut milk, rice flour, some water, and turmeric and mixed them together, and then added the beans. I pureed it into a batter, and got some of the black steel pans used for making this dish that Smythe kept under lock by his desk. I heated the pan until it was almost smoking. Yoon was next to me frying spring rolls, and a sheen of grease kept forming on my face. I added oil to the pan and ladled some of the batter in. It did what it was supposed to: It bubbled up in the center and the edges turned brown. I used a spatula to flip it, but the crepe stuck to the bottom and tore. After a few more seconds, the batter had toasted, then burned, and I upended it into the trash. Streaks of the burned batter still covered the bottom of the pan, so I scraped them out and tried again. The same thing happened. I tried another pan. The same thing. Another attempt, another mess. I tried once more. *The definition of insanity, I remembered reading, is doing the same thing over and over and expecting a different result.* I called out for Smythe. He came over to me.

"What's the problem?"

"They're sticking. I've tried five times." A trickle of sweat ran down my back. Service was about twenty minutes off.

"Well, the problem is, these pans aren't seasoned." He was picking at the crust on the bottom with his fingernail. "Okay, well, here's how you season a pan. Heat it up. Keep it heating. See how it's smoking? Okay, now we want to rub some oil into it. Now, wait for it. Wait for it. Okay—it's smoking again. Rub in more oil. We want to keep doing this for a while."

So we kept doing it for a while. Ten minutes. Fifteen. Twenty. He stood there with me at his elbow seasoning the pans.

Service started and had been going for ten minutes. He was still with me, seasoning. Finally, he asked for the batter. He poured it in, waited until it bubbled, then went to flip it. It stuck and tore and began to burn.

"Shit," he said mildly. He tried with the other pan. Same thing. "Dammit." He pushed the pans off the burners. "Did you rest your batter?"

"For a few minutes, I guess. But not for all that long."

"It might be the batter," he said. "But these pans really need more seasoning. But it's past 6:00 now. Well, no crepes tonight." He walked away. Maybe it *was* the batter. It didn't matter, though; I had nothing to do now during service. I went over to the sink and washed some dishes.

Later, I walked by his desk and saw his clipboard out. It had our daily grading sheet on it. I saw something marked next to my name and—though it was hard to decipher his handwriting—saw the words "bad" and "burnt crepes." I was getting marked down for that whole thing. I felt a dull hysteria rise up shrieking from my gut. I breathed in and out for a few seconds.

After we were done cleaning, we had a lecture. It started off at 8:30 p.m. about Vietnam and colonialism, covering the war through the fall of Saigon, then the rise of the Khmer Rouge in neighboring Cambodia, but through some miraculous stream-of-conscious improvisation, had, at 9:50, veered into the world of hotel management. Smythe was waxing about the price of towels, then about linens. He had been on about napkins for a few minutes and he lost my attention. I wasn't sure how many more tanks of gas I had left in the bank account, and Christmas was just a week away. A pain right below my eye, near my sinus, began to pulse. I really needed money. I had no writing prospects on the horizon. I had just taken a hit on something that I had no idea how to fix. I wondered if I could have done something different. I wondered how many points I was losing. I heard the word "napkin" again. My jaw was clenched tight enough to hurt.

———

FATE SOMETIMES PATS YOUR head: The next morning, when I checked my e-mail, I was offered a big freelance writing job. It would cover some expenses for a couple of months. It did, however, mean taking a little time off from school. Because the CIA schedule was broken into three-week chunks, it wasn't difficult to take a break here and there, and many people did. But it also meant that, if I took more than one three-week block, I would be assigned to a different group when I came back. I spent the morning walking through the house and thinking. I texted Adam and asked him to meet me about an hour before class and he agreed.

He was at a table in the cafeteria when I arrived, eating black bean soup from the Americas kitchen. After I sat down, he scraped the bottom of the cup, licked his spoon, and pushed them away.

"Hey there, fuzzy britches," he said. "Feeling better today?"

I told him about the money drought. Then I told him about the writing job.

"Oh, man," he said. "I think I see where this is going. How much time are you going to take? Are you going to be in Quantity Foods with us in January?"

"I think two blocks. When I come back from externship, wherever the hell that's going to be, I'll have to take the Quantity Foods course before I can keep going. So . . . me . . . this group . . ."

"Shit. Really? Shit. I had one ally."

"With these guys it might be a lost cause. I've never read Sun Tzu, but if I had, I bet there's an appropriate quote."

Fate gave me one more little pat on the head: My assignment for the last two days was to cook korma.

The first night I cooked the korma was an experiment, noting problems that cropped up and then noting how to fix them. I hadn't used the woks much during the Asia class and didn't comprehend how powerful the gas jets were, burning the hell out of my onions within a few seconds. The cashew nuts, which were supposed to be soaked, then ground into a paste, needed to soak longer. The recipe called for fifteen chopped Thai Bird chiles, but upon tasting, my tongue and throat felt seared. I wrote on my recipe card that three would probably do the job.

We took our final that night, tasting all the same bean pastes, fish sauces, and soy sauces we'd been training ourselves to recognize for the last two weeks. It was easy.

Smythe gave his final lecture that night, a review of trade routes, wars, colonialism, and commerce that tied all the countries we'd looked at together. He gave an extensive history of Indian vegetarianism that led to a discourse on how the real money in restaurants came not through big savings but by saving a few pennies here and there so they added up. He talked about the capsaicin contents of different peppers. Then he sent us home.

The final night was an anticlimax. It was the last class before Christmas break, and very few students came in to eat. We served maybe ten of them all night. Which was a shame, I thought, because my korma had come out really well. I'd heated the water for the cashews and simmered them for a few minutes, leaving them to soak for a good hour. I monitored the temperature of the wok really carefully so the onions turned translucent and golden, not brown. I cooked the ground cumin, cardamom, coriander, and fennel in oil until they were fragrant. I simmered the lamb at a low temperature for an hour and a half, twice the time the recipe indicated. I seasoned, tasted, and reseasoned at a dozen different points. The result was terrific. At least, I thought so. At dinner, Gio and I were the only ones who had some. After dinner, Smythe told us that since it was Christmas break, all the food needed to be tossed and we could take home what we wanted. I packed up a good bit of the korma into a take-out container and decided to give it to Nelly's parents, whose house I passed on the drive home.

Smythe called us one by one up to his desk. He was giving us our grades for the course. When it was my turn, I steeled myself. Given the e-mail he sent out on our second night, and the episode with the crepe batter, and given that, as far as I could ascertain, he'd never tasted anything I made (and I wondered: "Did what I do *look* so bad that he couldn't bring himself to try it?"), I was expecting a poor showing—C, maybe, or a C–. I stood next to him at his stool, looking at the computer screen.

"You did a good job this block. You did really well on the final, you kept yourself organized, I noticed that you and your partner each cooked the same dishes over and over and you seemed to be very interested in refining them. Here's your grade."

I craned in to see the last number on the spreadsheet: 91. An A–.

"Good luck, and I'll see you around," he said. He shook my hand and called up the next student.

At the end of class, we all clustered in the hallway outside the kitchen door. I wished everyone a happy holiday, then got in the car and drove off. With a couple of exceptions, it would be the last time I saw any of them again.

I FINISHED THE WRITING assignment, and I got paid. I wrote checks for rent, checks for utilities. I paid back money I borrowed to buy some Christmas gifts. I'd taken six weeks off already—two blocks—and to do the job, I'd need one more block. I called the CIA registrar's office and explained what was going on. They were sympathetic. But I knew I needed to get an externship soon, or it would affect my GPA. And I'd have to return to school to take my cooking practical—a sort of midterm for the entire degree—before I could start the externship, and to take the practical you needed to be enrolled in a class. They suggested that I come back and take my Garde-Manger class and the cooking practical after those three weeks were up.

Garde-Manger wasn't an easy class, but it didn't have the pressure of a daily production schedule. You learned how to make sausages and terrines. You played with foie gras. You learned to smoke salmon and cure whole legs of pork to make prosciutto. You learned to compose classical hors d'oeuvre plates and make more contemporary hot appetizers. Most of this stuff took time; a terrine was a two-day process, and the sausage recipes took three or four days. The prosciutto took more than a year; the ham we prepared now would be eaten by some other students in fifty-two weeks' time.

John Kowalski, an alumnus of the class of 1977, ran the morning Garde-Manger kitchen. He was a stout guy with a mustache, and he smiled constantly, always affable and warm. Unless you asked the wrong question. If you couldn't figure out how to put the meat grinder together, or if you needed some help lining a terrine mold, or you weren't sure how to affix casings to the spout of a sausage machine so they didn't tear, he was right by your side with a detailed explanation and demonstration. But if the answer to your question could be found in your recipe or the Garde-Manger textbook, or if it was something he'd covered during lecture, his voice rose with irritation.

He played music during most of the class over speakers on his computer, always the Dead, the Stones, or Dylan.

I liked my cooking partner, a woman named Liz. She was around nineteen years old, with long, straight, sandy brown hair and blue eyes. She played at being tough and callous; she loved extreme heavy metal and quizzed me constantly on bands I'd seen: Napalm Death, Godflesh, Pain Killer, Slayer. She had what she called "a pilot" of a television show on YouTube, in which she made Black Metal Cookies. Mainly this meant a camera was on Liz as she mixed a standard cookie recipe in her home kitchen to a soundtrack of Norwegian Black Metal, banging her head and throwing the devil's horn sign. I thought it was so cool, I e-mailed the link to almost everyone I knew and watched it a dozen times.

Even though the class began at 7:00 a.m., which meant another round of getting up way too early to make the hour commute from Saugerties in the chill of early March, it was an almost idyllic place to be with the music playing and the relaxed pace. Garde-Manger put a premium on refinement rather than speed, and it was a nice change to be able to concentrate on finessing a dish without a deadline.

But the phantom of the cooking practical was hovering like a threat.

It's ritual, a rite of passage. And difficult. You walk into a special kitchen constructed for just the purpose of the test and draw one of six menus out of a metaphorical hat. You know exactly which dishes make up each menu, but you don't know anything else. You'll need to make a soup, a protein, two vegetables, and a starch. Since you don't know what you'll get, you need to know six soups, six proteins, six starches, and twelve vegetables down pat. You've got two and a half hours to make the meal happen. You're watched and graded at every step of the way. You need to score above a 65. Failure happens, though, even to perfectly good cooks. If you blow it once, you pay $150 and take it again. If you blow it a second time, you pony up $150 more and take it again. If you fail it three times, you're screwed; you get an automatic fifteen-week suspension—but that's probably the least of your problems. This is basic stuff. Can you roast a chicken? Can you deep poach a piece of salmon? Can you make a good beef stew? Each menu component is something you've done a few times before in the Skills II and III classes, and you've presumably had some success with them. As an added bonus, you have to pass an oral exam given a few minutes before the test too. All this is why I never thought ill of people who fail it the first time around, or who scrape by with an insanely low score. Sometimes you simply have a bad day, and sometimes that bad day is when you're taking your practical.

There were all sorts of stories about the practical, some of them true, some of them CIA lore. The stories about people breaking down in tears and leaving the kitchen midtest were true. The story about someone once fainting was pretty possibly true; I couldn't get it definitively confirmed or denied—the instructors at school, all of whom took turns proctoring the test, seemed to enjoy keeping the rumors alive. The stories about people pissing themselves because of nerves were probably not true.

Failure almost always came down to poor organization. To prepare yourself, you needed to write down all the recipes—every one—leaving nothing out; it's too easy if you're in a rush to forget some crucial ingredient or vital technique. It was recommended in the strongest terms that you create a detailed timeline for each one of the menus, listing which tasks needed to be done and by when. You were also given a study guide for the oral component. It had about a hundred questions on it that you might be asked, like: name five of the most popular seasonings in Chinese cooking; describe how to prepare sauce piquante; list five differences between sautéing and panfrying; what are the five basic color pigments and how does the presence of acid or alkaline affect their colors and textures during cooking?

I had been scheduled to take my practical on the second-to-last day of Garde-Manger, so I used extra time during the week to study. And get nervous.

Liz was scheduled to take it two days before me, in the afternoon, after class. The next morning after she'd gone, Liz stood unpacking her knives and tools when I came to our station.

"How'd it go?" I asked.

"Shut up."

"No, seriously—how'd it go?"

"Seriously—shut the fuck up."

I changed the subject. Later, I asked around: Liz had failed. She hadn't told anyone why, and no one knew. She'd have to take it again a couple of weeks later. Liz was a solid cook, and I thought this was a chilly omen.

The night before my practical I stayed up until almost 1:00 getting my menus in order and going over and over the oral questions. I was up four hours later for class. I was incredibly nervous for the entire day.

At 2:00 in the afternoon, I arrived at the practical kitchen, along with the five others who'd be taking the test that day. I knew three of them from class. The kitchen was pretty small: a few equipment racks, a pair of refrigerators, shelves of ingredients and sanitation supplies, and six workspaces with six burners each and a small, reach-in fridge (a.k.a., a lowboy) below them. There were no sinks at any of the stations. Each work area was segmented from the others with a blue-tiled barricade.

I was prepared for every and all contingencies: I had all the possible recipes written out, a timeline for each of the possible menus, "shop-

ping lists" with all the possible ingredients. My stack of index cards
was about an inch thick.

I was very much hoping I would not have to make hollandaise, one
of my least favorite things to do. And if I could avoid making salmon—
one of my most hated foods—I'd feel okay about it.

The start times were staggered by fifteen, twenty minutes or so. If
you're the last to go, you would have been waiting for nearly two hours
before being allowed to start cooking.

We were given a tour for thirty minutes, and then loosed to go
exploring, just to see where everything was. The instructor, Joseba
Encabo, a gentle-seeming Spaniard with a soft voice and an occasionally impenetrable accent, called the first student over. It wasn't me. But
as I walked by I caught a glimpse of his clipboard and noticed my name
was last. I felt unsteady on my feet from exhaustion and suspected this
would be a long, long afternoon. I wasn't able to tell what the menu
would be, but as the time passed and the others began cooking—one
person got the roast chicken with mashed potatoes, gravy, and consommé, another (mercifully) got the salmon and hollandaise, also with
a consommé—the possibilities got narrower.

An hour passed. I spent that time walking through and observing
at a distance, from time to time bumping into Encabo, who was doing
the same thing. He'd stop, watch from over someone's shoulder, staring at a pile of scraps or dirty utensils or pans. He'd watch how they
stirred, how well they seared a piece of meat, and then make a mark
on a paper on his clipboard.

The next-to-last person was called, a young woman I'd never seen
before but whom others seemed to know. She did not appear to be a
favorite of any of them. They muttered about her being incompetent
and unpleasant. Apparently, this was her third time taking the test.
She was assigned a shallow-poached fillet of fish. This meant that I
knew exactly what my menu would be: beef stew, mashed potatoes,
sautéed green beans, blanched root vegetables, and a beef consommé. I
had never had much trouble with consommé—it always just seemed to
work for me—but I'd witnessed others make a mess with it.

"Hey, Jonathan," I heard. "Come here a minute, please." Encabo told me he was making a switch. "Forget the consommé," he said. "Do a cream of cauliflower soup instead."

Then he started asking me questions, each one worth a few points: "What are the five mother sauces?"

"Velouté, béchamel, tomato, espagnole, and hollandaise," I said.

"Good. And can you tell me what an emulsion is?"

I was anxious to get cooking and found my mind suddenly slippery. "Uhhh . . . when oil and a liquid are forced to coexist."

"What does that mean, 'coexist'?"

Words failed me. "When the oil molecules are forced to bond with the other molecules . . ." I was interlocking my fingers to illustrate this.

"But what holds them together?"

God? Destiny? "Uhhhh . . . another medium? Something in which the two incompatible molecules are suspended?"

"Maybe you mean a 'stabilizer'?"

"That's exactly what I mean," I said with confidence.

"And how is an emulsion formed?"

"You . . . you . . ." I put my hands to work for demonstration purposes. "You beat the hell out of it." I whipped my hands around. I was seriously tired.

He looked like he was pondering the nuances of the word "hell." "Okay," he said after a moment.

Thus it went for a while. He gave me a 100 on this part of the test. And I was given the go-ahead to start cooking.

I immediately preheated the oven to 375.

There were a few ingredients stowed in the lowboy: some cubed beef, green beans, a turnip. That was about it. I looked at my menu cards—stew, vegetables, potatoes, consommé—and then rocketed over to the storage fridge and commenced scavenging: small carrots for the root vegetables, a rutabaga, a whole lot of butter, red wine, and ingredients for the consommé: ground chicken (there was no ground beef), eggs, a few plum tomatoes, and so on. I grabbed potatoes to mash. There would be other things I'd need, but I could get them later on.

About ten minutes had passed.

Beef stew and soup both take a while. The soup could just sit on a back burner, so I figured I'd start it first. I started making the raft for the consommé: a rough chop of the onions, cutting up the tomatoes, separating the eggs. I beat the eggs and folded the other ingredients in. I went back to the fridge to get some stock. And it occurred to me that I had just made my first error.

"Forget the consommé," Encabo had said. "Do a cream of cauliflower soup instead."

Fifteen minutes had passed. Fifteen minutes had just been squandered. Nothing I'd prepped for the consommé could be salvaged for anything else. I toyed with the idea of just going ahead and making a consommé, but decided that could backfire. It hurt, but I tossed the ingredients.

Five students had gone prior. The pots and pans at the dish sink had piled into a small Everest. I would need a few of them, because there weren't that many left on the shelf. One of the first people to go had finished and was beginning work on the pile. I told him which ones I needed and he said he'd take care of me.

I then made my second big mistake, the one that would truly come back to bite me on the ass. I didn't get that at the time, though.

The base of a cream soup—broccoli, cauliflower, mushroom, whatever—is velouté, a sauce made of a roux and a stock. I had noticed that there was no espagnole sauce in the storage fridge. Espagnole sauce is a crucial component of the CIA's beef stew recipe. It is something of a pain in the ass to make if you're in a hurry. I was starting to be in a hurry. You need mirepoix, tomato paste, a brown roux, and stock. I'd deal with it in a minute, after I got the velouté going.

I looked at the clock and, man, a lot of time had passed. I started making a roux, enough for the velouté, working on a higher heat than I really should have. But I got it done, and added the stock bit by bit. I felt I was regaining that time. I let the sauce simmer.

I cranked the heat under a large sauteuse, poured in the oil, and started browning the beef. As it browned, I worked on mirepoix for the espagnole, and skimmed the velouté. Once the meat was done, I deglazed with the red wine, poured in the stock, added a bay leaf, brought it to a boil, and put it in the oven. I'd gotten the time back. One hour, forty minutes to go—more than enough, way more—to finish everything else.

I cooked the mirepoix until it caramelized. I spooned in the tomato paste and let it turn a nice, rusty red. I added the stock, pushed it to the back burner, and let it simmer. The espagnole was under control. I started boiling water for the cauliflower, cut it up, blanched it, shocked it, and set it aside. I did the same with the green beans in another pot. I fabricated the vegetables. I was in great shape again. For a few minutes I just stood and watched things steam and bubble, entranced by all the alchemy I'd just worked. I went to skim the espagnole and noticed there wasn't much flour rising to the top. I skimmed the velouté. I got the blender and made the cream soup. It was really good. One hour and ten minutes to go. I thought it was strange that there was still nothing to skim on the espagnole, but not strange enough to keep me from pouring it in with the already-simmering stew. I'd skim it later. An hour to go. I'd mash the potatoes last minute. I had the beans and the root vegetables set for a quick stay over the heat with some butter, salt, and pepper.

The dish sink was still mounded, and there was no place to take my dirty dishes. I tried to neaten the dirty pans at my own station as best I could. I wiped down what I could around the stove. Leaving the mess was mistake number three.

With forty minutes to go, I checked on my stew. I pulled it out and pulled the top from the pot. It looked watery. I tasted it. It tasted thin and almost acidic. Something had gone amiss.

It hit me just then: I had never gotten around to making the roux for the espagnole. I'd just forgotten. This was the root—the bedrock—of the problem. There was a significant paucity of flavor and texture to the stew. The forty minutes suddenly seemed very short.

I could make a roux, I thought, and get at least a twenty-minute simmer, maybe a few minutes more. I turned the heat to high under a pan, added some oil, and went off to get more flour. The flour went into the pan, and I whisked it into the oil. I should have done it in increments. I also should have paid more attention and not turned my back to deal with the potatoes, because it took just a few moments for the roux to burn beyond salvaging. As I tossed it out, I realized too that Encabo had been watching me for the past ninety minutes. I had no idea what he'd seen.

I looked over at him and he was looking back at me. I might have just imagined it, but I think I saw him—very slightly—shake his head in a sort of rebuke. Something unpleasant bloomed in my stomach.

I needed the quickest possible fix here. When Encabo was busy evaluating one of the students who'd just finished, I dashed to the fridge and the dry storage. I took a bottle of balsamic vinegar, a bottle of soy sauce, a rind of Parmesan, and some cornstarch. I put a good shot of balsamic into the stew, followed by a few dashes of soy sauce, and then the rind. Soy and Parmesan add depth of flavor—what the Japanese have dubbed umami—and I thought I'd get some sweetness from the balsamic. I left it on the stovetop and brought it to almost a boil. The meat was not going to be that tender, but . . .

I got the potatoes in the boiling water. I was really pushing it, timewise

I made a slurry of cornstarch and water, and, with fifteen minutes to go, added it to the stew. It thickened immediately. It still tasted off. I dumped in an immense spoonful of butter. It tasted passable.

Ten minutes to go. I speared a fork into one of the potato quarters and it felt done. I dumped them into a colander, put them into a food mill and started turning. That solitary potato piece was the only one of its brethren that had fully cooked. I scraped off the usable parts of the other potatoes and found I had about a serving's worth. I turned the mill again, with great vigor, and squeezed another quarter portion out.

I mixed in the hot cream and the softened butter. I seasoned the potatoes and realized I simply did not have enough for the two servings I was supposed to present for evaluation. I eyed the cream of cauliflower soup, pondered my situation, and dumped a large ladleful of the soup into my potatoes. I mixed quickly, tasted—actually, they were fairly tasty—and put them into a pastry bag. I piped them onto the plate in one of the silly curlicue designs the CIA seems to like.

It was just about time to be evaluated.

I plated the stew, one small serving on each of two plates. I cranked the heat under the root vegetables and then under the green beans. When I saw there was some activity, I plated those, too. I carried two cups of soup to a surface near the evaluation table. I had put the plates into the oven to heat up, and I took a side towel, grabbed the side of it, and carried the food over to Encabo's desk. I was thirty seconds early and I took slow, shuffling steps. When I reached the instructor, he was still evaluating the young woman who'd cooked right before me. The thirty seconds passed. Then thirty more passed. Then a minute, and then another.

I wasn't quite close enough to hear what was being said, but the woman did most of the talking. As she spoke, she gestured a lot with her hands and kept worrying her fingers.

I had been waiting for four minutes at this point, and she showed no signs of stopping. I could tell my food was cooling. Now I was pissed.

And she kept going. It became obvious she was arguing with Encabo. He bore an expression of solid patience, an almost kind look, and made no effort to cut her off.

I started tapping my foot. Then I shifted my weight from one foot to the other. I kept putting my plate down and picking it back up. I slapped a stuttering rhythm against my leg. I cracked my knuckles. Six minutes late now. I had a sudden vision of upturning my food over her head.

Encabo turned and looked at me. We made eye contact and he held it. The woman turned to follow his line of sight and I saw that her eyes were red and watery.

She'd failed. This was her third time.

Everyone else who had finished was at work cleaning the kitchen.

Abruptly, the young woman stood, turned, and walked with quick steps over to the kitchen door. She gathered her stuff and walked out.

Encabo watched her leave, then motioned me over. I sat and slid his plate toward him.

"My food's cold," I said.

"Yes, I've kept you waiting. My apologies. It couldn't be helped. I know you were ready, so no penalty. Now," he said, reaching for clean utensils, "let's see what we have here."

He took a bit of the stew. He chewed for a moment and looked up at me. He smiled, but it seemed rueful. He took a bite of the potatoes, then another. He nodded to himself. He took one forkful each of the root vegetables and the green beans. He tasted the soup. Then he pushed his plate away.

"So, Jonathan." He leaned back and crossed his arms behind his head. He still seemed kind, almost friendly, but I was beginning to detect a slight hue of pity to his bearing. "What happened here tonight? I watched you at the beginning of the test and you were so efficient. I thought for sure you would ace this. But something . . . something went bad, no?"

"Yes." He waited for more, but I couldn't think of any way to elaborate.

"Well," he said, finally. "What went bad?"

"I . . . I . . . I burned something. I had to start it over and I never got the time back."

"Yes, you burned your roux." Shit. He had seen that. "Also, your station looks like a pigsty. Why didn't you take your dishes to the sink instead of just leaving them?"

"There was no room."

"Then why didn't you put them on someone else's station? Someone who was done? No room? What kind of answer is that? That's just silly. Come on."

He stared at me. I figured this was, in essence, a rhetorical question. I shrugged. He held the stare.

"All right then. Your stew is terrible. This is . . . it's . . . edible. That's about the best I can say and that's not saying very much. The meat isn't quite tender enough. Your braising liquid is thin, sour. This is not what I want to eat for dinner. Not at all. But I very much like your potatoes. Your vegetables are cooked perfectly. Really perfectly. But I cannot get past this stew. Edible. Passable, but that's it."

He tallied up my score and wrote it down on a piece of paper that he slid across the table to me. I looked. I had passed. Not by much of a margin, but I passed. I felt no sense of triumph, no sense of accomplishment. Every piece of me, every cell, felt flushed with mediocrity.

"Thanks," I said, and stood up. He shook his head.

"You have talent," he said. "But this was disappointing." He pushed his plate to me. "You have quite a mess to clean up. Get started."

I walked back to my station. One of the others came up to me. "How'd you do, Jonathan?" he asked.

"I passed."

"What did you get?"

"I'd rather not say. I passed, though."

"You pissed?"

I thought for a second. "Yeah, I'm pissed." I grabbed some dishes and started carrying them to the sink. "Not at him, though."

The next morning was the last in Garde-Manger. We emptied the refrigerators of our things, scrubbed them out, froze extra sausages, put terrines in storage, wiped down the room, and took our final. I found it difficult because I'd expended most of my recent time preparing for the practical. I couldn't remember, right then, the basic ingredients for a whitefish mousseline or the technique for putting it together. I couldn't recall the essential difference between nitrites and nitrates.

I was the first one done. Kowalski shook my hand and told me if I ever needed anything—any advice, a recommendation, a lesson on how to make guanciale at home—to get in touch. I was slightly sad that I wouldn't be there the next day listening to the Dead and grinding foie gras for a terrine. Actually, I wouldn't be back at school at all for a long time. I was way overdue with my externship; five points had already been automatically deducted from my externship grade by that afternoon. I really needed to land a gig.

10

FLOYD CARDOZ, THE EXECUTIVE chef and co-owner of Tabla, sat down across from me at a small round table, saying by way of apology for being twenty minutes late, "Sorry it took me so long. You wouldn't believe how many retards there are in the Holland Tunnel."

We sat underneath Tabla's grand, curving staircase in near darkness. It was mid-May. Sunlight shone through the windows facing Madison Park. A few servers flitted around the tables in the downstairs dining room, arranging napkins and silverware. Mosaic pieces covered the vaulted ceilings—representations of grains, fruits, animals—and a bit of Miles Davis's *On the Corner*—from the first side, when the sitar kicks in—played over the sound system. Tabla was, in essence, two separate restaurants. The ground floor housed the Bread Bar, the casual, street-food-inspired yin to the finer dining, tasting-menu yang of the upstairs. The Bread Bar's kitchen was tiny and open, occupying just a corner of the long curving bar area that took up one entire side of the dining room. Anyone sitting at the bar could observe all the cooking being done. I considered that was very likely a nerve-racking proposition.

"Why don't we get right to it," Cardoz said. He wore shorts, a polo shirt, and sandals. He didn't smile much; a look meshing worry and wariness clouded his eyes. He had a defensive posture, hunched over his arms, sitting back and turned slightly away from me. "Why do you want to do your externship at Tabla?"

In the Asia class, we played with spices. I'd never encountered many of them before—asafetida, fenugreek seeds, black cardamom—but each had a role in recipes for *bondas* or *dal sambar* or *massaman* curry that saw them teaming up with other ingredients to become a whole lot more than the individual parts. My interest was piqued then, too, but we'd never really learned how to use them with a confident hand. There was too little time. Tabla, I'd read, had a small room in its pantry devoted entirely to spices. They used dozens of them and spent thousands of dollars every month to keep the supply up. That was one reason I wanted to do my externship at Tabla, and I told this to Cardoz.

I'd studied their menus beforehand, seen the pictures of dishes on their website. Crab cakes on a round of Goan-spiced guacamole with chutney. Naan bread stuffed with house-cured bacon. A sandwich of lamb braised in yogurt, with turmeric mashed potatoes. This was idiosyncratic, vibrant food. It was familiar—we've all had crab cakes; we've all had lamb stew—but I was captivated by the twist on them, serving the crab with that guacamole, braising *anything* in yogurt. It seemed like fun food. That was another reason, and I told this to Cardoz too.

I really needed to land an externship. Per Se had blown me off—and in retrospect, I'm not even sure what I'd been thinking, given what and where my skills were at the time—Gramercy Tavern had said no, the Modern had said no. The guy from Grocery, in Brooklyn, had been such a prick on the phone that I never bothered to follow up. During my search, I had read an article Cardoz wrote for the *New York Times* about how he views Tabla as a teaching kitchen, a place to really train people, and that he sees the mistakes people make every day as a perfect opportunity to further that training. I'd never had serious experience, so I needed the training. The chances were pretty good that I'd fuck a lot of things up, so I needed the restaurant's patience. That was a third reason. I kept that one to myself.

But it was something very small that ultimately made me want to go to Tabla. I had Cardoz's cookbook—*One Spice, Two Spice*—on the shelf at home and the first time I leafed through it, I'd stopped on a recipe that called for a roux made from chickpea flour. I loved the idea. Tabla had an eye on tradition. But the roux was made from chickpeas. Tabla also bristled against strictures. In my mind, this was the best of two contiguous worlds. So that was the real reason I wanted to be there.

"You use a roux made from chickpea flour," I answered. "How could I not want in on that kind of thinking? I've spent a lot of time looking at your menu, and I really want to eat this food. So if I want to eat it, naturally I'm going to want to know how to make it. You said in that *Times* article that you've staffed the kitchen with your employees' education in mind. You worked with Gray Kunz, and his cookbook is one of my all-time favorites, and then you took that and started this . . ." I waved at the expanse of the restaurant. "So you and your cooking represent something I think is romantic, interesting, and unique, and I want to learn it."

The CIA had phoned me just two days prior to ask if I was withdrawing from school or not, because I was so overdue in landing my externship. I had called a friend who knew Cardoz and asked for a favor to get this interview. Cardoz asked me more questions—if I understood the nature of restaurant work, was willing to do it, what I wanted to do after school was over, on and on. He told me they paid $7.25 an hour. He said that he expected externs to pull their weight but understood that this was the very beginning of a culinary education, and he didn't like expecting *too* much or working his externs like mules.

When we hit a lull, I told him I thought it was really cool that Miles Davis had been playing earlier, and how much I loved the man's electric music from the '70s. Cardoz shifted upright in his seat, lost the wariness, and we talked about Davis for a minute. Then, he took me up the staircase, flanked with softly burning votives, through the dining room, which was arranged around an open circle looking down on the Bread Bar, and into the kitchen. It was fucking immense. Immediately inside the door was the pass, and running perpendicular to it were the kitchen's stoves. The garde-manger station stood next to the pass, and next to that were two enormous steam kettles. A tilt skillet big enough for me to lie in stood near the kettles, right next to a deep fryer and another even bigger kettle, and in a room beyond that there was a long workspace where vegetables were prepped and meat butchered. The whole thing must have taken up about a quarter of a city block. We stopped at the back of the kitchen, looking toward the door and all the activity going on around the stoves. He told me to show up two days later at ten a.m., and spend the entire day—and night—trailing in the kitchen. He'd make his decision then.

I SHOWED UP AT ten on the nose. I was immediately directed to the locker room, where I found a uniform to put on. A guy named Ross—one of Tabla's four sous-chefs—gave me a whirlwind tour in and out of various storage areas. He explained the Tabla philosophy—American food, Indian spices—and that everything was local and seasonal. I wondered why, in May, there were four cartons of tomatoes on the shelf, but didn't ask. I was nervous, and I wanted this to go well. I put it out of my mind.

I liked Ross. He was warm and slightly hyperactive, moving quickly through his explanations, but genuinely interested in communicating. He made direct eye contact. He seemed honest.

He introduced me to a few of the cooks and showed me to a table right near the garde-manger station.

"Wait here for a second," Ross told me, "and we'll get you started. Did you bring knives?"

"I did indeed," I said.

"Let's see." I pulled out my main knife, a Global *santoku* that I had bought on sale for $80 and that I loved. Ross held it up to the light and tilted it back and forth. He dragged his thumb perpendicular to the edge, held it aloft again, and tilted a few more times.

"Good. Nice. I'll be right back." He put the knife down, pivoted, and dashed away, apron billowing, clogs slapping against the floor.

I spent a few seconds observing, trying to take it all in, process it, and use what I could to salve my nerves. I suppose it was natural that my nerves were making a low shriek; the environs of the CIA kitchens were relatively safe: They were a place for trials, errors, and utter fuck-ups. The stakes were low. Tabla had been given three stars in the *Times*. It was presumably not a place for trials, errors, or utter fuckups. I wanted some visual clue that what I was would fit here. After a minute I wasn't any more certain: It was like watching a colony of ants at work. The room was near silent, just the sound of blades against cutting boards. Everyone wore the same uniform and moved through the flow of their prep in a sort of anonymity. I had difficulty telling people apart.

Ross buzzed back in with a metal pan brimming with peeled ginger and told me to follow him. We arrived at a meat slicer.

"You ever use one of these?" he asked.

"Just once," I said.

"It's like riding a bike," Ross said. "To do ginger the way *we* do ginger, you set the slicer to number seven. Put the ginger here. Turn the slicer on here. Pull it back here. Slice it like this. If you hold your hand *here,* the slices will just pile up in your palm. Keep it neat. And for the love of God, please be careful. Come find me when you're done."

It took me twenty minutes to slice all the ginger I'd been given, but I was, for the love of God, being really careful.

When I finished, I unplugged the slicer, wiped it down, and brought the many hundred opaque slices of ginger to Ross. He led me to a cutting board and in a single deft move laid out a handful of ginger in an overlapping line, like a single row of fish scales. He took my knife and assaulted the slices, turning the whole pile into tiny filaments. He gave all the filaments a quarter turn and brought the knife down on them again. Now there was a fluffy row of minuscule ginger dice. He gave me my knife back.

"So do that"—he looked at the pan of slices—"a few dozen more times. And come find me."

And so I chopped, and chopped, and chopped some more. I chopped methodically. I was after precision and exactitude, two qualities that were taking me close to fucking forever to approach. Many, many minutes passed. The pile of ginger slices eroded very, very slowly.

Behind and all around me, lunch service was in full swing. I smelled spices and melting butter and grilling meat. I heard a gnarled aria of sizzles and clattering pans and Ross's persistent voice calling out phrases like, "Ordering one skate, fire one lamb." I'd turn and look and all the cooks stood in one place, rocking maniacally back and forth, reaching for ingredients, pushing and shaking their pans, laying food on plates, garnishing, handing off the plate, and starting the processes over again—a tight and orchestrated freak-out.

Afternoon arrived. I'd completed the ginger. The cooks who'd been there when I arrived were replaced by the evening shift. All the frenetic prep work started anew. I spent some time cutting up lemons for chutney. I sliced cucumbers lengthwise on a mandoline. I ran back and forth to the various walk-ins fetching meats, fish, and produce for others. And then I ran into Ty.

Ty was tall, thin, and in his midthirties. He served as Tabla's chef de cuisine, which meant he was the Waylon Smithers to Cardoz's Mr. Burns. Cardoz had told me that if he was out of the kitchen before dinner service, Ty would run the show. He came off as affable and welcoming. It was a pleasure to meet me, he said, and he'd heard from "everybody" that I was holding my own so far that day.

I was pleased to hear it. "I'm trying to be more asset than liability," I said. But I was still nervous.

"Well, how about you knock off for a bit? I want you to hang back and observe. Go from station to station and see what people are doing. Take notes. If anyone needs help, just do whatever they need."

For the next ninety minutes, I drifted around the kitchen. Tabla's lunch menu was mostly à la carte, but dinner featured two tasting menus. They constituted the majority of the nighttime orders. In addition, a whole crew of cooks and one dedicated prep person worked on getting the Bread Bar set for the night. The Bread Bar would typically sell its chicken *tikka, naan* breads, and lamb sandwiches to some two hundred fifty people on a bustling night.

It wasn't solely that dinner service is usually more intense than lunch, just in terms of sheer volume. There was something else in the air that I couldn't quantify or qualify. The vibe of the room seemed a little more shrill than the morning. Motions were a little more frenzied, a touch more deranged. A tension had settled like a slight chill over the kitchen; I noticed that Ty used a brusquer voice.

Most of Tabla's press had been favorable over the years. Ruth Reichl had awarded them those three stars in the *New York Times*. But they were undoubtedly rankled by a subsequent *Times* review in which William Grimes rabbit-punched the place, stating, "It's getting harder to remember what all the fuss was about." And just recently Cardoz had been slapped a little bit by the *Times*'s Frank Bruni for his *taqueria* at the newly opened Citi Field.

These knocks were small scale, really, and Tabla had mounds of adoring press beyond those, but I wondered if every dinner service at Tabla felt like an audition or competition.

Ty worked the pass, where the food moves from the line cooks to the food runners, who take it to the tables. He expedited—or managed—all the orders, firing this table's order, then that one, and gave the once-over to every plate leaving the kitchen, garnishing with microgreens and salt. The spice room stood next to the pass, and Ty told me to stand there in the doorway and to watch for the duration of the service. It was 7:00. The kitchen would pull the plug at about eleven, which meant I'd be standing and watching for a long time.

And it was a long time. By eight, I'd been in the Tabla kitchen for nine hours, in all the whirls of motion and heat, and hadn't eaten anything for eleven hours. I was exceptionally thirsty. It's more physically difficult to stand in one place, immobile, than to keep moving. My back bitched at me, and the bones of my feet murmured obscenities. But the orders started coming steadily at 8:00, first in small bursts announced by the ticket printer in staccato coughs, then in a quick steady stream. Ty was calling out, "Picking up one crab cake, picking up a watermelon salad. Fire another bass. Ordering one vegetarian tasting," functioning as a conductor, and each station like a string

section or brass section or percussion section, operating apart and join-
ing together, at a precise moment to see six different plates arrive
simultaneously at the pass.

I observed a lot of moments of harmony between the stations, but I
benefited from any mistakes. If anything sat under the heat lamp for
too long, Ty explained, it usually got discarded and cooked again.
Instead, tonight they came to me. I ate a samosa, spicy skate, a cheese-
stuffed naan bread, a small, ever-so-slightly overcooked piece of lamb,
a too-brown crab cake, and a really good layered vegetarian entrée of
rice, sautéed greens, spices, and nuts. I'd later calculate that I'd eaten
around $120 worth of food.

While I was watching frenetic action by the fish station, Ty
appeared in front of me. "We don't stand like that in the kitchen."

I was puzzled. "I thought you told me to stay here. Should I go
somewhere else?"

"I did tell you to stand here. But we don't stand like *that*." He
motioned toward my feet. I had crossed one foot over the other.

"Okay," I said. I uncrossed my foot.

"If you stand like that, you're off balance. If I bump you you're going
to fall. I might trip over you if you fall, and what if I was carrying
something?"

"Okay, got it," I said.

"You need to stand with both feet firmly on the floor."

"Okay."

"Like this . . ." He demonstrated what both feet firmly on the floor
looked like.

"This way, if I bump you"—Ty went ahead and bumped me—"this
way, you're not going down." He bumped me again.

"Right," I said. "Okay."

At eleven, Ty informed the kitchen that all the orders were in, and
it was time to clean up. He gestured to get my attention. "Okay—
interview time. Let's chat." I followed him to an office that was only
marginally bigger than an elevator.

We squeezed in and sat down. The questions started, many of them and with much rapidity. I knew it probably wasn't prudent to indicate from the jump that I had no designs on a restaurant career. Otherwise I told the truth. I acknowledged that, yes, I was older, but argued that only underscored the seriousness I had about learning—this wasn't a dilettante thing. I admitted that, yes, I was a writer and would always write and while I planned to document my experiences at Tabla, I wasn't here to write. I said that my focus here was on cooking. Eleven became eleven forty.

At midnight, he told me to go change, that I was done for the night. What had to happen next, he said, was that, tonight, he needed to do some serious thinking. Depending on what he decided—and, he informed me, he was really on the fence—I'd have to come in and trail one, probably two more times. Then, he and Cardoz would make a decision. After I changed, he led me to the exit and said good night.

As I walked to the subway, I asked the phantom of Ty in my head, *One, probably two more times? Are you serious? Are you fucking kidding?*

I went back upstate and waited to hear something from Cardoz. A week went by, and I started approaching restaurants in the Hudson Valley about externships. The farms and farmers' markets were in full swing, and I targeted a few places that sourced their food from them. I figured doing an externship someplace that was closely allied with the food sources would be a real education. Another week went by, and I received word that the position at Tabla was mine and I'd start five days later.

I'd spend Tuesdays through Saturdays at Tabla and venture back to Saugerties on Sundays. Nelly wasn't thrilled with the schedule. She'd really liked the idea of my working upstate. "All I get with you is about an hour a day. I already feel like I've been single for a year now. I had really been hoping we'd have this great summer together. Well, now I'm definitely going to be living like a hermit for four months."

On Tuesday, June 9, at 10:45 a.m., I presented myself at Tabla to start my externship.

Ross was cutting up skate at the pass when I walked in. He looked up, smiled broadly, greeted me, stripped the latex gloves off his hands,

and took me past the garde-manger station, to a steel worktable standing next to a large bank of refrigerators and directly across from the
tilt skillet. This was my station for the next four and a half months. I
was, he said, to be the prep cook for the Bread Bar. He told me that
each morning I'd get a checklist of some thirty-seven possible dishes
and tasks to undertake and I could expect to do about a third of them.
Some of the tasks were simple: julienne green papaya, or boil finger-
ling potatoes. Others, as I saw from the book of recipes he issued to
me, required a bit of work, like the chickpea chole or eggplant bartha.

I spent that day and the next training, during which I followed first
Nicole, whom I'd be replacing, then Chris, another of the sous-chefs,
as they performed various tasks on the list. I took notes and annotated
my sheaf of recipes. Today—the third day—I was on my own.

I got to my station and put my things down. I grabbed two bains-
marie, one for garbage, one for my equipment. I got a cutting board. I
got out my knives. Then I reached for the clipboard. My prep list read:
make cucumber raita, make spicy yogurt, make lamb marinade, mari-
nate lamb top round, cut asparagus, soak beans for sprouting, sprout
already soaked beans, make foogoth base, make mushroom korma,
make lamb stew, make chole, make green sauce for halibut seviche.

My stomach pitched as I read the list. This was a lot of work. I cross-
checked some of the tasks with the recipes. Just the chole, a dish of
chickpeas served to customers like a stew, for instance, required the following: simmer five pounds of the chickpeas until done. Make a small
dice of ten onions, slice forty-five cloves of garlic on the mandoline,
small dice twenty tomatoes, and julienne a 9-pan (a vessel holding
about three cups) of ginger. Toast spices for a mix: cumin, coriander,
green and black cardamom, cloves, cinnamon sticks. Grind all of them,
along with fifteen dry red chiles. The onions needed caramelization,
the ginger and garlic had to be sweated, and the tomatoes cooked until
they "broke down." Everything got mixed into a steam kettle, and
cooked for twenty more minutes. The stew was finished with a 9-pan
of tamarind paste and some mango powder. Upon completion, it was
decanted into a large hotel pan, put on ice, cooled, and put away.

Line cooks were moving quickly and steadily past, and one of them bumped me. I dropped the clipboard and picked it back up.

I felt a pulse or two of desperation. I wanted to succeed. Cardoz walked by and said hello. He asked what I was working on and I told him I was about to start the chole. He nodded, looked around at my equipment, and left.

I poured the chickpeas into one of the steam kettles, filled the kettle with water, and turned on the heat. I stood over the peas, watching the water start to bubble, and reminded myself that I'd need to get the lamb seared for the stew. I had no idea how long it would take, but I knew that it needed to braise for at least four hours. I had the tomatoes and onions to dice, the spices to toast and grind, fingerlings to cook. And there was much more coming after that.

I discovered that as soon as water boils on chickpeas, a thick scum of starch forms and comes together on the water's surface. It needs to be skimmed constantly. As soon as one layer of scum disappears, a new one appears immediately. The steam kettle with my peas stood about twenty-five feet away from my station.

While they cooked, I turned on the tilt skillet to heat up, diced the onions, then the tomatoes. First Ty, then Cardoz, then Chris walked by the kettle and had a tiny conniption about whatever starch was presently at the top of the peas.

I'd been told to waste nothing. When an onion is diced, there's always some waste; there's the base of the onion that acts as support while you're actually doing the dicing, and a few scraps always turn out to be too long or too big. I worked with large yellow onions, cutting them in half, carefully making several horizontal slices, cutting—very deliberately—fifteen or so perpendicular slices, then making the whole thing into chopped dice. I did this with a number of them, the fumes rising up, stinging my eyes, making them weep. I chopped the waste into the approximate size of the dice and mixed it in. This stuff would be cooked down to translucency, and then cooked some more. Exactitude of shape, I reasoned, wasn't a primary concern.

Chris arrived, leaned in past me, and ran his fingers through the bowl of dice. He found some of the imperfect pieces, announced they were "unacceptable" and told me to go through and cull them out. I dumped my onions onto a sheet tray and plucked the offending pieces away. After a few minutes, Cardoz arrived, dismayed by the several tablespoons of onion I was about to get rid of, and told me to incorporate them back in.

Ty shouted that the peas needed more skimming—right that second. I dashed over. Cardoz kept inspecting the onions and then moved on. From somewhere out of sight, Chris wondered aloud—fervently— why the lamb wasn't being seared.

I retrieved twenty-five pounds of cubed lamb from the meat refrigerator, poured oil into the tilt skillet, tossed a cube in to test it, and, when it spit and sizzled with a violence, dumped about a third of the meat in and spread it around.

Ty stood by the peas, telling me to skim again, and after I walked over to start skimming, he went to the tilt skillet. "Whoa! Whoa!" he shouted. "That is way, way too much lamb!" He began poking at the pieces, many of which had taken on a nice brown color. The meat sizzled very loudly. "You're never going to get *any* color on it. It's not going to sear, it's going to steam. And listen to that—you shouldn't be able to hear me speak right now because this pan should be *that* loud. You just completely wrecked this meat. Maybe we can salvage it. I don't know. Dammit."

He scooped a healthy amount of the meat out and with a great flamboyance plopped it into a perforated pan I'd set up so the oil could drain away from the cooked pieces.

"Ideally," Ty said, looming up in front of me, "we'd sear one piece of meat at a time. But obviously we're on a schedule." He surveyed the meat. "Well, we *were* on a schedule." He walked away. He walked back. "You know, the speed you're operating at is *not* acceptable. You shouldn't be *walking* anywhere. You should be at a full sprint. And I shouldn't have to tell you those peas need skimming. I shouldn't have to tell you that you put too much meat in the skillet. And you haven't even started caramelizing the onions. This is three-star dining.

Three-star dining. This isn't the CIA. Got it?" Away he went. I started caramelizing the onions as the peas continued simmering and foaming and the lamb kept searing.

A few minutes passed by and then so did Cardoz. He stopped by the tilt skillet and looked incredulous. "Jonathan—what are you doing?" He put his hands on his hips.

I'd been at Tabla for about one hundred minutes that day and while I was being upbraided—the whole time—my mind had been curiously blank. I'd felt very little. I'd acted on whatever orders were given with an almost reptilian detachment. But deep in my head, a small black node began to pulse with the first faint stirring urges of violence.

"Do you know how long it's going to take you at this rate? Look at this—why do you have so little lamb in here? This job should take you thirty-five minutes from start to finish. It's going to take you three hours." He dumped the lamb Ty had removed back in. "Don't throw the fat away. There's a lot of flavor there. When you cook down the garlic and ginger and yogurt, emulsify the fat back in. We can skim it after it's been braised." He went away.

A few minutes later, Chris appeared next to me at the skillet. He wore what I was beginning to understand as Tabla's default posture: a look of incredulity

"Listen to me, and listen really carefully. You better start doing exactly what you're told. If I tell you I don't want you doing something, don't do it. And I told you about the onion scraps.

My arms fell dangling by my sides and my hands shook. I enunciated every syllable: "Chef Cardoz told me to put them into that pot." Chris said nothing, then walked off.

Later, Ty intervened as I mixed the lamb fat back into the garlic, ginger, and yogurt, asking, "What are you thinking?"

And later still, Chris handed me a tray with ten bunches of asparagus. He pulled a stalk free. "You hold on to the tip here," he said. "And you hold the very end of the stem. Bend it. It'll naturally break where it's tender. The rest is too woody to use." He snapped the asparagus and it broke a little more than halfway up the stalk; what had been eight inches measured about three and a half. "Toss the rest—we can't do anything with it."

I went through all ten bunches, breaking the stems, turning long stalks into short ones. I was supposed to begin slicing the stalks on a severe bias, but I went to the bathroom first. I had almost gotten through the kitchen door when Cardoz's voice—full of crisis—boomed across the room, calling out, "JONATHAN!"

He and Ty stood over the kitchen's blue bin, positioned right near my table, where all the food waste went. Cardoz looked as if he was on the verge of tears and also like he might want to kill me. He held a few of the spent stalks in his hand. Ty stood behind him, face impassive.

A dam broke in Cardoz's throat and the deluge poured out: "Why would you waste asparagus like this? Do you have any idea—*any idea*—what this stuff costs? How could you just throw it away? How could you do that? What the hell? We cannot afford to work like this— we cannot—*cannot*—afford to make waste like this. What were you thinking?"

Ty had his arms crossed over his chest, shaking his head.

I told them this was how I was shown. I didn't mention Chris's name. Their expressions said I was an idiot. Cardoz demonstrated how I should cut with a knife—not break with a snap—right at the point where the stem turns from tan to green. They left me alone.

Ty came back ten minutes later. I was slicing asparagus on a severe bias, my cutting board full of bright green scraps, working three or four stalks at a time.

"No," he said. "Nope. Uh-uh. You don't do it like that. You need to do one stalk at a time to be sure they come out perfectly even. And you need to do it *right now*. They'll need the asparagus at the Bread Bar in a few minutes." Ty went back to the pass, but Cardoz showed up to inspect. "You're going to be here all night that way," he said. He grouped four or five stalks together and sliced them on the bias, all at once. Chris ambled over a few minutes afterward. "I heard Ty telling you to do that one stalk at a time. You need to start listening."

For every end result, there are a dozen different ways to get there.

Everyone in the kitchen had their preferred method to attack any given task. My problem was that I wasn't fast enough to cross the finish line before anyone and everyone had the chance to comment on the method.

My first week ended, my second began. The days melted together.

Tabla was a lonely place. I arrived, started prepping from the list, got reprimanded and lectured, finished the list, and went home. I had no expectations of my shifts being filled with hugs and lollipops, but I thought it strange that after two weeks, no one had asked a single personal question.

"No one laughs here," I told Nelly on the phone. I usually called her the second I was out of Tabla's door.

My behavior at home took a ritualistic bent. Each evening, starting from that first day I worked on my own, I'd come back to Brooklyn, sit at the apartment window, drink beer, and watch traffic. I'd eat Trader Joe's Mini-Chicken Tacos with a side of sautéed snow peas. I'd watch reruns of *The West Wing*. I'd fall asleep on the couch, fully clothed, with the lights on listening to Lou Reed's *Street Hassle* on repeat. I'd wake up during the noisy parts, coming to and hearing Lou bellowing, "Gimme, gimme, gimme some good times . . ." The clock would tell me I had to be up in four more hours and I'd turn the lights out, pushing my face into the cushions. I did this night after night without deviating. Starting on my third week, when I woke up in the morning, my stomach was in knots.

According to Ty and Chris, and Cardoz himself, I was slow, slow, slow, slow. According to Ty and Chris, I verged on incompetent. I didn't—and possibly couldn't—think. I didn't understand the basic nature of food. I didn't listen. Other people had applied for the externship spot, been turned down, and deserved it much more than I did.

"It isn't until someone knows their station inside and out that we let them try another one," Ty said to me. "But it's pretty unlikely that will be of any concern to you."

"I think they're trying to motivate me," I said to Nelly on the phone. She was always sympathetic. "Like the army: break 'em down, build 'em up. It's exhausting. What they're really doing is making me not give a shit."

I had, admittedly, some pretty bad habits. I was slow, slower than I should have been. And I was a slob. My cutting board—my whole station—looked like the beach at low tide, covered with detritus and scraps. Everyone was on me to speed up and clean up. But at the end of that third week, no one was on me more than Dwayne Motley, one of the sous-chefs who had just returned from some time off. Since Dwayne ran the Bread Bar, I'd be spending most of my time with him.

Dwayne was tall and broad, wore his hair in tight cornrows, and seemed perpetually pissed off. He walked slowly, deliberately, as if he hurried for no one. If Barry White had a handsome younger brother without the girth, he would look like Dwayne.

On his first day back, he approached my station and put his tools away on a nearby shelf. He didn't acknowledge me; he just slowly arranged his things.

"I'm Jonathan," I said, offering my hand. He turned and looked at my hand. Then he gave it a perfunctory shake.

"Yeah, I know who you are." He picked up the prep list and read it. He put the list down and looked around my area at the stove, at the steam kettles, into the tilt skillet.

"What time did you get here today?" he asked. His size and his presence filled a lot of the small space, and I took a step back.

"Around ten," I answered.

And then he blew up. "What the fuck?" he yelled. "You've been here for an hour today and all you've gotten done is some boiled pota-toes and some chickpeas? What about the mushroom korma? What about the saag paneer sauce? You even start that? You haven't started the kalonji, either, have you? This is not fucking right. This is un-fucking-believable. You need to get all that started *now!*" He snarled the last word. "You need to get it all done—all of it, all of it done— right now because I've got things to do and I'm not going to help your lazy ass."

I stood stunned. I tried recalling the last time I'd been spoken to like this, in that tone, with that language. I couldn't remember. Maybe by a bully when I was twelve. And an anger similar to what I'd felt at twelve—a brooding helplessness mixed with outrage, crossed with indignation—stoked up and metastasized into a feeling my whole body experienced as bitter.

My head said to me, *There is nothing here in the world of this restaurant for you. Or in the restaurant world, period. Fuck school. Get out. Fuck your obligations. Go, now. Leave.*

But I didn't walk out. I stayed and finished the day. I hurled myself—every bit of myself—into all those delinquent jobs. And I felt a strange mix of things while pureeing tomatoes with a giant stick blender, and sweating garlic and shallots in butter with twenty spices: like a martyr, like a fuckup, like a marathoner with twenty-five miles to go. Like an asshole for not being able to hold my own. I felt ridiculous, too, for the brief flash of wanting to get the fuck out of there: everyone who ever started at the bottom in a restaurant does this, has this done to them, and what makes me think I had the privilege of being any different?

By 7:00, I had all the jobs done. I checked them off one by one and, at day's end, handed my prep sheet—stained with droplets of oil, streaks of pureed tomato—to Dwayne. He read it, handed it back to me, and said, "Fine. Go home." I spent the rest of the night wondering what, if anything—and I assumed there must have been something—I'd done wrong or forgotten about that I'd answer for tomorrow.

The next morning, I saw Dwayne, standing in a cloud of steam. He was boiling corn in the stock kettle next to the deep fryer. He skimmed off all the silk floating at the top and had a grapefruit-sized pile on the head of the strainer. Someone called his name and he turned; he tilted the strainer too far and all the silk fell onto the floor. It lay there puddled and steaming. He looked at me.

"Pick that up," he said, and turned his back.

I picked it up.

"I keep playing these movies in my head," I told Nelly on the phone. "Snuff films, really. I have a baseball bat and there's Dwayne and I keep beating him until I don't feel angry anymore."

"You always have these extreme reactions to people," she said. "You hate them, then you wind up loving them. Look at Viverito."

"Viverito was acting. I think Dwayne has a cellular-level sadism."

Later that night I put Led Zeppelin on the stereo, and played "When the Levee Breaks" five sequential times. I imagined that each beat of John Bonham's kick drum was a mallet pounding the heads of everyone in Tabla's kitchen. But especially Dwayne.

My weekends—Sundays and Mondays—were paradisical. I'd arrive at Tabla Saturday mornings with a suitcase and catch a train back upstate as soon as my shift ended. Nelly would pick me up at the station and we'd both forget all the angst, all the irritations, both of my own and hers at being alone upstate. Nelly would read to me from the novella she'd started, set in the world of her childhood dollhouse, about Barbie and Ken as underworld vigilantes trying to rescue two young mice kidnapped by the Sunshine Family.

I'd gotten very interested in Mexican food, bought a copy of Rick Bayless's *Authentic Mexican,* and was cooking my way through it. I had great successes with the moles. On Sundays, Nelly and I went to farmers' markets and bought ingredients. We went hiking, or just drove around the Hudson Valley, knocked out by the sharp pitch of the mountains as they rose up verdant all around us. We'd cook dinner, relax, and try to forget that Monday's time was limited, that I'd need to catch a train back.

The drives to the train were like driving to the dentist when you knew something painful would occur on arrival. The distance closed up too fast.

On Tuesday mornings, I'd be back at Tabla, covering the two blocks from subway to restaurant with forlorn steps.

On a Tuesday night in mid-July, right around my thirty-ninth birthday, I finished everything by 5:15. I'd glided through the day at peak efficiency. Everything tasted great; everything looked great. There was no waste of food or effort.

"I don't know what got into you this past weekend," Dwayne said as I checked out for the night. "But your big mistake was showing me you could do it. Now, if you fuck up, I'm *really* going to be all over your ass."

A few weeks passed and my days were getting shorter. I was getting home—not just leaving the restaurant—at 6:30, occasionally six. I could cut a lot of onions quickly. I could manage a stovetop and pair of steam kettles full of different preparations. Chris was leaving me alone. Ty was on vacation. Dwayne had loosened his grip on my neck's scruff.

At 3:00 one afternoon, Cardoz asked to see me in his office. His voice was soft, and his face was quiet. He was always that way. He sat me down right across from me, knees almost touching, and asked, "Why are things going so badly for you? Why have you not shown any improvement?"

"I thought I had shown improvement." I felt blindsided.

"You haven't."

"But I'm leaving earlier, I'm getting more done."

He waved his hands, dismissing what I was saying. He was quiet for a moment, then changed the subject and asked, "Is the experience what you expected?"

I instinctively knew what he wanted to hear, and, admittedly, it was true. "It's more difficult. There's a big difference between the CIA kitchens and here."

"I mentioned that would be the case."

I wanted the subject back where we started. "But I thought I was doing—"

"I wanted to say you really need to start showing improvement."

I thought about what he said on my subway ride home that night. Ty and Cardoz both spoke very highly of Dylan, a CIA extern with whose tenure I'd overlapped. Dylan often stayed later, after his morning shift was over, to do extra work or trail Ty. He came in from his home in New Jersey on his day off. He was dedicated to Tabla, or at least dedicated to the experience of learning at Tabla. He launched himself headlong into everything he did at the restaurant. The ways

Dylan conducted himself were likely at the root of the improvement Cardoz was talking about. I told myself, if I was Dylan's age, I'd probably be doing the same things. But I'm almost twice that age, and I have a relationship. I get tired. I need to be with Nelly on my weekends, not in the restaurant. But I knew there was an element of horseshit there; in Viverito's class, I stayed at school afterward to use the library; I spent hours doing the homework that he never even collected. On some nights after my Americas class, I came home and I cooked, just to test out and reinforce something I learned. I still fit my personal life in. I was stuck in a slightly vicious—and petty—cycle. I refused to be constantly admonished and not respond in kind. But neither side was benefiting in the least that way.

I TASTED EVERYTHING I made—every chole, every lamb stew—and tasted it multiple times. I dipped a tasting spoon in, blew on it, put it in my mouth, and let the flavors announce themselves, play around, then fade. I auditioned everything to ensure it wasn't over- or undercooked, and that the seasoning was right. Once I was satisfied, I took it to a sous-chef to taste and he signed off on it. Sometimes Ty tasted things; sometimes, Chris or Dwayne; once or twice, Cardoz. Maybe I'd be told to add a little more salt or a pinch more sugar, but no one ever tasted a dish and grimaced, or said it was bad. Mostly, they just nodded and said, "okay." One afternoon, I made tomato chutney and took it to Ty. He sampled it and stopped. He tasted it again. He looked shocked. "That's . . ." He paused. "Really *good.*"

Whether the food was good or not really had little to do with me. Cardoz's recipes were, as far as quantity of ingredients went, very finely calibrated. All I did was gather and prep the ingredients the way I'd been taught, both at the CIA and at Tabla. There was a point when an onion was cooked, and a point when a chickpea was done. I used my head. I was just a facilitator. If a dish failed, it was my doing. If it succeeded, I had just shepherded it along.

———

ONE AFTERNOON IN LATE July, I had a mound of thirty-two red onions in front of me. They needed dicing. I wasn't exactly rocketing through the task. My mind and energies were visiting other places. My feet hurt. I kept looking down at them and noticing all the smudges and films on my rubber kitchen clogs. Dwayne appeared next to me, muscled his way into my space, moving me so my left shoulder was pressed into the side of the refrigerator, and said as he took out his kitchen knife, "You'll be here until midnight at this rate."

He cut one of the onions in half, stripped away the paper, and laid the halves facedown on the cutting board. His knife became a glinting blur, up and down as fast as a sewing machine, making perfect slices. He turned the onion forty-five degrees, undertook a few deft slices, and the onion fell apart into small dice. I laid my own knife down and stared.

"That is seriously impressive," I said. "How the hell do you do that?"

He just stood silently. After a few seconds, he reached for the other onion half, bumping me, and did it again.

"Seriously," I said. "That's pretty amazing."

He laid his knife flat and moved to give me a little more room. "It's a matter of practice," he said. "Man, you just do it enough and you get fast like that. Keep it up and you'll get there. Mostly, it's a matter of wanting to get the boring shit done as quickly as possible." His voice was softer, conversational. It was the first time he'd really talked to me. I wanted him to keep going.

"So where did you do your practicing?"

"A couple of places around D.C., at first. Then I came here to New York. I worked in a shit Italian place downtown, worked here and there. And I wound up at Tabla. When I started here, I loved it. But I remember, I walked in thinking I was hot shit, pulled my knife out, and cut myself open. I literally hadn't been here five minutes. Most places, when you cut yourself, they think you're incompetent. All they said here was, 'Well, at least we know your knives are sharp.' That was it. I stayed. I worked every station. Then there was an opportunity and they opened the books. I got the sous-chef position. Here I am, and here you are."

I looked around me to see who might be in earshot. We were alone. "What do you think of the food here?"

His knife was still laid down and he had a tight grip on the handle. He looked around too, and his voice dropped. "It's good food. Interesting food." His tone was measured. Then he got more animated. "Is this what I want to be cooking for the rest of my life? No. What I want to do is—I'm a big fan of the Lee brothers. My big huge dream is to do food along those lines. I want to do clean Southern food. I love Southern food. I love it. But Southern food—that food's not so clean. Boiling the shit out of collard greens until they're gray mush? Until every damn nutrient is cooked out of it? Do you see any rationale there?

"Look, I'm going to help you finish this up. Then I need you to help me with family meal. All you have to do is be heating up tortillas on the flattop. Do, I don't know, about a hundred of them. Use a pair of tongs. I've got big, manly hands and I don't need tongs. You've got small, girly hands, so use a pair."

From that moment, Dwayne never got visibly pissed at me again. If there was a problem, if I made an error, he took the attitude of *Okay, let's figure out how to fix it* and let those mistakes stay quiet.

I never knew what flipped the switch in his head—maybe it was simply a matter of my having survived the initial hazing—but I started feeling relieved and happy when I'd see Dwayne walk in. I'd ask him what was going on, and he'd tell me about who had gotten drunk at a nearby bar after service ended the night before, or about an encounter he'd had with some freak on the subway home to Rego Park at three in the morning.

We began talking quite a bit. He taught me how and why spices combined, about building flavors by breaking a recipe down into phases of cooking, and concentrating on bringing each phase into full and total completion, and all sorts of tips and tricks. He had strident views on pop culture (he did vicious and pretty much unprintable parodies of Patrick and Gina Neely from the Food Network); he had an unsettlingly deep knowledge of horrible '80s synth-pop bands. He was about to propose to his girlfriend, and we compared notes about our respective relationships.

As we got to know each other, it dawned on me that he was, hands down, probably the smartest person in the place. He was dedicated to Tabla, but not a disciple. Which was likely the reason he got the continual short end of the stick. His mind did its pinwheels with too much independence, and it seemed to make some of the others uneasy and Dwayne into a lightning rod.

One morning he walked in and I almost didn't recognize him. He was wearing a do-rag, a red football jersey, jeans, and unlaced Timberlands, and walked slowly across the kitchen with great resignation. His iPod was blaring. He looked at the prep list for a moment.

"Shit. Fuck. Dammit," he said.

"What?" I asked. He didn't answer. I shook his arm and asked again.

He pulled one of his earbuds out; I could hear a soprano singing part of an opera. "Chris was supposed to make lamb haleem yesterday, I knew he was going to dodge that bullet. He sighed and looked down at the cutting board. "So guess who's going to help me?" He clapped my shoulder, affixed his earbud, and went to change.

One day, Dwayne stood next to me, taking up all the space in front of the station. I was cutting onions and had to keep moving around him to place the dice in a bowl and grab new ones to cut. He was staring off into the distance in some existential reverie.

Two of the Bread Bar cooks ran to him in a panic. Service started in an hour and they couldn't find the pears they needed for a salad. He said nothing, just kept staring off. They scurried away to continue the search.

"There's a twenty-five-pound box of pears in the walk-in," I volunteered.

He ignored me, too. Finally he stirred. "Look at them," he said, "running around in a tizzy, crying out, 'Lordy, Lordy, we have no pears! We have no pears!'"

In August, I got promoted. It was a dubious promotion, but I remembered Ty telling me that until a person mastered his station, he wasn't permitted to do anything else. Despite my irritations, I felt a shimmer of pride. I *was* doing well. I was finishing everything on my prep list by around 4:00. I'd spend my remaining two hours helping Dwayne or Chris with whatever projects they had going, and I got ahead by prepping vegetables for the next day.

Ty had called me into his office and said that from now on, two nights a week during dinner service (Tuesdays and Thursdays), in addition to my regular Bread Bar cooking, I'd run the amuse-bouche station. My responsibilities included seasoning and serving soup and deep-frying onion rings and squash pakoras to order. It took Nicholas, who usually ran the station, about two and a half hours to prep everything: deal with the soup, make batters for the rings and squash, cut the onions and squash on the slicer, and fill the deep fryer and heat it up. Dinner started at 6:00, but the station was to be set up by 5:30.

I trained with Nicholas for an evening and he showed me how to get set up and undertake the frying. He also demonstrated how to make samosas, which were hard to do. Ty couldn't really do them, neither could Chris, and I'd never seen Dwayne try. The dough was made with so much butter that you had to work incredibly fast, or it fell apart on you. I never did quite get the hang of it.

Also around this time, other cooks began talking to me. I guess I'd passed some kind of test, or just been around long enough. I found myself liking most of them a lot: Sam, the morning garde-manger guy; Akhil, who took over for him at night; Woodrow, the daytime fish cook; Carmine, the pastry chef; Stan, one of the Bread Bar cooks. Sam and I talked music and books; Carmine and I talked about poetry; Akhil, Woodrow, and Stan had all attended the CIA (as had Ty, Sam, and Ross) and we'd swap stories.

I'd been promoted. I was working well and efficiently cooking for the Bread Bar. I met people I liked. On the day I debuted on the bouche station, I experienced the first day since I'd started that saw me entirely content to be going to Tabla.

And the debut went well. I worked two areas: next to the deep fryer where I had my batters and coatings for the onion rings and squash, and right up front by the pass, where the soup and a garnish of herbs sat chilling on ice. Not much happened the first half hour, but at around 6:30, Bolivar, one of the waitstaff, appeared and called out an order for onion rings. I made for the deep fryer, reached into a refrigerator for a handful of onions, dipped them into a mix of water and chickpea flour, dredged them in spiced chickpea flour, and lowered them into the oil. For a minute I stood watching the oil bubble fiercely up and over the rings, pushing them around the fryer until they turned brown and the turbulence calmed. I watched them transform, and I listened to what they sounded like as they cooked because the noise changed the longer they were in the oil; I wanted the ability to simply hear what the fryer was doing if my back was turned and know what stage the onion rings were at. The oil, which at first made a small roaring sound, barely murmured as the rings took on a nice brown coloring. When they were done, I turned the rings out onto a rack to let the oil drip off, then mounded them in a bowl and took them up to the pass. A food runner picked up the bowl, showed it to Ty for quality control, then carried it off to the customer.

For the whole of the dinner service, I bolted between the soup setup and the fryer. Bolivar, the chief food runner, would pop his head around the corner from his position in front of the pass and order, maybe, three soups and two rings. I'd go for the fryer and start a double handful working. While they cooked, I crossed the red tiled floor back to the soup. I put a pinch of cilantro and a few dice of celery hearts into the tiny bowls—they looked like outsized thimbles—then poured in the cold soup. I dusted a sprinkling of crushed fennel seeds on top, arranged all the soups in a line, signaled to Bolivar, and clipped back to the fryer to lift the rings from the oil.

The evening was busy, but not so busy I ever felt the weeds growing up around my ankles. Busy enough for someone working the station for the first time to need to push themselves a little faster than they normally operated. The area around the fryer looked bollixed up: small pools of spilled batter, drifts of flour, a scattering of rings that had lost their coating or tanned too much. Ty and Chris came by a few times to tell me to get the area tight. But service went smoothly; Ty never asked for anything to be refired, he had no complaints, and didn't have to wait very long between when the order was called and when the rings went out. At the end of night, he took me aside and, for the first and only time, gave me a compliment. "You did a really nice job tonight," he said. He clapped my shoulder. "Keep it up."

I kept it up. At least, for the most part. One night, I made my onion ring batter too thin, and the rings emerged from the oil denuded of coating, greasy and shriveled. Ty kept asking me to refire them and soon enough, I was way behind. I got sloppy behind the pressure, and the station disintegrated into chaos and litter.

But I kept it up.

One afternoon, the cooks pulled all the vessels out of the ice bath, added more ice, and topped it off with water. Someone was leaving Tabla to go work elsewhere, and he was being dunked into the ice bath on his last day. When the departing cook was coming back into the kitchen after family meal, the rest of them pounced. Two people had him by each arm; two had one leg. The other leg flailed as they carried him through the kitchen, knocking a pan onto the floor, kicking utensils across the top of a workstation. They got him to the ice bath and heaved him in. He rose up shrieking, streaming with frigid water, pink skin showing through his soaked white jacket. Everyone laughed and he started laughing too, and someone dunked a bain-marie into the bath, filled it with more water, and upended it over his head.

Ty and I stood a few feet off, just on the periphery of a puddle of water and ice. Ty asked if I'd ever seen that done before and I told him I hadn't.

"It's a tradition," he said. "And it's a sign of respect. They do this to you when you leave if they respect you."

———

AUGUST FADED TO SEPTEMBER, and the nights began turning cooler. My stint at Tabla was winding down. My samosas were still terrible, but I had a solid handle on the amuse-bouche station and had the Bread Bar prep down to second nature.

On an early September afternoon, Dwayne was standing next to me while I trimmed tendons from pieces of chicken, trying to explain why football was worth watching. "It's about the strategy," he said. "Every player has a function, every player has a purpose and it's a matter of—"

"Jonathan," Cardoz said, stopping as he passed by. "I'd like to see you in my office." He turned and walked from the kitchen, pausing at one of the steam kettles to check the progress of a saag paneer sauce I had going.

"Go ahead," Dwayne said. "I'll cover this."

I pulled the latex gloves off my hands and tossed them in the garbage, untied my apron, and tucked it onto a shelf underneath the work area. I had no idea what he wanted, but figured maybe this was about training someone to take over my spot when I left. I walked up to Cardoz where he stood at the kettle.

"Okay, come on," he said, leading me out of the kitchen and signaling Ty as we walked. Ty followed behind.

Cardoz opened his office door and sat down, motioning for me to take the seat across from him. Ty took the seat nearest the door. His eyes seemed to run over the spines of the cookbooks lining Cardoz's wall.

"I had something I wanted to say," Cardoz began. "I think it's time for you to consider other career options, because this one is obviously not working out for you."

I looked over at Ty, but he didn't meet my gaze. He stared at his hands. I looked back to Cardoz. His face was neutral and he held eye contact with me.

I felt dazed.

"Wow," I said. I started picking at the cuticle on my index finger. I didn't look up. I began to experience a sense of foundering, of sinking and shrinking and cracking apart. My stomach began to bleed out small, burning nauseas, and I could perceive my pulse quickening. Cardoz was still looking directly at me. "Wow," I said again. "I guess there's no sugarcoating anything for me today." I laughed a little and looked at my feet. My eyes had a sensation of swelling in their sockets. I could hear the whirring of the fan on the computer and the chair creak as Cardoz repositioned. I looked up and he was still staring. I held my hands out, palms up, and shrugged. I put my hands in my lap and looked back at him, waiting for him to continue. I hoped my eyes weren't reddening.

"There are a lot of people with less ability than you who are able to pick things up a lot faster. You just aren't getting it."

I reflected on the work I'd done recently, banging out the Bread Bar cooking, working the bouche station. Cardoz kept talking, but the words never reached my ears. For two minutes, I sat watching the screen saver on his computer cycle through its geometric permutations. And I noticed that there was a photo right above Cardoz's head of him and Martha Stewart.

I came back to the moment as he was saying, "I'm not firing you. But right here, right now, if I don't see more effort on your part . . . so that's it, plain and simple." He paused. "Do you have any questions?"

"No, I don't."

"You understand why I'm telling you what I'm telling you?"

I smiled. It was completely fake. "Sure."

"No, I need you to tell me you understand."

I looked again at Ty, who looked at me for the first time but then turned his head away.

"Yeah, I understand. Thank you for your honesty." I stood up. "Okay. I better get back to the chicken."

I got back to my station and it was clean. Akhil walked by and said, "Dwayne put the chicken into the walk-in for you."

I went back to the walk-in and stood leaning against the wall with my head down. I ran through all the progress I'd made, all the days cooking as fast and as hard as I could, the nights at the fryer. At that moment, that precise second, I gave up.

Other than for professional reasons, I didn't speak to Ty or Cardoz for weeks, and when I did, it was strictly kitchen business. I kept my head down, shift after shift, face angled into the steam of the kettles and skillet, or focused entirely on my cutting board, trying to work as hermetically as I could.

I confided in Dwayne. As he was taking an inventory in the Bread Bar's walk-in one evening after service I finally told him about the meeting with Ty and Cardoz. I'd held off for a few weeks because I had difficulty getting my mind to process it. He leaned back against the wall, the two of us standing in the deep chill under a few bare bulbs, and he just shook his head. "I'm guessing that's their interpretation of a motivational speech," he said.

"Am I that incompetent? You can tell me. Seriously."

"No. No, you are not incompetent. Do I wish you were just a little bit faster? Sure. You're new to this, though. I've watched you since you came here. You didn't know what the hell you were doing. Scrambling around one hand not knowing what the other was doing. It took you ninety hours to get that list done. But here you are. You've made huge, huge steps. You're on your way.

"You're not ever going to get positive reinforcement here. You're as good as your last service. Doesn't matter what came before. They're not ever going to tell you you've done a good job. It's always going to be, 'what have you done for me lately?' But on your last day, which is coming up, they're going to take you aside and tell you what a great job you did. Watch. And, by the way, you might want to start bringing in a few changes of underwear to keep around. It really sucks to come out of that ice bath and not have anything to change into. They'll probably do a couple test runs on you, too. Be forewarned."

Nelly and I had arranged for someone to sublet our apartment so we could save some money on rent for a couple of months. The sub-letter would be moving in a couple days after my externship at Tabla concluded. One night, I sat in the window with a beer and was going over the calendar, trying to figure out when we could get a cleaner in for a few hours to give the apartment floors and walls a good scrub. The CIA's externship program requires the externship to last 126 days. I was scheduled to do my last day at Tabla on October 10. I counted backward. October 10 meant I would have worked 127 days at the restaurant. *No, uh-uh,* I thought. *They cannot have one more day from me than I need to give them.*

Ty and Cardoz were on a business trip during my last week. They'd be returning two days before I left. Chris was in charge of scheduling. I told him that I needed to make a change to the staff calendar, that Friday the ninth, not Saturday the tenth, would have to be my last day. It took some cajoling, but he finally agreed and made the switch. Someone else had asked if he could pick up a few more hours, so Chris gave him my Saturday slot. In my gut, I knew this was a shit thing to do, with both Ty and Cardoz away, but it was hard to shake how angry, how bereft, I felt after Cardoz's talk.

During that week, whenever Dwayne mentioned I had just four then three then two days left, I'd break out in an ecstatic, spastic dance, something akin to the way Deadheads danced, but as if they were cranked to the gills on meth.

Ty and Cardoz were back toward the end of the day on Thursday, jet-lagged and wired from traveling.

I was cleaning my tools at the end of my shift, and wiping down my station, when Ty bobbed up behind me. He got right up close, causing me to take an involuntary step backward, but I was up against the worktable and there was nowhere to go. Ty was pissed.

"What's this nonsense about you leaving tomorrow? You're sched-uled to be here through Saturday, and we have an event Saturday afternoon."

"Stan's taking over." I paused. "I'm sure he'll do a better job."

"Why are you leaving early?"

"We have a subletter coming. I have to make sure they get in. I've got to make Friday the last day."

Ty made a gesture that signified *I'm done listening to your bullshit* and walked away. I could almost feel the anger streaming off him. I finished cleaning up, waited until Ty was away from the pass and kitchen door, and left quietly for the night.

I woke up ecstatic on my final day. Even my dreams during the night had been easy. I drank coffee and sang to myself. I packed three extra T-shirts and three pairs of boxers, because I had no idea how many times I'd be dunked. The plan was, Nelly would have already arrived from Saugerties and handed off the keys to the subletter by the time work was over. All my things were packed. I'd leave Tabla at around 6:00, be home by 6:30, and we'd drive back upstate, arriving around 8:30. We'd head out for a celebratory liberation dinner. I selected music for the ride up.

I left the house at 9:30 and got to Tabla at a few minutes after ten. I entered the old MetLife building, said hello to the same security guard I'd seen every morning since June, and wished him good luck. I climbed the stairs, changed into my uniform, and strolled into the kitchen.

Ross stopped cutting herbs when I walked in. "I hope you enjoy frigid, ball-shattering cold water baths," he said. "What *I* think needs to happen is that we test out the ice bath with a few different levels of ice. So prepare yourself. I'm envisioning, I don't know, at least two dunks in the bath. Oh, by the way—you'll never know when it's coming." I made my way through the kitchen. Woodrow, Sam, everyone kept up a constant warning of how cold the water was going to be. I was actually looking forward to it.

I got to my station and looked at the prep list. It was a simple day: kalonji, lamb stew, and a bunch of busywork.

Thank you, Dwayne, I said to myself. The butcher wasn't done with the lamb so I set about the grunt work. I peeled some papaya, put it on the slicer, and julienned it. I made green sauce for the halibut seviche. I prepped the kalonji, and got it going in the steam kettle. It was about

11:30. I wiped down my cutting board, swabbed the worktable, and Dwayne arrived.

"This guy," he said, extending his hand. "This fucking guy. Last day. I didn't give you much to do because I figured you'd want to get out of here right before family meal. Plus, you'll need to change your clothes several times today."

I was opening bags of chickpeas and soaking them for the next day's prep when Ty arrived. He moved through the kitchen saying hello to everyone, but walked past me without a word.

The butcher told me the lamb was ready. I put the meat in a large mixing bowl, seasoned it heavily with salt, and plunged my hand in to mix it up. I cranked the tilt skillet to high and gathered garlic, ginger, pepper, cloves, and cardamom, making a paste with the garlic, ginger, and some water. I opened the dairy refrigerator and pulled out six quarts of yogurt, poured it into a bowl, and whipped it until it was smooth. I went to the bathroom. I bullshitted with Akhil and Woodrow. I went downstairs to the Bread Bar and hung out for a minute with Dwayne, who was checking the status for the lunch service.

When I went back upstairs, I passed Ty on the way. He didn't look at me.

"Ice bath! Ice bath!" people called out as I walked back through the kitchen. I poured some oil into the tilt skillet, and it immediately began to shimmer and dance. I tossed the spices in and stirred them in the oil. When I could smell the spices, I threw in a portion of lamb. Dwayne walked past me, with Ty on his heels.

Ty stopped. "That skillet's not hot enough."

I looked in. It was exactly as hot as it had been every time I made the lamb stew. *Fuck this,* I thought.

"It's *not* hot enough. Take that meat out, dump the oil. Scrub it down and start over. Now." He moved over to the kalonji. "This is too hot. It's already starting to burn. Pour it out and put it into the other steam kettle. Scrub out this one. And watch the heat this time." He walked out of the kitchen.

I turned to Dwayne. He looked shocked.

"What the fuck?" I asked. Dwayne moved over next to me.

"Listen to me: Everything you do today, you need to do perfectly. He is on your ass, and he's going to make you miserable. Do everything right. Don't take any shortcuts."

I turned the skillet off and took out the meat. I poured out the oil into a bucket, put an inch or so of water in the skillet, and let it soak. I moved the kalonji from one kettle to the other. It splattered all over my apron.

It took around twenty minutes for the skillet to cool down enough for me to scrub it. I turned it back on, all the way up, and let it heat. In the meantime, I diced some ginger. After thirty minutes, I poured some oil in. I grabbed a cube of lamb and tossed it in. It jumped and sputtered and began to sear. Dwayne was nearby, meticulously cleaning the tops of some okra. Ty passed and said, "It's still not hot enough."

Dwayne looked up and shook his head. I started cutting up tomatoes. The tomatoes were to be put into one of the steam kettles and boiled with a bit of water. I'd strain them later and give the liquid to the Bread Bar. They'd use it to make rice pilaf.

I finished cutting the tomatoes, about seventy of them. My fingers were shriveled from all the liquid, and my cutting board sat in a puddle of it. I put them into a steam kettle, stirred the kalonji, and went back to the skillet. It had been on for an hour.

I tossed the lamb in.

"It's still not hot enough," Ty's voice came from behind me. "Get it out, scrub it down, and start again." I didn't turn around. My head hung. My eyes watered a little, out of sheer frustration. I took the lamb out and then looked at the clock. It was around two. I knew there was a meeting between Cardoz, Ty, and the sous-chefs. I waited until I saw Ty and Dwayne and Chris and Ross leave the kitchen, then I put the lamb back in. I finished half an hour later and turned the tilt skillet over to Woodrow, who was waiting to make soup.

At 3:15, everyone had been back for a while. This was when the morning and evening shifts turned over, and usually when the ice bath dunkings occurred, so everyone could participate. But the bath was full of bains-marie holding sauces and my kalonji. I roasted the okra while I waited to get dunked.

After an hour, the bath was still full. A lot of the morning guys had gone home. Twenty more minutes passed and it was just about time to eat family meal. I would need to stick around until the lamb stew came out of the oven and I could ice it down. I noticed no one was talking to me anymore. I strained the tomatoes and went to eat something.

After dinner, I stood by my workstation, waiting on the lamb. I had packed up most of my stuff. Stan came by and handed me a note. It was from Dwayne. *I need you to deep-fry cashews for salad. Do a week's worth.*

"Is he kidding?" I asked Stan. This would take a while.

"No, he's not kidding."

Every burner on my stove was in use by garde-manger and pastry. It was too close to service to use any of the line stoves. I'd have to wait. It was also, I realized, too close to service for me to get dunked. The ice was still full of sauces.

Ross came by and shook my hand. "I've enjoyed your being here," he said. "You helped us out a lot. I think when you get back to school, it's going to be nothing. You'll be running circles around most of your peers."

"You never got to dunk me," I said.

He gave me a sort of sad smile. "Yeah, we got a little too busy today. You lucked out."

No one had seemed any more busy than usual. I saw Ty come into the kitchen, and it hit me why I hadn't been dunked. I remembered standing next to him a couple of months back, watching someone get tossed in. "They do this to you when you leave if they respect you," he'd said.

I was actually surprised as I stood at my station how hurt I felt.

At 5:30, I took the lamb out, put it into hotel pans, and iced them down.

At 6:00, service started.

At 6:30, a burner opened up on the stove and I deep-fried the cashews.

At 7:45, I finished changing in the locker room. I put my stuff in a corner and went back into the kitchen. I said good-bye to a few people, but dinner service was in full swing and they couldn't really engage. I walked to the front and thanked Ty and shook his hand. He wished me luck at school. Cardoz had already gone home.

Downstairs, I went to the Bread Bar and found Dwayne. He thanked me and told me I'd done a good job.

"You're not going to disappear, right?" he said. "You're going to let me know how it's going at school, correct?"

"Of course. I think I'm actually going to miss you."

"Yeah, I imagine you will."

"Hey—did Ty tell you guys not to dunk me?"

"I don't know," Dwayne said. "I think it was something like that."

And then I left. I stood outside on Twenty-Fourth Street for a moment, waiting to feel liberation. I just felt exhausted.

There were delays on the trains, and I got into the apartment at 8:45. Nelly was pissed, but when I explained, she softened. "Well . . ." she said. "You never have to go there again. You never have to put up with that shit again."

"I can't believe I didn't get dunked." I looked at her. "My feelings are really hurt."

She rubbed my shoulders. "Do you want to have a beer before we hit the road?"

"No," I said. "I just want to go home."

The following week, I sat down at my desk in Saugerties and I e-mailed Ty, Chris, Ross, and Cardoz. I wrote very nice, fawning thank-you notes. I got very nice responses from each of them.

Two more weeks passed. We had our first frost.

11

AFTER THREE WEEKS OF lying around, processing the flow and ebb of the summer, watching the foliage turn luminous and then fall from the branches, it was time for school to start up again. My desire to go back was only moderately stronger than my desire to be given a catheter.

I started Quantity Food Production, twelve days of, basically, cooking food in huge quantities, on November 9, at 3:45 in the morning. I'd be doing the morning shift for six days, then switching over to the dinner shift for six more.

For the first day and the next five afterward, I got up at 1:30 in the morning, usually the time I went to sleep. The school hadn't revalidated my parking pass, which unlocked the electronic gates of the lots near Roth Hall, so I had to park in the open areas half a mile away. My body shook with exhaustion; I was near delirium. It was turning cold.

The first morning, I arrived at 3:30, fifteen minutes early. I went to the QFP breakfast kitchen and found that class had already started. I looked at my watch and at the time on my cell phone. They were both correct. I walked in, stunned that I had missed something as big as the start time on my first day. I had made a point of arriving *early* on day one.

Chef Joe De Paola, a tall guy about my age, was in midlecture as I came in, and he stopped.

"You must be Jonathan Dixon. Well, I think it's just a great way to start this class by being fifteen minutes late. Way to get off on the right foot."

"I apologize," I said. "I thought—I was *certain*—that class began at three forty-five. I thought I was early."

"Your group leader sent out an e-mail the other day announcing class was at three fifteen the first day."

I was coming back from externship. I had never even met anyone in this new group before. I had no idea who the group leader was. And I hadn't gotten an e-mail.

"I never got that e-mail," I said.

"I'm so sick of hearing how people didn't get an e-mail."

"I'm really sorry, but I never got it."

"Well, since you're here now, you can get this: You fail for the day."

I sat down. This was beginning to feel too familiar. The mixture of resignation and resentment, of feeling that the flow of things was passing just beyond my reach and comprehension, of feeling *fucked* before I even started—it made me want to cry. I thought about—later—pulling De Paola aside and explaining that being late wasn't who I was, that I was exactly the opposite, but the persona he was wearing for this class was stern and unblinking. I didn't see the point.

We started cooking half an hour later; my assignment was to do eggs Benedict. I attempted to poach one hundred eggs, but my water wasn't hot enough, and I screwed them up; the pot became full of a yellow-gray slush. Someone else had to make my hollandaise for me as I struggled to right my error. Another person split and toasted my English muffins. All that I knew I'd accomplished at Tabla had turned to nothing.

On the ride home I had a thought. Maybe it was time to consider the idea that I just wasn't a cook.

The thought hung there echoing, and I pulled off the road, into a convenience store parking lot. I sat idling. I turned the music off. Other cars came and went. What if this was true—and a small voice said, *hey, it probably is true*—what do I do? I felt deeply embarrassed and humiliated. Is this another waste of time, like my entire twenties? I felt embarrassed and humiliated on behalf of my parents, who had been so excited when I made the decision to attend school. I felt embarrassed and humiliated on behalf of Nelly. Did she know the whole time what I was now suspecting, and was too tender to lay it out? All her support and all the sacrifice she'd made while I basically went off hunting unicorns . . .

Nelly was right then down in the city, teaching. I wanted to call her, but I knew she was in class. I wanted to apologize and make the apology so heartfelt that I'd break down, and maybe in the dismantling, I'd get a glimpse of what the real nature of things was.

I started the engine and drove the rest of the way home. I got back to Saugerties at noon. I'd been up for more than eleven hours, and I'd be going to bed in six. I decided to have a beer, then decided to have several more. At some point, I talked myself back into thinking that I was just having a bad spell of it. But the initial suspicion I'd had on my drive lingered. Like a scar, or a lesion.

On the third morning, I peeled fifty pounds of potatoes and put them into a steam kettle to boil. They'd be turned into home fries later on. I got lost in other activities, and overcooked them until they fell apart.

After the sixth day, we began the evening portion of the class. We'd be making dinner under Chef Eric Schawarock's tutelage. I was working with a woman from Wisconsin named Aziria, or Azzy for short. Each team had a different entrée assigned to them; there might be a choice of five or six entrées available nightly to each diner. We were to come up with our own recipes for the meatloaf or spaghetti and meatballs or baked sole or roast beef served starting at 5:00 in the afternoon. Schawarock, a New Yorker with hawkish eyes, a head of gray hair, and a thick Long Island accent, threw out our recipes and explained how he expected the dishes to be executed. We were cooking for around two hundred people a night. The second night, Azzy and I were to make sole topped with bread crumbs. It was disastrous. We baked the sole in the convection oven, sprinkled bread crumbs on top, and put the fish under a broiler to quickly toast the crumbs. We underestimated how powerful the convection ovens were, and the fish lost every bit of moisture. Broiling the bread crumbs just compounded the error. Schawarock's comments on his grade sheet that night simply read, "All bad."

Five more days passed, pretty much without incident, but without any progress or triumphs. Thanksgiving came. The beginning of December arrived, and so did L-Block.

DURING THE SIX WEEKS of L-Block, there's no cooking. All the classes— Restaurant Law, Cost Control, Menu Development, Nutrition, Intro to Management—are book based, everything purely academic. I was back in my khakis and polo shirts, arriving most days at 7:00 a.m., downpressed by the frigid winter temperatures, enduring the slack erosion of my time on campus.

"If you divide the cost of sales percentage with operating expense percentage, you get the variable rate for your restaurant. . . . Determining the break-even point is to divide the occupational expenses by the contribution margin percentage. . . . Protein contains 4 calories per gram and should make up 10 to 35% of your daily diet. . . . The fat-soluble vitamins are A, D, E, and K; they occur in foods containing fat and get stored in the liver or fatty tissue until needed. . . . There are four basic theories of management: scientific, human relations, participative, and humanistic. . . . Success in leadership means focusing on a 'return on the individual,' a philosophy that blends imagination, initiative, improvement, interaction, innovation, and inspiration. . . . Judy, a caterer, signs a contract for a party with David for $1,500.00 for October 5. The day before the party, David calls Judy and tells her to cancel the party. Judy decides to sue David for the contract price. Judy then finds out David is seventeen years old. Can she still sue?"

To Nelly and me, money was now just a fabled thing that other people had. We were low on oil to heat the house but couldn't afford more. Nelly had taken on additional teaching, which meant many hours of additional reading and time away from her writing, and her synapses were beginning to smoke.

There was a single bright spot. Raimundo Gaby was a handsome and nattily dressed Brazilian man who taught Menu Development. In a lightly accented voice, he bounced from one side of the room to another, shouting, singing, waving his hands, cracking jokes, always wearing a beautiful suit and wildly colored tie. "Look at this! Look at this menu!" He'd have a picture of the Café Boulud menu projected on the overhead. "Awesome! Excellent! Bringing it! Brrrrrrrrriiiiinnngggiiinnng it! But then . . . but then . . . now, look at this! It breaks your heart!" He switched to a projection of the Balthazar menu. "Not bringing it! Not bringing it! Does your eye know where to go? Mine doesn't! Off balance! Too crowded! If they just moved this . . . if they rearranged this. . ." His hands swooped all over the place. "They'd be bringing it! Three simple changes! Easy, breezy, beautiful, Cover Girl!"

He was better than television.

Gaby gave us an assignment to create a menu for an imaginary restaurant. I came up with an idea. I owned a book called *British Grub,* a garishly illustrated collection of recipes—full of Day-Glo, psychedelic colors and grotesque drawings of English people eating—for traditional British blue-collar food. I had looked through it a lot as a little kid, enraptured by the colors and the food itself. And what little kid wouldn't want something called Toad-in-the-Hole for dinner? I'd been given a copy of Heston Blumenthal's *The Fat Duck Cookbook* and had acquired Grant Achatz's *Alinea* a few months prior. I decided that my menu would take all those traditional British foods and give them the Blumenthal/Achatz treatment—sci-fi, high-tech interpretations of salt-of-the-earth classics. Ridiculous foams, gels, and powders; bizarre deconstructions and groan-inducing puns. I spent an entire weekend pouring myself into the menu—sublimating the prior five weeks of L-Block tedium. I was surprised: I really got into it. It was the most fun I'd had in ages.

I had dishes on the menu like Scotch Woodcock, described as: egg yolk drops and crème fraîche spheres on anchovy-Parmesan toast; "Potted Shrimp" Pousse Café, which was butter and prawn parfait, English pea mousseline, honeydew-cucumber sorbet, and sauternes gelée; and Deviled Varieties, grilled variety meats with braised mustard seeds, mustard-honeycomb-apple compote, and Pommery mustard gelato. I'd look at the components of the traditional dish, break them down, see if Alinea or Blumenthal had handled similar ingredients in interesting ways, concoct flavor and texture ideas, and there I'd have the finished dish. I wound up ripping off my two source materials a lot less than I'd anticipated.

When I showed it to Gaby, he loved it. It was sophisticated, he said. Vibrant. Fun. Exciting. I explained how I'd "invented" the dishes and his response thrilled me. I hadn't been thrilled in many months.

"I know those books. I see the influence, but you've also got your own thing happening. I want to eat this food. Really—I want to eat this food."

"Oh, Jonathan Dixon," Nelly exclaimed, when I showed her the menu. "Will you make some of these?"

I never did.

At Christmas I had to borrow $200 from my aunt to buy presents for my parents. I considered that this might be a new low.

The holidays ended, and L-Block limped almost imperceptibly to a close. I waited for it all to end.

ON DAY ONE OF the Baking and Pastry class, signs started going up around campus announcing that the Bocuse d'Or finals would be held at the CIA in just a couple of weeks.

I've heard cooking and baking compared to the difference between jazz and classical music; cooking requires an intuition and ability to improvise, but baking is all about exactitude, a science. I did poorly in science classes when I was younger and felt a little intimidated by the idea that it was preternaturally easy to screw up baked goods.

Baking and Pastry classes run in the Baking Center, a separate building connected to Roth Hall by a walkway. It was the same building where incoming students eat those first few formal meals, and where the Banquet and Catering course occurs; it was an area most of us enrolled in the culinary arts program steered clear of. There wasn't much of a rivalry between the culinary students and the baking students—although it went unspoken that each thought their program superior and more rigorous and difficult—but the bakeshops, as they were called, felt like uncharted territory. When I looked at a campus map, and saw the representation of the baking center, I always had it in my head that it should read like an ancient map, where unexplored areas bore the words "Here there be dragons" except ours could read, "Here there be Germans." That was the association I had of the place: that it was staffed by stern Teutons with an appropriate love of order. On the few occasions I was in that area (usually to use their bathroom, because it was really nice), that's pretty much what it seemed like.

The weekend before class started, I pored over the textbook. I was hungover from L-Block and the crawling damage of the winter. My snuffed-out enthusiasm hadn't rekindled.

I was really beginning to worry. I had a while yet to go to get my degree, and I believed that the only way to really get the most one could out of it was to go through it headlong. Why the hell stay—why bother? Why waste the time and resources?—if I didn't burn to do it? Wouldn't it make sense to maybe cut my losses?

Gaby's project had felt good. It reminded me of the way I was before I'd started school the year before: excited, brimming with wonder, open to every scrap of data. That menu had been like a shot of L-dopa, with a burst of life but then crucial diminishing returns. I remembered all those forays through the really high-end cookbooks in my collection, almost giddy when I'd look at French Laundry recipes that I knew were out of my reach and think, *I'll be taught every technique I need to know to do that.*

I sat on my bed with the textbook open. Beer bread dough . . . chocolate cherry sourdough . . . meringues . . . croissants . . .

It would be pretty cool to understand how these get made, I thought. I flipped back and forth, looking at the pictures and stopped on page 231, the recipe for puff pastry dough.

Just a short time ago, I'd been having a Proust moment, thinking about these Pepperidge Farm goods I used to eat, a broccoli-cheese mix encased in pastry. Pepperidge Farm had long since stopped producing them. I associated the taste with my first months in New York City because I'd come home late from work and buy some from the supermarket, heat them up, eat them, and drink beer while watching the news. *I wish I could have one of those right now,* I'd thought that short time ago, and then a second thought came: *Hold up there—you're in cooking school. Why don't you make some?*

I drove to the local Price Chopper and bought ingredients— broccoli, cheddar, and frozen puff pastry. I balked at the price of the puff pastry because it was ridiculous: $4.99 for two small sheets of it. Still, I took two boxes home. Back in the kitchen, I made a Mornay sauce by cooking up a light béchamel and shredding the cheddar into it. I blanched the broccoli and sweated some onions and garlic in a sauté pan. I chopped all the vegetables fine, mixed in some of the Mornay, and gave the whole thing a generous hit of salt and pepper. I spooned the broccoli mixture onto one of the sheets, folded the pastry over, and cut them into rounds. I got about three per sheet. The bundles baked until they were golden. I let them cool, and then sampled my efforts. Not exactly what I remembered—and it occurred to me even if I had an actual Pepperidge Farm pastry in my kitchen, it wouldn't taste like I remembered—but pretty good. Then I broke it down: probably about $2 worth of broccoli and cheddar, and $10 worth of puff pastry. $12 for the whole recipe, meaning each pastry cost $2. That was pretty steep for a trifling snack.

But staring at page 231, I noticed that the recipe yielded almost nine pounds of puff pastry. It called for almost three pounds of butter and three of flour, but I'd get ten times the amount of puff pastry for the same cost.

I closed the book. I willed myself to think, *That will be really cool to know how to do.*

ON TUESDAY AFTERNOON, JANUARY 25, I arrived at Bakeshop 8 a few minutes early for class because I wasn't sure where the bakeshop was, and I'd be starting with an entirely new group of people again. I'd finish the program out with this group, and I wanted to get a read on them. They had all arrived before me, and when I walked in, they turned to look at the new guy.

I nodded and forced a faint smile, moving past the four large wooden-topped square workstations toward an open seat right at the front of the room. I put my things down and the other students started coming up to me, introducing themselves. Leo, Micah, Sammy, Rocco. Jessica. Gabrielle, Margot. Stephen. Bruce. Sabrina. I shook hands with everyone. It was nice to meet them, too. Just a minute before 2:00, our instructor arrived.

Rudy Speiss killed off every preassociation I had with not only the building, but the whole art of baking within about five minutes of entering. He was Swiss, not German; he wore kindness and patience like a nicely tailored shirt; and as soon as he began talking, baking suddenly became accessible, leagues from the esoteric science I'd always thought it. He was about fifty-eight or so, on the short side, with a full head of brown hair and a carriage that indicated that he wasn't completely averse to sampling his own wares. His voice was soft and even and impossible to imagine rising. He smiled constantly.

He spent a few minutes laying out the rules—three absences equal a failing grade, two tardies equal one absence, and all the rest of the disciplinary calculus—that we knew by rote.

As he spoke, I swiveled in my seat to get glimpses of my new classmates. Man, they looked young—really young. Baby skin. Inner glow. Full of energy. They looked incredibly earnest, too. Everyone leaned forward into Speiss's words, taking careful notes. These kids had no dust of cynicism on them. One student, Carol, caught my eye and smiled and bent her head back over her notes.

Speiss was saying that from now on, we were to forget about cups and half cups and all the systems of measuring we used in our old kitchens. Here, we worked by weight. Our recipes would call for, maybe, thirty-two ounces of flour—regrettably, Speiss said, we were not on the metric system, which was even more exact—and sixteen ounces of water. We were to weigh this stuff out, even the liquids.

Next, he explained all the differences between the flours stored in bins under the worktables. Bread flour, all-purpose flour, cake flour, whole-wheat flour—they all had different levels of gluten in them, and they were employed in different recipes to exploit those differences, and in different ratios to refine the end results even more—heavier on the bread flour for a certain texture, more durum for another texture. Most people, he lamented, have a single type of flour in their pantries at home. You'll never experience the wonders of baking and all its variety with a single type of flour. He gave a lesson on the nature of yeast. He talked about how salt toughens up gluten, how too much salt will make the dough irreparably sticky and impossible to work with. Then, as if cued by the word "sticky," he said something really interesting.

"Students ask me, 'How long do I mix a dough for? When is it ready?' They think that baking is that precise, that you mix and knead for an absolute amount of time. No more, no less. This isn't so. You know in the kitchen *approximately* how long it takes to sauté a chicken breast, but you can't say it is for exactly four minutes and thirty-two seconds. At a certain moment, you sense it is done. Stoves vary with their heat, pans vary with their thicknesses. There are differences between each and every chicken breast. Baking is like that too. You need to be more careful with amounts, but you need instinct, also. A dough will tell you when it is just about ready. You can see the sheen on it, you can feel the stickiness. But you will also learn to feel with your gut when that dough is done. You will just know."

Speiss divided us up into teams: laminating, desserts, custards, and bread. I was assigned to the laminating team. Just as I was about to raise my hand and ask exactly what laminating was, he explained that we would be making doughs of butter and flour for pie crusts, croissants, and puff pastry. I perked up. Then he handed out one recipe sheet each. I glanced at mine and saw "Puff Pastry" across the top. I perked up some more.

We broke apart and started gathering our ingredients. I weighed out five pounds of butter, eight ounces of flour, and then cut the butter into tiny pieces.

"Good, good," Speiss said, standing at my elbow. "Now everything into the mixer. Use the paddle attachment. Mix it until there are no more lumps. No lumps, no lumps."

I did as I was told. As my flour and butter mixed, I watched Speiss. He moved from team to team, person to person, with a genuine excitement. He loved this. He obviously loved his students—he made his explanations and corrections ("No, I think you might be just a *little* short with the flour weight" he said to Margot, whose dough was, the first time she tried it, a sopping mess. "There we go . . . good, good, great, beautiful.") with concern and warmth. His whole manner seemed to communicate that we weren't screwing anything up; we just hadn't yet learned the right way to do things.

This was a different way of passing on knowledge than Viverito or Perillo or Coyac. A raised voice wouldn't have suited Speiss any more than a paternal kindness would have fit Coyac. But the endgame turned out the same: You wanted to do things well.

All around the four tables, there was motion and noise. Giant Hobart mixers growled and thumped; clouds of flour rose up in drifts; people grunted behind the effort of kneading; whisks stirring custards rang against the sides of steel pots. When it ended a few weeks from now, I'd understand how to make bread, how to make flans, how to make croissants and puff pastry. Mysterious things were being made clear. I started to feel good about being in the class.

On the other hand, baking was slow business. The butter-flour compound I'd mixed was divided into four pieces and molded into squares, then set into the refrigerator to chill overnight. Speiss handed me a recipe for pie crust, and I started in on that.

"There are all sorts of factors that bear on bread and baked goods," Speiss said to us as we worked. "Especially breads. Temperature is crucial. Yeast and gluten are both influenced by heat. What's the room temperature? What's the water temperature? What's the temperature of your flour? When you mix dough, you will encounter mixing friction, and you can assume that the temperature of your dough will rise two degrees for every minute of mixing you do."

"What should I do for a pie filling?" I asked him when I was done making the crust; it sat resting in the refrigerator.

"Whatever you want to do. Anything you want. Chocolate pudding, apple, we can order some blueberries . . . it's up to you." That wasn't a sentiment expressed very often at the CIA. For a second, it threw me. I didn't know what I wanted.

"I will say," he continued. "I saw some really nice apples in the walk-in. Come here." He led me to the walk-in and we went inside. He pointed to a pan full of Empire apples. "What do you think?"

"Yeah, I think I want to do apple pie."

"Good, great, beautiful. Peel them, cut them up. Do what you can to make the pieces even. We'll make a syrup with sugar—just a tiny, tiny bit of water to get it melted." Speiss was lighting up as he walked me through the process. "Add some spice—a pinch of nutmeg, some cinnamon. Some lemon, but not too much. I want to taste apple, not citrus, right? Right. Then we bake it. And we'll send it out to the faculty lounge later for their dessert."

My classmates had been together as a group for a while, spoke in their own shorthand, and obviously weren't sure how or if I'd fit into the dynamic. For the first few days, most of our interactions were on the level of, "May I have that flour when you're done, please? Are you finished with this pan—can I take it to the dish sink? Is there any more room in the oven for this pie?" Polite, businesslike. When I was around, they were formal with each other. When I moved off, they reverted to a more natural state.

After about a week, I started to be included.

I stood at the dish sink one afternoon, scrubbing out a pan. Bruce was cleaning something next to me. He was a quiet, seemingly serious guy from Atlanta. He and I had nodded at each other but hadn't had an exchange. He turned to me and asked, "Are you a Deadhead?"

"I love the Dead. How did you know?"

"I saw you pull into the parking lot in your truck and I saw the skull-and-lightning sticker on the back. I'm a Dead fan too." We started talking about our favorite Dead songs (we both agreed on

"Wharf Rat") then about our lives outside of school. He got excited. "I write too," he exclaimed. "I'm really interested in comedy writing. That's what I do when I'm not here." We talked about Woody Allen and Larry David. I was surprised, because he had come off as so serious; when he smiled, his lips barely seemed to move. We wound up doing routines from the *Chapelle Show* for each other.

Gabrielle, or Gabi as she liked to be called, was one of the four people on my team. She was a pretty, slender woman from Queens, and we had spoken briefly to each other about New York City. She sang to herself as she worked. One day, she sang something over and over. I liked the melody and asked her what she was singing.

"It's a song from *Wicked*. Do you know that play?"

"No, not at all. But you have a really nice voice." From that moment on, she was friendly and talkative.

But no one was more talkative than Leo. He was twenty years old, from Mexico, and irrepressible. Within the span of sixty seconds, Leo might burst out into song—often Sinatra—then ask anyone in range what they thought of Sinatra, then what they thought of his singing. He'd free-associate words and say them aloud. He bounced from one worktable to another, hugging people, asking them what they were doing, how they were feeling. He'd yell out a question for Speiss, interrupt the answer to ask an unrelated question, and then ask Speiss how he felt about Sinatra. He just never stopped.

At first Leo had kept his distance, but his curiosity seemed to win out. He began addressing me as "Jonny" and, for days, fired question after question at me: Where was I from? Did I like Lee Marvin? What about Charles Bronson? Had I ever studied martial arts? Do I like bread? What's my favorite kind of bread? Do I prefer classic rock or metal? Did I think Carol was pretty? Gabi? Margot? Did I have a girlfriend? What was she like?

He began getting on my nerves. At most points during class, I could hear Leo's voice somewhere in the room.

"Wow," I said to Gabi. "That kid just never slows down, does he?"

For a day or two during our second week, I tried focusing on my projects—rolling out croissant dough, making crème anglaise, shaping pretzels—but no matter my concentration, Leo's chattering would seep in. It became something akin to a toothache. One afternoon as I was trying to shape a baguette, his attention shifted to me.

"Jonny—I need to know which you think is the best *Star Wars* movie. Which one does your girlfriend like? Where did you live in New York City? Which restaurants did you like to go to? How far is Brooklyn from here? I have a thousand friends on Facebook. Have you ever seen *It's Always Sunny in Philadelphia*?"

"Leo, I'm trying to work. Can you interrogate me during dinner?"

"Jonny, I want answers. My favorite drink is a martini—"

"Leo . . ."

"One time, in Mexico, I used to play soccer—"

"Leo—"

"Yes, and there was this opossum—"

I exploded. "Leo, do you ever shut the fuck up?"

"What?"

"Leo, do you ever stop? I am getting this new vision of hell and that vision is being trapped in a car with you for a really long ride. Why are you talking to me about opossums?"

"I have ADD. But also because the opossum bit one of my team-mates, and so I got a tennis racket and put on cleats and . . ."

"Okay. No more. You must stop."

"We will talk about the opossum during dinner, yes? Tell me you love me, Jonny."

He had worn me down. I started laughing to myself in disbelief, wiping my hands together to get the flour off.

"Will you hug me, Jonny?"

"No."

"Yes, you will." Leo swooped in and hugged me. "Jonny, will you be my Facebook friend?"

I noticed two things as Baking class progressed. One, we actually did a lot more work than was apparent. It seemed as if most of our class time was spent watching our recipes cook through the glass of the oven doors, but Speiss, in all his placidity, influenced us through a number of different tasks every day. We had our main project—rolling out the croissants, for instance—but he might suddenly hand you a recipe for biscotti just twenty minutes before dinner and with his quiet enthusiasm have you scurrying to mix it together, all without any resentment. One day, I worked on croissants, made chocolate biscotti, did a crème anglaise, rolled up a strudel whose patina of dough stretched and tore in about six different places, helped twist together a dozen challah breads, and piped whipped cream on a few dozen plates of desserts. Others in the class did just as much and more. If Speiss asked you to do something, you did it because you really couldn't stomach the idea of disappointing the guy. When things went wrong, you felt bad.

Most of the goods we baked and desserts we made got sent out to the Banquet and Catering dining room, or to the dessert table in the cafeteria. If we screwed something up—like when the strudel dough split—Speiss wouldn't send it out, he'd stand next to you, looking down on your baked mistake, wordless until his hand went on your shoulder and he said, "You weren't careful enough when you were stretching it out. Remember how I showed you? But it's okay, Jonathan—we'll just eat it ourselves. Why don't you cut it up and we'll put some out for everyone to try?" I remembered as he said it to me a time when I was little and broke a favorite lamp of my mother's, purely by accident. She didn't yell. "It's okay," she said. "You didn't mean to do it." But, on a very low frequency, her face broadcast her distress. Speiss was like that.

The second thing I noticed was that by the middle of the second week, everyone was excelling. It was rocky, at first, for a lot of the group, whose culinary experiences were centered around sauté pans and open flames. Bread dough had gotten overkneaded until the gluten gave up and died, starters wouldn't start, ice creams had turned out rock hard, and the kitchen would often be permeated by the smoky odor of goods being baked until black. Stephen, a Texan whom I recognized from some of my L-Block classes, and whom I really liked, had, I think, been born under a bad sign. If he walked through a room that was completely empty except for a glass in the far corner, Stephen would somehow find a way to accidentally break that glass. On the second day of class, we had sat down for Speiss's lecture and Stephen pulled out his notebook and his pen. He uncapped the pen, began lowering it toward his paper, and the pen exploded in a pool of ink. The third day, he stood in front of one of the Hobart mixers staring forlornly into the mixing bowl. I arrived next to him and started pouring ingredients into the second mixer.

"Hey, Jonathan, how's everything going?"

"Good, Stephen, and you?"

"I can't figure out why my dough is doing this . . ."

I looked into the bowl. The dough was splotched with different shades of tan and looked like soft wax. "I've never actually seen dough act like that," I said. Speiss happened by.

"Stephen, what did you do to that dough?"

"I have no idea, Chef."

Speiss stared at the mass as it turned and the motor buzzed and whined. "I honestly have no idea either."

But by the middle of the second week, Stephen's unlucky streak had ended, he was making great focaccia and fantastic biscuits. Jacky, a sweet, offbeat kid born in Hong Kong and raised in New Jersey, who had been constantly knocking things off the counter, scorching his crème anglaise, or burning caramel into a searing epoxy, turned quick and efficient. Margot, who always wore the expression of someone who had just screwed up and was about to have to answer for it, was making these perfect pie crusts, and her croissants were delicious. Everyone—Sammy, Rocco, the rest of the class, including me—had bloomed, and quickly. It might have been unfamiliar territory to all of us, but we grasped it in a way that I hadn't seen occur in other classes before this.

I understood why as I walked to class that second week, having arrived early for no other reason than I wanted to get into class; it was my day to make ice cream and I planned to add crumbled-up Kit Kats to it. We had bloomed because no one had to duck and cover; no one had to be on the defensive. None of us worried about covering our vitals in the face of an attack from a loud, abrasive chef. It wasn't a vacation in Bakeshop 8—we worked. We had the same two hours to get things done as we'd had and would continue to have in other classes. We got everything done on time. I'd gotten lucky for the most part when it came to my instructors. No one had ever taken me completely apart. But there was always the threat that your next instructor might be one of those chefs who did have a reputation for relentlessness—Turgeon, Roe, Pardus, on and on. And threat contributed to a constant case of anxiety. It was just floating on the air of the campus, like an incredibly pervasive pheromone. But with Speiss, you knew you weren't going to be eviscerated, so you could focus—really turn your faculties like a laser—on what you were doing and why you were doing it. I felt as if I were truly learning under Speiss's charge.

I was on a small upswing at school. There wasn't a ton of time left, either in Speiss's class or of classes, period. I resolved to ride it out, to enjoy what remained of Baking, to try and take the most I could out of my remaining classes.

IT WAS THE NIGHT before the Bocuse d'Or finals. Twelve American teams would be competing to see who would go to the actual Bocuse d'Or in Lyon, France, in 2011, and the CIA was hosting the event in the school gymnasium. A prestigious competition, with all the noblesse of the Olympics, this event is taken pretty seriously in the culinary universe. Teams from around the world compete biennially in Lyon; each team is notified in advance of what fish and which meat they'd be cooking with, and they spend months concocting menus, refining them through practice, refining some more, practicing some more, and then meeting for the actual competition. Here at the CIA, the competing chefs had two and a half hours to get their dishes done the day of the competition (they got three hours the day before to get the grunt work accomplished), and their dishes would be judged by renowned chefs—like Keller and Boulud—grading on presentation and taste. Also, each team could earn a significant number of points if the Kitchen Supervision Committee saw those teams working cleanly and hygienically. I didn't know who was on the Kitchen Supervision Team, or who chose them, or what their criteria was, but I found the concept funny. I kept thinking of the Taliban's Ministry for the Promotion of Virtue and Prevention of Vice.

I got ready for bed a little earlier, the alarm set for 5:30. I told myself that I would see all of the competition the next day, from beginning to end. My journalist training was kicking in—it seemed like the sort of event that begged to be experienced that way. Some of the best cooks in the country would be at work tomorrow, judged by a few of the best chefs in the world. The ones doing the judging had once been just like those doing the cooking, who had formerly been just like those attending the school. Some of those best chefs had literally been like those of us currently going to school. Grant Achatz is an alumnus of the CIA, as is Eric Ziebold, and both were French Laundry alums. I'd been taught to sauté in just the same way as they had. At some point, that knowledge began working differently for them than for most others with the same education. I wasn't sure that it was strictly a matter of experience, although that certainly helped. I wanted to see what people did tomorrow. I wanted to see all of it. I wanted to compare movements, gestures.

I arrived at 7:50 because the gymnasium began letting people in at 8:00. I'd been thinking the whole ride over that there would probably be lines and crowds and mayhem, but at that hour, the parking lots were empty and I didn't see anyone. The Rec Center was still dead. I sat down in the second row of the bleachers, right in the middle, settled in, and began watching. All six kitchens were occupied with a competing chef, his or her assistant, and then a third helper, a *commis,* who lent a hand wherever needed. Many of the commis were CIA students—they wore their uniforms—and I wondered how they landed the job. For a second I felt a brief flash of envy—it would have been kind of cool to be that close to the action—but within a blink, I began thinking that I would never want the gig. What if one gaff on my part caused a break in the action that the cooks could never recover from? How could those kids handle that responsibility?

The cooks had been going since 6:00 and had two and a half hours, so the first round of presentations would be in thirty minutes. They had to present a Scottish salmon dish and a lamb dish. I sat back, watching, but there was very little to watch. They bent over their counters or stoves, reaching for a tool, grabbing an ingredient. A few different camera crews trawled along the length of the kitchens. Sometimes they'd stop, and what they shot showed up on the video monitor. I looked up and saw the cooks chopping vegetables, whisking something in a pot, plucking leaves from stems of herbs. Right then, none of them seemed rushed or panicked. No one appeared rattled.

More spectators arrived; clusters of people gathered at either end of the kitchens and the bleachers started to fill. I saw some of my classmates. I saw Gabriel Kreuther, executive chef at the Modern, where I'd wanted to do my externship, standing off to the left of the room, arms folded, watching the cooks at work. I saw André Soltner, of Lutèce, right behind Kreuther. Charlie Trotter, one of whose employees was competing, strolled from one end of the kitchens to the other. The judges started arriving in twos and threes: Grant Achatz and Thomas Keller, Daniel Boulud, Tim Hollingsworth, from the French Laundry, who competed a few years prior and had been written about in the book *Knives at Dawn*. Ziebold arrived. Tim Ryan. Jerome Bocuse.

The event was emceed by Gavin Kaysen, chef at Café Boulud, who competed in the Bocuse d'Or in 2007, and a woman named Kelly Choi, host of the television show *Top Chef Masters*. They discussed who the judges were and Kaysen riffed a little on the pressures of cooking under those conditions—"These are some of the most intense hours of your life," he said. "You have no room for error. You can't make mistakes. The judges pick up on everything." I wondered how the cooks felt hearing this. No one seemed to be paying any attention, but I couldn't believe they didn't take it in.

It occurred to me that the exciting stuff might have happened way before anyone was allowed into the gym, around six a.m., when the first set of cooks fired up their burners. At this point, they were just working steadily, honing things.

Because there was so little going on, Choi worked the room, picking her way along and up the bleachers, looking for young faces and inquiring, "Are you a culinary student?" She was on the money each time. She followed up by asking, "What do you think of the event so far?" And each time, the student underwent a mild freeze-up, looking up at Choi and at his or her face outsized on the monitor. For the four or so minutes Choi stalked the bleachers, every interviewee gave roughly the same answer, "I think this is just amazing." I wasn't sure what they were amazed by. She followed up with, "Do you think this is something you'd like to do someday?" She got an affirmative from each person. I saw Choi getting closer to where I was sitting. She's incredibly slender and her dress was very purple. I worried that when she asked me—and she really looked as if she was coming my way—I'd go blank and respond with the word "amazing," so I got up and clomped down the bleachers to the main floor and went off to stand by the doors.

I found a spot right by the table where the cooks would be plating their dishes for the judges. The weather around this table was full of coiled activity just about to spring. A small squadron of Certified Master Chefs stood expressionless with clipboards—I recognized them, I'd passed them in the hallways, and oftentimes, before I'd even seen their faces or read the CMC title embroidered on their chefs' jackets, I could intuit their rank. They walked differently, with a degree more bearing. Something about passing that monster of a test must alter your genetics. Alongside them were a knot of senior chef-instructors, whom I also recognized from the day-to-day traffic in the hallways. A group of students stood there with the CMCs and instructors, dressed in white shirts and ties and black pants, idling with their hands clasped behind their backs. And off a ways, standing behind them, was Sitti with a large camera around his neck. When he eventually looked in my direction, I waved and he picked his way through the islands of people. We stood there with a velvet cordon between us.

"I'm assuming you're taking photos here?" I asked. "Is this for the personal Sitti collection or is this a job?"

"I was asked to do this. The school paper asked me. I've taken 236 photos."

"Of what?"

"Mostly people just standing around. It's very boring so far. And people keep telling me I'm in their way, so I'm just trying to find a place to stand."

"Hey, Sit—do you know how all these commis got the gig?"

"I don't know. But I do think you have to know someone."

"I wouldn't want to do it."

"I don't think I'd want to either. Maybe too much pressure."

Someone came and told Sitti "Fifteen minutes." Sit nodded and said, "I'll find you later and show you the pictures."

Kaysen announced that in a very short time, the first platter of salmon, followed fifteen minutes later by a platter of lamb, would be presented to the judges. Only half the judges would taste the salmon, and the other half would taste the lamb. The first presenter was Jennifer Petrusky, from Charlie Trotter's restaurant in Chicago. She was in the kitchen closest to where I stood, but from my angle, I couldn't see inside or see the monitor. There was a small army of cameras trained on her, and Daniel Boulud and Thomas Keller stood behind them, watching. After a few minutes, Boulud and Keller strolled back to their seats. Kaysen told the room that Petrusky would be presenting momentarily, and I wondered how she felt offering the debut platter—every eye on her, establishing the tone for the rest of the day, having to face not just the judges, but the snap judgment of everyone in the room, assessing just how high she's setting the bar.

And then the platter came out, held by a pair of the instructors, gliding down and past the row of assembled judges, moving slowly, steadily, letting everyone take it in. The platter's silver caught the lights of the room and it turned incandescent. It arrived at one of the tables near where I stood, descended upon by Petrusky and her commis, surrounded by the CMCs and their clipboards, photographed by a dozen different people.

Petrusky, a twenty-three-year-old midwesterner with angled, pretty features, also looked subtly crazy right then. Her eyes were shiny and panicked, but it didn't show in the purls of her movement, with a small offset spatula in one hand, poised to address the four salmon preparations on the platter: a roulade, confit, cured fillet, and tartar. The platter itself invited a small, momentary reverence; it had a flow and structure to it that made me think of a Japanese rock garden or piece of Buddhist calligraphy.

Then, she had to plate the food for evaluation. The students in their waiter uniforms would carry the plates to the judges' table. I realized I was wrong: Things were beginning to show in Petrusky's movements. Her hand trembled, and a very slight sheen of sweat materialized on her brow. She began lifting the first piece of salmon and placed it at a precise spot on a plate. One of the CMCs leaned in and told her she needed to wear gloves. She slumped for a second, bit her lip, and, without a word, reached for latex gloves from a nearby box. Her commis already had them on.

The remonstration broke her moment, and she began having difficulty arranging the plates. So did her commis. Both of their hands had wills of their own; hers seemed to have a temper, darting and snapping, and his were sullen and uncooperative. Carrying a piece of fish to a plate, Petrusky's commis dropped the fillet awkwardly on the plate. He righted it, leaving a smudge on the pristine white of the china. Petrusky fixed it, murmured something, and the two kept on. When the last plate was done, she left the commis to clean up, and she dashed back to the kitchen to undertake the lamb.

It went like that for an hour. One team replaced by another. One platter of fish or lamb—and a number of the teams, from Petrusky on up, seemed to have been enticed by the idea of using Middle Eastern spices for the lamb—after another, and each of them a beautiful piece of architecture in miniature.

When the final chef presented, there was a break as the kitchens were scrubbed, refurbished, and stocked with the next team's preparations from the previous night. I wanted to watch the process of its being put together, in all its excitement or mundanity, by a single team. I headed upstairs to the deck and staked out a position at the railing overlooking the kitchens. I could see everything inside them. I looked at the schedule to see who was up next and found that a team from Eleven Madison Park was competing. EMP is a Danny Meyer restaurant and shares space in the same building as Tabla. Not too long after Cardoz had gotten a shin kicking from Frank Bruni, EMP was given a four-star review, which caused a stir and some dismay among the staff at Tabla. But I remembered reading the review and the descriptions of the cuisine—a slow-poached egg with brown butter hollandaise and Parmesan foam, a tomato salad made of liquid spheres—thinking of the elegance, the boldness, and the cleverness, and thinking it was definitely a cut above.

James Kent, a sous-chef at EMP, and his sous-chef for the day, Tom Allan, also from the restaurant, were rifling through their supplies. Kent and Allan, I noticed and remarked to myself, are fucking *kids*. I'd been seeing it for almost two years on campus: When individuals have just tripped into their twenties, they have an energy that isn't tamed, like a piece of charcoal before it waxes into an ember. These two had that. They weren't talking, but they still came off as boisterous. Yet at the same time, anchoring that energy and that silent noise was something I remembered seeing in punk or hardcore musicians whose bands have just taken the stage in a club, when they know they're really good and are about to unleash. It's a calm, determined passion, married to confidence and competence. And what they're about to do is for them as much as it is for you. This is a pretty charismatic blend, and it's usually mesmerizing to see. Their commis was a guy named Viraj, who came to extern at Tabla just as I was leaving. We compared notes when we next saw each other on campus. He had had a rosier time of it than I did.

Kent had five different timers set up on his station, each programmed to a different countdown. Taped to the walls were photos of each finished component of his platters, taken during one of his practice runs. He had an immersion circulator for sous-vide cooking bubbling and a mound of neatly folded towels close at hand. When he and Allan started cooking, it was like they'd already been cooking for two hours and I'd just happened onto it. There was no hesitation, no building up, just action—purposeful action—taken with an unconscious economy of movement and motion.

Kent's knife moved over pieces of his salmon, which disintegrated into a pink hash. He picked up a tiny circular mold, like a makeup compact, and filled it with the fish. He made twelve of them. He piped something white and creamy over each mold and, with a tiny spatula smoothed it over. He had a tray of tiny green strips the color of zucchini skin and he wove them on top of the molds into a basket pattern.

The thing that kept my eyes trained was this: it did not have the feeling of a sequence of steps, each with a start and finish. He didn't stop at any point to evaluate what he did. Each moment of this dish coming together was, instead, a continuum of reactions, a constant metamorphosis. Inevitability.

I had two thoughts: Even from where I stood, which was about twenty feet away and ten feet above the action, those little mounds of salmon look beautiful. I hated salmon, but I'd eat one of them. And then I thought, *I've never even attempted something like that.* But why not? Sure, there were practical considerations. These dishes take time. And, more—they take money. But that's a load of horseshit.

Nelly once said to me that it wasn't just failure I was afraid of, but succeeding, too. I didn't understand it at the time she said it—and I'm not sure I understood it fully while remembering the exchange as I watched the EMP guys—but after she said it, the sentence lay there newly born, glistening with truth. To do something right carries with it a set of demands that you be able to do it again, that you irreversibly elevate your standards. I had no idea why that should be unnerving.

Sitti was suddenly at my elbow with his camera. He angled the camera down and clicked away. He stopped and lowered it slightly and stood watching the EMP team. He laughed to himself.

"I swear, Sit, these guys are going to win. I've never seen anything quite like this in a kitchen."

"They are," Sitti said slowly, "kind of incredible." I noticed that the crowd out front had begun to form a knot in front of the EMP kitchen. And I started to notice a feeling of increased heat around me; people were gathering and pressing in up here, too. I looked off to my right and saw Speiss, too, hands in his pockets, glasses perched on his nose, looking down, expressionless but riveted.

Kent and Allan also looked as if they were enjoying themselves. Neither one was grinning, no high fives or anything, but—you could tell—they *knew* they were doing well, and their expressions and their postures spoke in a cant of confidence and competence. They'd worked for this moment for a long time, even before they ever knew they'd be here.

And in that small realization, that tiny truism, I started sensing something gigantic.

Their platter came together, element by element, exactly as all their work had progressed that day. And then activity just stopped; they stood for a moment, and they turned and looked at each other. It was their turn to present. A team of chefs took the platter from them and paraded it for the judges. I found out later exactly what was on it: roulade with Alaskan King Crab, relish of cucumber and Meyer lemon; chilled mousse with tartare and roe; pickled heirloom beets with crème fraîche, dill, and black pepper.

After a few minutes, they were back to arrange the lamb platter and present it: bacon-wrapped lamb saddle with piquillo peppers and provençale herbes; vol-au-vent of braised lamb with sweetbreads and preserved lemon; zucchini with goat cheese and mint; tart of tomato confit with basil, Niçoise olives, and fromage blanc.

To the right of them, the previous team cleaned up. To their left, another team continued to cook and began to put up their platter. With the motion stilled in the EMP kitchen, momentum and purpose were hanging like phantoms in the air. In a moment they'd dissipate like a scent.

I was thinking again of what I thought before: *They've worked for this moment for a long time, even before they ever knew they'd be here.*

And I started to move away; I was out of the crowd, rounding the corner of the upstairs deck, picking my way along, as far back as I could go. There were chairs there, but no one else was around. I sat down and put my face in my hands. I could feel my eyes pulsing. The hair on my arms stood up. I had gooseflesh. My body was so attentive, so pitched, that I could almost feel the light hitting my skin.

What I'd just seen was a philosophy of life in action. Two guys—two kids—who one day decided they would be excellent; who disciplined themselves, learned everything they could, practiced aggressively, and moved their thinking onto a whole other plane. They might have been musicians; they might have been dancers. In their case, it was about food. And they recognized that at each stage—from the second they set out their equipment through the moment they do their prep to the final assemblage—that there is a best possible way to do everything. Every gesture, no matter how small, was about the individual attempting to be great.

What those guys did—what they do—is attainable. You'll wind up bleeding to get there, but you can get there. But not me, at least not with the bruises and slights of how I think about myself, with all my hesitations, my timidity, my half-assed methodology of doing what was expected of me but little more.

This is why they yell at you. This is why you're forced to get up in the morning and go cut fish. This is why they will never give you a compliment. This is why.

And I disagree with so much of how they do it sometimes, the chefs, with their bullying, their brute force. But I understood now the impulse behind it. If you can get rid of all your mental baggage and distractions, all your own doubts and pettiness and bullshit, you can arrive at the clarity of mind with a diamond focus that lets all of a person's training and skill bloom. Then a person can be great.

I had gotten to see greatness today. Everything that had gone on for me up until now, the exhaustion, the being disciplined, the building angers, the energy of those angers, the nervous, racked nights of the last summer were all leading to watching this today.

I HAD A BETTER understanding of what people meant when they referred to being born again. I looked the same, but my body felt different. My mind had had a bypass done on it. I felt able. I felt electrified. I saw school and everything about it as an opportunity to try and touch perfection, to hone efficiency, to find at every moment a chance to be better, no matter the external pressures.

On our final night of baking, Speiss said that instead of going to dinner, he thought it would be a nice idea to stay in and make our own pizzas. He ordered mozzarella, Parmesan, and ricotta for us, and all sorts of meats and vegetables. "Do whatever you want," he said. "We'll all try each other's wares." He asked for a volunteer to make a tomato sauce, and he mixed the dough for us as we finished up baking our final loaves of bread and making desserts to take to the faculty lounge and the cafeteria. He cranked up the heat in one of the ovens, gave a quick demonstration on how to stretch out the dough, and then set us loose. It was another moment when our choices spoke loudly about culinary values and interests. Micah, a twenty-year-old from Alaska, tall, thin, with an impish face who had taken to very lightly tickling me whenever he walked by and I was trying to concentrate on something, set about putting herbs into goat cheese and caramelizing fennel. Rocco, a loud, likable kid from New Jersey, who constantly sang, danced, and kissed everyone's cheeks, covered his dough with sausage, pepperoni, and a little bit of every fresh vegetable Speiss had ordered. I went minimal. I wanted to do a simple margherita pizza. I stretched out my crust so it was thin to the point of tearing. I slicked the dough with a little olive oil and garlic, judiciously applied the sauce—which I had also put through a food mill to avoid any chunks—and laid down uniform slices of fresh mozzarella and a scattering of Parmesan. I tried to deduce where the hottest spot in the oven would be and put the pizza in to bake. I had a little time to think as my pizza cooked.

The world is glutted with mediocre pizza. Most dough is too thick and dense and tastes wet. Most sauces are either too thin and acidic, or too sweet after having been cooked for so long that they become concentrated and sugary. And, further, most mozzarella seems to have been pulled by the handful from an industrial-sized bag of shredded processed cheese sold by Sysco. It's usually rubbery. You can cheat a little bit by piling all sorts of ingredients on top—garlicky mushrooms, sausage, pepperoni—but if you leave the pizza nude, it's easy to tell what level your skills were. This was a key point for me. My mind took a sudden turn to a different endeavor, away from pizza and toward chicken.

My tastes often run to the simple. Like a lot of people involved in cooking, my favorite meal is roast chicken, preferably with roasted potatoes. I've been making it once a week for years. And I've seen a million variations on it in cookbooks: tamarind glazed; rubbed with Mexican spices or Indian spices; with all manner of things forced under the skin, from a citrus peel and bread-crumb mix to goat cheese and pine nuts to truffles. I'm sure that a lot of these are pretty good. But— I was asking myself as I checked my pizza; the crust had begun showing flecks of gold. I closed the door again—why mess with a naked chicken? Because a lot of people out there haven't ever really learned how to roast a chicken well. And many of us have always relied on Perdue for the chicken itself. If you simply shove a crappy factory bird in an oven—and do so without the right amount of seasoning, without the right oven temperature, and so on—the results will be bland for certain, and probably awful. It's almost as if playing with a roast chicken were similar to how spices were used in medieval times: with an ungodly heavy hand, all the better to cover the rank taste of off meat.

But also, I reasoned, simplicity is hard. Really hard.

I recalled that when Fernand Point wanted to judge the skill level of a cook, he'd have the cook fry an egg. Daniel Boulud allegedly asks him or her to make an omelet.

Once, I remembered, while I was working at Martha Stewart, I scoffed at a recipe we were putting online for basic boiled rice.

"Put the freaking rice in a pot," I had said, dismissive. "Pour in twice the amount of water. Boil it. Boom—you're done. What state have we reached when we need to spell all this out in recipe form?"

Melissa, one of my editors, said, "Actually, that isn't the right ratio of water. And furthermore, have you ever actually had a serving of perfectly cooked rice?"

"I don't know," I said. "I've never even considered it."

"Then you haven't."

An old Buddhist koan came to my mind as I pulled my pizza out: *How many flavors can you detect in a single grain of rice?*

I remembered Viverito saying to me, "So many of these kids tell me about things they want to try making: 'Oh, I want to do shrimp with a pine needle foam and pea gel.' I want to tell them, 'Okay, so you've made a foam. Now, explain what this adds to the dish other than demonstrating that you can make a foam? How about learning inside and out how to cook that shrimp so it isn't pure rubber?'"

The underside of the pizza was a beautiful light brown. I shoved a pizza peel under it to pull it out and slid it onto a cutting board to cool. After a minute, I used scissors to cut pieces of ripe basil over the top.

You get a perfect roasted chicken by following directions close to this: Dry the skin of the bird with a paper towel; you don't want moisture. Remove the wishbone. Salt the cavity of the bird. Truss the bird—there are a hundred dozen ways to do this; choose one—and salt the exterior of the chicken as well. Have your oven at around 425. Put your chicken in a pan, up and off the pan's floor. Some people use a rack, I roll aluminum foil up, wrap it around my fingers into a coil, and perch the chicken on top. Put it into the oven and let it go for twenty, twenty-five minutes, until the skin begins turning color. Drop the heat to 375 and let it go for another thirty-five minutes. Tip the chicken; red juices will run out. Close the oven on it for another four or five minutes. Tip again. There will be less red in the juices, and they will be darker. Close the oven. After a couple of minutes, tip again. The juices will be a dark, cooked red with some gray. Take the bird out; it's done. Let it rest, uncovered, for twenty minutes—no less. Then cut it up.

This represents an accretion of steps. None of them—in and of themselves—essential, none of them complex. Could you not truss the bird and still get a good chicken? Yes. Could you skip trussing and salting the cavity? Yes. Skip the trussing, cavity salting, elevation off the pan, and seasoning the exterior? Now you're pushing your luck.

If you do it right, the chicken is tender, juicy, and really *tastes* of chicken.

Culinary mediocrity is an accretion of shortcuts. *Take a shortcut now and you'll be taking them for the rest of your career.*

Kent and Allan knew that there is a way to handle every single element, no matter how small, that goes into a dish—*there's a right way to do everything,* Ty had said at Tabla—and they didn't take shortcuts.

Jacky was at my shoulder. "You had all those vegetables here, all those sausages, and you made a margherita pizza? You are so ambitious, aren't you?"

"Do you like roast chicken?"

Jacky looked puzzled. "Of course I do."

I lightly slapped his forehead. "Then eat the freaking pizza and shut the hell up."

The two of us stood eating my pizza. Maybe I could have taken it out a minute earlier, but it was really good.

We had spent that day and the day prior in a state of light heartbreak over leaving Speiss's class. "It was like a womb in here," I'd said, and everyone agreed. But we'd gotten good news on the morning of our final day. The next class was Cuisine of Europe and the Mediterranean. It covered basic Middle Eastern, Spanish, Italian, and French cooking. Everyone was excited. The best lunch and dinnertime foods came out of the Mediterranean kitchens. And our instructor was the recently promoted former Skills teacher, Robert Perillo.

12

"ALL RIGHT," PERILLO SAID. We were gathered in a semicircle around him in the Mediterranean kitchen, which looked identical to most of the other kitchens, except there were a few more ranges and ovens, each stretching parallel against opposite walls. Behind us there was a cart loaded down with that day's order, and trays of meat and fish on table-tops nearby. "A lot of you I remember from Skills I and II. But we're all going to get to know each other even better. I love teaching this class. I love the food, I love passing on what I know, I love learning tricks and techniques from you guys. You've all been out on externship, and you all picked things up. And I'm excited to see what you can show me.

"I think we're going to have a really great time together. Everyone has their assignments? Okay, then. Start cooking."

There is something difficult to describe about how different you feel working under someone who doesn't have too many other places he'd rather be, who wants you to do well, who is genuinely excited about imparting information, who loves cooking and assumes the same about you, who watches every move you make—not to nail you for an error, but to be sure you're doing it the best possible way—and who is having a truly good time doing it all. It's like being given permission to succeed, and you operate fueled by a low, constant ebullience. It was great working with Perillo.

Not that he was easy, or tender, all the time.

It's simpler to cut an onion in half and then pull away the peel than it is to cut off the tops and peel the whole thing first before slicing it in two. But it's cleaner to peel the onion first. Perillo told us to do it that way. He didn't just get excited when things went right; he was just as emotionally invested when things went wrong.

"Okay," I heard him say to Bruce, his voice animated. "When I say peel the onion first, how many different meanings does that have? I'm certain there is one meaning. I think there's no room for interpretation on this one. Peel. The. Onion. First. Please don't make me tell you again."

Or, a little later that first day, Sammy and I had finished our prep work and were putting together a demo plate for Perillo to critique. We were doing ghaliyeh maygoo, an Iranian dish of sautéed shrimp in a tamarind-tomato sauce. I was sautéing shrimp. I didn't have a spatula near me, so I was tossing the pan to make the shrimp jump and bounce and turn over.

"Jonathan," Perillo called out. "Have you ever eaten flying shrimp?"

"Are they a Mediterranean shrimp?" I asked. "I've never heard of flying shrimp before."

"Me neither. Keep the damn pan on the stove."

But then when things went right . . .

I'd been following the hummus recipe and noticed something. "Chef Perillo. There's no cumin in this recipe." He scanned my recipe sheet.

"Very good, Jonathan. You've assessed the recipe correctly." He started moving on.

"Can I put cumin in?"

"No."

"Why not?"

"Because . . ." He stopped and seemed to think about it. "Actually, I don't have a good reason. Okay, go ahead. Just don't make it overpowering."

I immediately toasted some cumin in a pan. The flavor of the cumin is intensified and transformed by toasting it—something I'd picked up at Tabla. I ground it up and put it aside. I minced some garlic, got the chickpeas out (someone from the previous class had soaked and cooked the beans for us), and put them right into a food processor. The recipe didn't call for my next step either. The skins of the chickpeas are tough, and usually make hummus grainy. I pulsed the peas into a paste and then put them twice through a tamis, which looks like a drum head covered with fine wire mesh. The flesh of the peas came out the other side; the skins stayed behind. I put the peas back in the processor with the garlic and cumin, some tahini paste, and lemon juice.

Perillo happened by. "And here's Jonathan, still laboring over the hummus."

I didn't look up. "I would love to banter with you, Chef Perillo, but right now, I am very, very busy and you shouldn't distract me."

"Oh, Jonathan, how I've missed you." He drummed his hands on the worktable and walked away.

I remembered reading that when making hummus, a very slow dribble of oil into the mix as it blends results in a smoother finish. I had my olive oil and began to drip it in, slowly, slowly, a thimbleful at a time, the food processor whirring and shrieking. I could smell the motor heating up. It took a while, but when I finally got the consistency I wanted, I turned the processor off. I tasted it. Before the texture, before the flavor of the hummus, the lack of salt and the need for some tartness hit me first. To leave some wiggle room, I added less salt than I thought I'd need, and then a squirt from a quarter of a lemon. I tried again. The earthiness of the chickpeas came through, the creaminess of the tahini; I could taste the ghost of the garlic on the back of my tongue, and the flavor of the cumin. A touch more salt, another two seconds of the processor. I called Perillo over to evaluate it. He picked up a spoon from a container Sammy and I had standing nearby, dipped it in and tasted. He dropped the spoon into a bin filled with other dirty spoons. Then he took a new spoon and tasted again.

"Man, that is damn good hummus," he said. "I was dubious, but . . ."

"Dubious?" I said. "Oh, ye of little faith."

He stared. "What can I say? I'm happy I'm wrong." He took another spoonful for good measure and went on to make his rounds.

I wasn't the only one doing well. I tried the falafel and it was great. The baba ganouj, too. The fresh-baked pita, the lamb dumplings with yogurt sauce in brown butter—everything was a success. And we were on time to open the kitchen at six. At quarter to, Sammy and I put a stack of eight sauté pans into a 450-degree oven to heat up so the shrimp and tamarind-tomato sauce would cook more quickly. We readied all the ingredients we'd need. When service started, Sammy pulled the sauté pans out from the oven and put them on a burner we weren't using. He would sauté the shrimp when an order came in, and I would take care of the sauce. When the door to the kitchen opened we got two orders immediately and fired them up, passing them off to the students within a minute. I reached for a new pan and pulled it toward me. It had been out of the oven for barely sixty seconds. I felt a sensation that I described later as being "blue" and a scream run from my fingers up my arm. I tried to let go of the handle, but my skin stuck to it. I thrust it loose and looked at my palm. It was a gleaming red. A lot of skin was gone. It hurt so much, my eyes welled up. Sammy turned to look at me.

"What's the problem?"

"I just fucking burned myself."

"How bad?"

"Pretty bad."

Perillo called out for three orders of shrimp. I wrapped my hand in a towel and kept cooking. The pain was grotesque. There were a series of refrigerators under our worktables and we had several metal bains-marie in ours. I kept reaching in and pressing my palm against the cold metal for relief. It would help for about five seconds.

I kept cooking. I didn't quite get why; this was a student kitchen, not three-star dining. Who cared if the students didn't get the shrimp as fast as they wanted it? Or at all. But I couldn't walk away. All I needed to do was spoon some of the tamarind-tomato jam into the pan, shake it with butter until the mix was loose and flowing, and toss in Sammy's shrimp. But I couldn't concentrate on anything other than the blaring pain in my hand.

Perillo came over and said loudly, "Jonathan, your sauce is like mud. What the hell are you doing?"

I didn't answer. I just kept going.

"Hey, come on—we need to fix this sauce!"

Sammy said, "I'll do this. Just serve up the rice. I got it. Don't worry."

I gave up my spot at the stove and addressed myself to the rice. Perillo kept looking over. After about fifteen more minutes, we'd served all our shrimp—about twenty plates' worth. I went up and told Perillo I needed to see the nurse.

"Is that why your sauce was so bad?" he asked, when I told him about the burn.

"I was on the verge of tears."

"Why didn't you leave?"

"I don't know."

"That's insane. Lemme see."

I held my hand out to him.

"That, my friend, is going to hurt."

The nurse debated whether or not to give me antibiotics, decided not to, salved the burn, wrapped it up, and told me to keep it dry. I went back to class; dinner service was long over. Family meal was finished. Everyone milled around, cleaning up. I did what I could with one hand.

I couldn't do anything the next two days, except spoon rice onto the students' plates. By the fourth day, the skin had blistered over, so I put on a latex glove and started cooking again.

But during that time, I was really impressed with how smoothly everyone was working together. Each night, there were a lot of dishes on our menu—six different entrées and about a dozen appetizers, in addition to freshly baked breads, everything to be prepared in two and a half hours. There were the usual problems: dropped pans, brief but vicious arguments over who got to use which piece of equipment when, the inevitable burned foodstuffs.

But in past classes, like in Americas, when something had gone horribly wrong—dropping a full sheet tray of eggplant Parmesan, for instance—the problem got solved by eliminating it completely. The eggplant got wrecked? Fine, we didn't serve eggplant that night.

Perillo wouldn't eliminate the problem. If something went bad—a tomato-pepper jam that got dried out in the pot beyond repair—he made you figure out a way to fix it, to make sure that item was available on the menu with all the others. He moved as if on fast-forward, and when Perillo kept that pace up, the rest of us followed suit. A year ago, when we had tried to effect that sort of speed, we looked like the Keystone Kops, a wake of spills and breakage and cinders trailing behind us. Now the tomato-pepper sauce got done again, and on time.

It became apparent that we had been the recipients of a pretty good education. We'd been taught every technique we'd need and been given the opportunity to practice and refine them. When mistakes happened, it was almost always the result of carelessness, zoning out. It was never a matter of *not* being able to do something. A lot of the nerves and angst we'd all felt when we'd start a new class had eroded away. We were capable, and there was a lot less to worry about.

On the fourth night, we made a selection of tapas dishes. Sammy and I did braised oxtails; others made paella, cod fritters, fried monkfish, tripe in a sauce of stock and wine, braised octopus, Serrano ham fritters, and at least six or seven more. Perillo was ecstatic with the results, and so we were too.

When I labored over an osso bucco one night, during each step, the past two years repeated itself in bursts and flashes in my mind. I thought of the trip to the CSA farm to dispatch the chickens when I was handling the veal, and as it cooked I remembered the duck. As I diced up onions and carrots and made a tomato concassé, I was retelling myself the story of Viverito and the blue bin, and also picturing the platters at the Bocuse d'Or. I tried to make every cut a model of exactitude. I tried to use every scrap. When I saw my cutting board getting littered, I remembered Tabla, and remembered it again when I'd look at the clock and see it pointing out the disparity between what needed to be done and the target time of 6:00. I'd taste my sauce and a phantom Coyac would arrive at my shoulder with bulging eyes; I worked for perfection with the seasoning. I tried to hit a harmony of mind and action that let whatever dish I was working on come together from nothing into a aggregate of small successes.

Perillo had really bloomed too. He mused to us one day about how fascinated he was with history in general, how it made up the bulk of his reading, and he reflected it in his lectures. Italy, France, Spain, and the Middle East each has, to understate the matter, a substantial historical record, and Perillo got animated and intense whenever he'd talk about the spice trade, or the Inquisition, or which foods came from the New World, or the fall of the Roman Empire. He had a theory of history that was based on economic exploitation, and he'd grow angry talking about blood spilled in the name of money, shaking his head, pursing his lips, waving his hands.

Before dinner service one afternoon, a few days before the end of the class, Perillo took each of us into the hallway for a short conference on our progress.

"So what happened to you over the last year and a half? I'm watching you zip around the kitchen with more confidence—more *competence*—than I saw in you before. You're really doing some cooking in here, and you're putting up great food."

"I don't know. I sort of had a born-again culinary experience a little while ago. It's a little hard to explain."

"Well, hallelujah, then," he said. He glanced down at the clipboard in his hand. "On the other hand, your sense of teamwork needs some help. You're not communicating with others well. Part of working in a kitchen is keeping a dialogue going with people around you."

"Okay. Fair enough. I'll give you that one."

"Thanks. That's kind of you. Especially since I'm the one giving the grades. Just as an example, the night you burned your hand, I shouldn't have to have been the one coming over to you and telling you how bad your sauce was. You and Sammy should have worked that one out." He gripped the clipboard by its corner and started swinging it, signaling we were done. "But really—you've come a long, long way. Keep going."

———

From Perillo's kitchen we went to Banquets and Catering, seven days of cooking in quantity for the incoming students—around eighty or so each night—who crowded into the same room I'd sat in the first weeks of school. But before we got near a stove, we would spend seven days waiting on them.

Ezra Eichelberger, the hospitality instructor, was a short, smart, jolly guy with a broad smile and a mustache, and he jumped right into the fundamentals, teaching us the first day about how to carry several full plates at once, about setting the table, taking orders on our dupe pads, learning how systems of tables and seats worked in restaurants, and the fundamentals of dealing with people face-to-face.

It was easy to take in the mechanics. I already knew where knives and forks went on a table because my mother had taught me. Seat one at each table in the B&C room was at seven o'clock. When you said "table 45" that did not mean there were forty-five tables in the room, but that you were referring to the fifth table in the fourth row.

But I had a very hard time interacting with our clientele—the students. On the first few nights, some of them were very pleasant. They asked questions not about the menu, but about the program, about my experiences at the school, which instructors they should be hoping to get for their Skills or Asia or Mediterranean class. But that was only some of them.

My threshold for rudeness is low. Rudeness is an entirely unnecessary mode of socializing. Being polite is effortless. And what made it difficult for me—the *demands* for another glass of chocolate milk, the absence of *please* and *thank you* in our exchanges, telling me, "This table needs more bread. Now."—was that it seemed like it never would have occurred to a lot of these kids to ask nicely for something and say thank you when they got it.

And, for culinary students, they were pretty unadventurous. Served a rack of lamb done to a very nice medium-rare, one table of guests looked horrified when Gabi and I placed their plates in front of them.

"It's raw!" they marveled, incredulous.

One young woman pushed the plate away. "I don't eat raw food." Her expression indicated we were the worst sort of morons for trying to slide this incompetence past her. She looked at her dining companions and snorted derisively.

I tried diplomacy. "No, no—it's not raw. This is when it's at its best. Also, this is how you guys are going to be cooking this stuff in class. Try it. That's why they have you coming here. This is your future you're tasting now."

"Well, this isn't how *I* cook lamb." Then she told me, "You can serve your other tables now."

Gabi's face looked as if she wanted to laugh. She kept looking from me to the students and back. I wanted to tip this girl's plate into her lap. I said nothing.

Leaving the table, I passed Eichelberger. "I weep for our future," I said.

"Oh, Jonathan." He ruefully shook his head. "You have no idea."

Eichelberger walked up to me on the sixth night. "Jonathan, I've been wanting to tell you all week that I haven't had as much fun in a long time as I've had watching you try and keep your composure with the students. It's been just hilarious. Thank you for that. And this is definitely *not* the career path you should be choosing."

We finally moved into the kitchen, which had been placed under the charge of Paul Sartory. This was the last class he'd be teaching at the Hyde Park campus. He'd been transferred to the San Antonio branch of the CIA and couldn't have been more excited.

"So this is a permanent move?" I asked.

"Man, I hope so," Sartory said.

He hadn't changed at all since Americas. He was still unflappable and relentlessly calm. The first day, there was some confusion about which menu we were following and, so, which recipes to use and I made the wrong sauce to accompany the beef tenderloin for dinner.

"Huh," Sartory pondered. "Well, Jon, I'll tell you what—there's no reason to do it over. Why don't we just go with what you've got. I should have been more clear. No big deal. The kids won't know the difference."

We also never gave him much reason to become flappable or get upset. It wasn't that dissimilar to Perillo's class: We knew what we were doing and we did it. We had our instructions and we followed them. The food came out well.

The third day passed, then the fourth and fifth. On the fifth day, before class got started, I was unpacking my knives and equipment in front of the same window I'd stood on the other side of my first day of school. And a young guy—he was maybe seventeen or eighteen— stood looking back at me. I raised my eyebrows and smiled at him, and thought, *You poor fucker; you have no idea what you're in for . . .*

IF YOU ASKED ANYONE who'd taken the wine course what parts of the textbook you *really* needed to know, they simply told you, "All of it."

Wines class—officially designated as Wines and Beverages—ran for three weeks, from 2:00 in the afternoon until 8:00 at night. It had the highest failure rate—30 percent—of any class in the CIA curriculum. The textbook took you from country to country, region to region, vineyard to vineyard around the world: the United States, Chile, Australia, France, Italy, Spain, Portugal. It numbered more than eight hundred pages.

For the tests on the United States (also including Mexico and Canada) and France and Italy, you needed to memorize all the major growing regions (or appellations) and the major vineyards. You were allowed to use the book—and any notes you could manage to fit inside the cover and frontispieces—for the final, which a lot of people still failed. You needed to know which wines were produced in a given region, which grapes went into those wines, how to read a French wine label as opposed to an Italian or American label, and have a good working knowledge of how all these wines were produced, fermented, and aged.

It was a deluge of information.

The evening class was taught by Steven Kolpan, a man Eichelberger described as "brilliant." He knew, Eichelberger said, everything there was to know about wines and could also discourse knowledgeably on literature, art, and music.

When we arrived for the first class, Kolpan was seated behind a podium down on the floor of the lecture room, which was ringed by tiers of seats attached to long tables. He said nothing to anyone until the precise stroke of 2:00. He gave a few introductory remarks about the class, the necessity—and he gave the word necessity a very dire cast—of studying, of reading *everything* and of reading ahead. He stressed that one of the class's main components would be the pairing of foods and wine. Wine, he said, could not be fully enjoyed without food. He stood up at that point. He was a large guy who looked as if he'd put his philosophy of wine and food to the test. He spent a little while orienting us to the world of viniculture, giving us basic definitions of concepts like fermentation and the influence of weather on a wine grape. He kept us on the edge of the vat for a few more minutes, letting us test the temperature with our big toes, and then he pushed us in. He turned on an overhead projector, and a map of Northern California appeared on the screen.

"California has three major regions: the North Coast, Central Coast, and the Interior/Central Valley. You only need to worry about the North and Central coasts. Let's look at the North Coast first. You'll need to know about Napa, Sonoma, and Mendocino. The Napa AVA, or American Viticultural Area, is divided into fourteen sub-AVAs. The most important are Oakville, Rutherford, Stags' Leap, and Los Carneros. Now, the important vineyards in the Oakville sub-AVA are . . ."

He lectured for four hours, until 6:00, limning out the history of California wine growing, the importance of the cabernet sauvignon grape, which wines were made by which vineyards, who had the best chardonnays and why.

I sat in the front row next to Zach and Sabrina, and I took down as much as I could. By six, my hand was cramping and moaning from writing so much. We took a forty-five-minute dinner break, and when we returned, several students were dispatched to pick up racks of tasting glasses. A bunch more were ordered to open bottles of wine. Eight of the glasses were put in rows in front of each seat, and tasting portions of wines poured into them.

"Okay, wine number one," Kolpan said. "Sauvignon blanc, from the Honig vineyard, from Napa, from 2007. What do you get by way of the wine's nose? Anyone? No one?"

We all had our faces jammed into the tops of our glass. It smelled like wine. White wine. Kolpan paused. He got a slightly weary look on his face.

"Okay. How about citrus? Does anyone smell citrus?"

We all agreed that, yes, come to mention it, we smelled citrus.

"What about green apple?"

Yes, indeed, green apple.

"How about something a little less pleasant?"

We continued sniffing. It still only smelled of citrus and apple.

"Does anyone get a hint of cat pee?"

I sniffed deeply. There actually was that hint. "Wow," I exclaimed. "I actually do get a little bit of cat piss."

"Okay, good, good. But let's refer to it as 'cat pee,' just to keep it civilized in here. Now let's taste it. Acidic, fruity. A long finish. What do I mean by finish? How long do you keep tasting it after you've swallowed? That's the finish. Most of the wines we taste in here will have a long finish. It's been twenty seconds and I'm still tasting this one. What foods do you think this would go with? If you said seafood, you're right. If you said goat cheese, you're right too."

So he led us, wine by wine, day after day, into a working vocabulary of tasting. An Anderson Valley gewürztraminer had a lychee nut/ cream soda nose, and a honey, hops, and cardamom flavor. A chardonnay from the Russian River Valley gave up a horseradish nose with buttery, tannic, almost potatolike flavors. We moved into red wines, from California and the Hudson Valley and Finger Lakes region of New York. Onward to Washington State, up into Canada. We got hints of plums, pepper, leather, blackberries.

On test day, before he lectured, Kolpan gave us our first exam. Fifty questions, multiple choice, on a sheet where we filled in the little circles with a number two pencil. I barreled through it and all the queries about which vineyard grew exemplary chardonnay grapes, which wine would go best with goat cheese tortellini and lamb jus, or lobster, or fried calamari.

During dinner, Kolpan fed the Scantrons through the computer and gave us our tests back after the break. I got mine and read the score: a 70. I began attending tutoring sessions.

The score notwithstanding, a friend of mine e-mailed me, saying his parents were in town and he was cooking lamb that coming Sunday; did I have any wine suggestions, since I'd been taking this class. I wrote back: "Okay, keeping in mind we've only done wines from California, try something with a lot of tannins in it—try a cabernet sauvignon from the Napa Valley (look for St. Helena, Stags' Leap, Mount Veeder, Rutherford, or Oakville) or a syrah. We had a really amazing syrah tonight that retails for about eighteen or nineteen bucks called Syrah 'Le Posseur' from the Bonny Doon winery. It was better than any one of the wines that was three times the price."

After sojourns in Chile, Argentina, Mexico, Australia, and South Africa, we arrived in France.

"France and Italy," the tutor told us, "are ridiculously hard."

She didn't lie. We studied the wines of the Loire Valley—the western, central, and eastern parts—and its muscadets, the Pouilly-Fumés, the Sancerres; on to the Champagne region and then to Bourdeaux. Bourdeaux got really complex; yes, it was primarily known for dry reds—mainly cabernet sauvignon—but you needed to know that Château Latour, Château Lafite Rothschild, and Château Mouton Rothschild all came from the Pauillac commune in the Left Bank of Bordeaux. There were eight other communes to know, each with their Châteaus, plus Bordeaux had a Right Bank, and another section— Entre Deux Mers—to contend with. Then we went to Burgundy, to Alsace, and the Rhône Valley.

We tasted wines from all these places, Kolpan leading us in figuring out what we were detecting as far as flavors went, and how to talk about them. There was, at no point, a single question he wasn't able to answer at length—what type of oak an obscure vineyard in Alsace used to age its wines, how the different vineyards all varied from one another as far as weather went, which vineyard had more chalk in its soil than another. We all liked him because he obviously knew what he was talking about. He was, in fact, as brilliant as Eichelberger had told us. And he seemed to really enjoy hearing what we had to say, at least, once we had the words to say it.

We moved on to Italy: Tuscany, Piedmont, Campagnia, Sicily, Sardinia, Venice, Lombardi. Dozens of grapes, innumerable vineyards, infinite wines.

On the second test, covering France and Italy both, I studied until my brain foamed and my eyes ran with glycerin and blood. I got a 75.

"I'm not stupid," I told Nelly. "Shit, I don't know. I really studied."

"Honey, you manage to forget what you're going to the supermarket for. Plus, I honestly believe when you're younger, doing rote memorization is a lot easier. I don't know that *I* could memorize all this stuff."

I ran into Eichelberger in the hallway the day after the test and he stopped to talk. He asked me how I liked wines class.

"Kolpan is everything you said he was. He's kind of awe inspiring. There's nothing he doesn't know. But I have the same problem with this class that I've had with meat and fish: You're given an insane amount of information to memorize in a very short time. And it's good information, it's useful information. But we're cramming all of it in there, and we're just going to forget most of it because we'll be on to the next class."

I used to go into wine stores and buy according to price. It didn't matter what I was planning on drinking the wine with, I knew two things: I wanted red wine, and I wanted to spend about $10. All the names and terms and abbreviations on the label might as well have been in Hittite. But now I had begun understanding what those labels meant. I could look at a zinfandel, see where it was grown and bottled—which appellation, which sub-AVA—and make an educated guess. I was pretty broke, so I wasn't buying much wine, but within a stretch of two weeks, I got three bottles, mainly because I wanted to flex my knowledge. I was on the money with two, dead wrong with the third.

By the time the final rolled around, we had tasted almost 150 wines. We had two days off between our last class and the last test. I'd been to all the tutoring sessions. I spent hours copying my lecture notes and tasting notes into any blank space I could find in the textbook. I had Nelly quiz me using flash cards.

On test day, those who looked nauseated and dyspeptic were screwed. Some of those who looked at ease and confident were probably screwed too. I figured the rest of us who fell somewhere in between might have a fighting chance. A handful of the group—and we numbered around fifty or so—was taking the class for the second time. One woman was on her third attempt. There were more than one hundred questions. I went through and answered every question I didn't need to look up first; that left me with around seventy questions to go. I had tagged various sections in the book based on region, so I could flip right to whatever information I needed. But the questions weren't always black and white: Given two different regions, which one would most likely have the best merlot? What about the best gamay? They might both produce those wines, but which one had the edge? The book wasn't always clear, and you had to read carefully to get a hint and answer the question. We had two and a half hours, and I used up almost all the time.

I got a 75 on the final, and a 79 for the class, the lowest grade I'd gotten so far in school. And I felt lucky.

FOR THE FINAL THREE months of the program, the CIA used to send each of the students through each of the four restaurants on campus that were open to the public: Caterina D'Medici, the Italian restaurant; American Bounty, which specialized in regional American food; St. Andrew's, which had started out as a health-food restaurant but changed its focus to serving locally sourced and sustainable foods; and the Escoffier Room, which served old-school, classic French cuisine inspired by its namesake. Every student did a short stint as a cook and a short stint as a waiter in each place.

Our group was the first to see this policy changed. Now we would choose two restaurants and spend three weeks in the kitchen of each, followed by three weeks serving its customers. We were assigned a randomly generated number—mine was thirty-six—and on the appointed day, we chose in order according to our numbers. Even with a relatively good number, I still didn't get what I wanted. I chose Caterina and Escoffier; I got into Escoffier, but Caterina was full. I'd be going to St. Andrew's instead.

For most of us, it was beginning to sink in that things were just about over, that graduation was coming up fast. People were beginning to put feelers out for jobs. Some had already lined up work; a few were returning to their externship sites; others had interviewed at restaurants in New York City, Boston, Yellowstone Park, and Nantucket and were set to begin in just a few weeks. The future was arriving and it felt wide open.

But there was an edge of weariness, too. It sprang, I think, from a sense of impending emancipation. The weight of the rules and regulations, of the chefs' shouting and reprimands, suddenly felt a lot heavier. We were sick of being yelled at. And since we were now cooking for the public—for actual paying customers—I suspected there might be some more yelling to come.

Some of the people I'd been with since Baking were still in the group—Dan, Jessica, Bruce, Stephen, Gabi—others, like Jeff, who was now the group leader, were familiar faces, but I was meeting them for the first time. Leo, Zach, Rocco, and Micah had all gone to Caterina, and I was sorry to see them go.

On our first day we met in a classroom underneath St. Andrew's. The kitchen was run by Chef Robert Mullooly, who had only been at the CIA for a couple of years. I had asked Viverito what he thought of Mullooly and he'd said, "He's a really nice guy. He's very well received by everyone who works with him. I think you'll have a good time."

Mullooly was a forty-year-old Long Islander who stood about six foot five and had about him the air of someone who had lived pretty intensely when he was younger. He smiled a lot, but as he talked, sometimes you weren't certain what he was smiling about. Occasionally, he'd trail off in midsentence, as if he were stopping to read a postcard his mind sent him from some trip of his youth. He also told us that he'd been working double shifts for a few weeks. I couldn't tell which accounted for the lapses, but I did instinctively like the guy.

I was paired up with someone I'd never met before—Laura—and we were put on Sauté 2, which meant we'd be cooking panfried trout with grain salad and an apple–brown butter sauce, and a pork dish—the exact preparation changed every few days—with asparagus and a pork jus.

I still had never done any line cooking before, and I was about to make my debut. No fanfare, no training—just tossed onto the line and expected to perform. It made me uneasy.

During the same conversation in which I'd asked him about Mullooly, I confessed that I was a little nervous about my lack of experience to Viverito.

"Please," he said. "How many are in your group? Eighteen? And there are, what, seven stations? So two people per? Do you really think you're going to have weeds growing up around your ankles? Most students say it's actually too easy, that it's kind of boring. Don't worry about it."

Laura and I set up at our station, which was in the middle of a bank of ranges running along a wall visible to customers in the dining room. If I did screw up, I thought, I'd get to do it in full view of everyone. I was more nervous than I'd anticipated, and I tried to think of what Viverito had told me, of what Perillo had said, and told myself, *Just concentrate and just cook.*

At 5:30, Mullooly came to our station and showed us how to cook the trout—into buttermilk, dredged in flour, sautéed in a pan. The grain salad got reheated with some butter in another pan, and the sauce, made with butter, apple cider, apple pieces, thyme, and lemon juice, was done in a third pan. The pork was shredded, braised, and wrapped in caul fat. We were to give it a quick sear, put it in the oven for five or six minutes, emulsify the jus with butter, and reheat the asparagus—already blanched—with some butter too. We'd get gratin potatoes and some sweet potato puree from the station next to us, which was responsible for most of the side dishes on the St. Andrew's menu.

At 6:00, we watched the first diners filing in. Tommy, the teaching assistant, was at the pass up front, expediting all the orders. A few moments after the first diners were seated, the ticket machine sputtered out the first orders: soups, tortellini, a hamburger, and two trout. Laura and I looked at each other; we hadn't stopped to figure out how to divide the labor.

"I'll do proteins," she said. "You do everything else."

"Deal." She waited for a few minutes until Tommy, now having told us the order was in, commanded that we go ahead and fire—start cooking—the trout. When he did, Laura dredged and sautéed the trout fillets, and, just as they were done, I melted butter in a hot pan, scooped in some of the grain salad, and melted more butter for the sauce. When we were done, we plated it and waited as Dan, running the grill station, finished cooking his order for a burger.

"So that's it?" I said to Laura.

"Yeah," she said, looking relieved. I guess she had been a little apprehensive too. "That's it."

The whole kitchen had a few snags; we were lit up with first night adrenaline, and just fired our orders as they came in, forgetting that some dishes took a lot longer than others. So if we didn't bother to ask each other how long a burger that went with our trout might take, or how long it would be until the chicken breast was finished searing, someone's tortellini or pizza might be sitting up at the pass waiting and getting cold.

For the first few orders and the first few screwups, Mullooly kept his cool. But when someone couldn't keep up—and Stephen, who was on the side dish station, was having a hard time (he had the most difficult job there because every single dish came with some sort of side dish, plus they could all be ordered à la carte)—Mullooly got vocal.

Stephen seemed to make a dozen fits and starts and stops and do-overs, and after a few moments of this—as dishes sat cooling, waiting for their accompaniments—Mullooly reared up next to him.

"I need those vegetables," he said. He waited about five seconds and, when they didn't materialize, he screamed, "Give me those vege-tables right now!"

I turned and watched the guests in the dining room craning to look through the glass at the commotion. Everyone in the kitchen kept their heads down.

I thought, *I can't believe these guys think that works.* I wondered how the poor guy would be doing right now if, instead, Mullooly coached him—I mean, we were *students*—if he stood right next to Stephen and directed him—*No, don't do that. Try this. Or this. Now, do that. Do the other thing. Okay, now . . .*

When things didn't improve, Mullooly kicked him off the line and sent him home.

Bruce took over and, because he'd had some experience, there weren't any more flubs.

The rest of us kept putting out the food. Stephen was back the next day, and within another day, was doing fine. We always had some bumps—had them every night, in fact—something done under or over, a forgotten component for a dish. When it happened, Mullooly's voice would rise and thunder. In the middle of service on the fifth night, my sauce for the trout kept breaking; the apple cider and butter kept separating. Mullooly was on me, howling in my ear, as I stood over the stove, heat baking my face, sweat running down my back. I tried tuning him out, but he was like an itch. I did the sauce again, and it broke and he made me toss it. Again, and it was thrown out. And again. And again. Until I finally got it right.

"That's it! That's it!" Mullooly yelled. "That's what I want!"

And that's how it went, night on night—things like that with me, with Laura, with everyone in the class. But they were minor bumps.

Each evening, from 6:00 to 9:00, we just cooked. By this point, we weren't bad at it. Every night was one more step in our evolution.

"There's a difference between 'service' and 'hospitality,'" Philip Papineau told us. "Service is a transaction. Hospitality is an experience."

The group had moved from the kitchen to the front of the house, meaning that we would be serving actual customers—not just our fellow students—and trying to provide them with a pleasant dining experience.

We sat at tables that ran in a ring around a room in St. Andrew's basement. Papineau had just arrived. He was well over six feet, with dark hair, and was impeccably dressed in a dark suit and sleek shoes. Each of us wore the CIA's goofy service uniform: black pants, a white shirt, a black vest, a tie, and a long, brilliantly white apron, in the pocket of which we carried a corkscrew, a table crumber, two pens, and a dupe pad. Except for me. I had on a suit because my assignment for the first day of service in St. Andrew's dining room was to act as maître d'. It was precisely the second time in my entire life I'd worn a suit, and I felt weird.

"Why do you feel weird?" Jess had asked me before class began while we were waiting around.

"Yeah, Grampa Dix," Rocco said. He had recently taken to calling me this. "You look downright sexy."

"Hey—I've made major life decisions around not having to wear one of these things." I said it as a joke, but I realized I wasn't lying.

Papineau spent a good while trying to put us at ease over what we were about to do, but I hadn't known there was anything to be nervous about. I figured we'd go out there, take customers' orders, bring them the food, ring up their checks, and send them out the door.

But there was actually a bit more to it than that. He didn't want us "auctioning off" the food orders; there was to be no "Who had the fish? Who had the beef?" so we really needed to be up on our seat numbers. Depending on the order, a customer might need a soup spoon, a fish fork, a steak knife, whatever. All these things had to be there on the table before the customer realized he or she needed them. We had very little idea, he told us, how awkward it could be asking someone for an ID when they ordered alcohol. The computer system, too, where we entered the orders, was somewhat complex. The customer is pretty much always right, Papineau explained, unless they're drunk or abusive. And, he told us with a wry expression on his face, it could be difficult keeping that in mind when we dealt with students, who were allowed to make reservations on weeknights and eat one of their two daily meals there. "They love sending food back, because they think they know everything there is to know about cooking it. And they love to point out to you what you're doing wrong."

Because the CIA was a destination spot in the Hudson Valley, we saw a lot of tourists. And because St. Andrew's was the least expensive of the school's restaurants, a lot of them ate there.

"This is a real attraction for them," he said. "They *love* that students are waiting on them and making their food. But keep in mind, they also love it when you screw up. It gives them stories to tell. But I don't want them to be able to tell *those* stories. I want them telling a different story altogether."

As he walked us through a history of fine dining, the different types of table service—English, Russian, butler—the basics of face-to-face interactions ("Don't tell people what your name is. They don't care. Unless they ask, which means they do."), it grew apparent how much Papineau loved the whole flow of service. He didn't seem to look at it the way someone like Danny Meyer did—with an unfathomably deep devotion to customer comfort, although Papineau certainly wanted his customers comfortable. Instead it was like a game, or a psychological operation. The challenge was to control the customers' experience without them realizing what you were doing. This required you to read their body language very closely, to detect nuances in their speech to determine how much attention they needed, whether they wanted their water glass filled every two seconds, what was making them happy or unhappy and how to maintain it or fix it. Serving a customer was not unlike a complex dish from a kitchen; you didn't notice the individual components or the seasoning; you appreciated it as a whole.

As maître d', the sum of my duties was to answer the phone and take people to their tables. My very first customers were an elderly couple. I greeted them, saw their reservation was assigned to table 41, asked them to follow me, and set off. Papineau intercepted me when I was about halfway through the dining room. "Jonathan," he whispered. "They're moving at about two miles an hour. You just left them in the dust."

I turned and saw that the couple had barely crossed the threshold of the dining room and were very, very slowly following in my wake. He and I waited for a while at the table for them to arrive. "When you're dealing with the elderly, you have to move like they do. Next time, not so fast." He watched their approach, which was still a ways off. "I love elderly customers," Papineau said. "They know how to behave. Although I find you often have to replenish the sugar holders after they leave."

When he later saw me leading a trio of customers toward the wrong table, he silently swooped in, put a hand on my shoulder and influenced me to the right spot, then darted away. I don't think the customers noticed a thing.

Papineau just seemed to be having a great time at his job, and he treated us as if we were in on those psychological operations with him, sharing the secret. That first night—with everyone screwing up the table numbers, putting all sorts of wrong orders into the computer, forgetting to give guests essential silverware, I saw his expression go stern just once, when Jon, a guy I hadn't met before that evening, spilled a tray of water glasses onto two of the guests. It wasn't just that they'd gotten a splash that needed to be blotted up; they were soaked. Even then, Papineau was much more concerned with drying the guests off than in upbraiding Jon. His one comment on it later when he did a postservice critique was an assertively enunciated, "We really need to be careful."

I was out on the floor the next night, as a server, taking orders, bringing food to tables, clearing them afterward, and talking to the customers who did actually seem to care what my name was. They asked a lot of questions about the school, what I was doing after graduation—which was, at this point, just a few weeks away—where I was from, and so on. Strangely, I found that I was really enjoying myself. Papineau's enthusiasm was catchy, and playing the game with him was fun. From a few moments of conversation, I was able to tell whether people would be more interested in hearing that I'd taught before coming here, or hearing about Martha Stewart. I liked watching people as they ate, seeing some hint in their behavior—a gesture, an unconscious facial expression—and arriving at the table to see if there was anything they needed just before they were about to put their hands up and signal me.

I also liked a good percentage of the customers. It seemed as if they recognized that part of having a good experience dining out was dependent on us, the servers, and that they'd get a lot more out of those servers by being courteous and friendly.

But the good customers weren't alone in the dining room. There was always a healthy number of nightmarish ones—people who let their kids run like maniacs around the tables, screaming; people who walked in dressed like they were just coming from the beach; people who snapped their fingers or whistled at us for attention; people who were condescending or hostile; people who made ridiculous demands, requesting that there be less ice in the ice water, or asking that we immediately remove a few scant crumbs they had just dropped on the table. People who seemed to enjoy fucking with us.

One night, I stood in the doorway watching a table of ten. They were loud and raucous. They were finger snappers and whistlers. I watched one woman eating most of her meal—steak and potato gratin—with her fingers. Papineau was standing next to me.

I asked him: "Is it me or do you think people's manners keep getting worse?" I had been reminded of some of the kids in the Banquet and Catering dining room as I watched this party carry on.

He didn't answer for a moment. The woman had her steak in her hand and was tearing a piece off with her teeth. "It's a whole new philosophy of dining out," he said.

"The new philosophy sucks," I answered.

"It does. It really does."

On quite a few nights, there weren't many people in the dining room, and we had a lot of downtime. We'd do what we could to appear busy, but you can only fill water glasses so many times. So we stood off to the sides, hands behind our backs, appearing attentive, and talking among ourselves. Jeff told me that in addition to cooking, he wrote poetry and loved Rimbaud. It was surprising, not because he didn't seem like he was incapable of writing poetry, but because these sorts of conversations never happened much. We all knew where each other was from, had heard all sorts of stories about one another's externships, and often talked about experiences in past classes, but there were whole layers to one another that we never bothered sharing. I found out Micah wrote too, loved South American magical realist fiction, and was going to blog about the trip to Japan he and his girlfriend, Natasha, were taking after graduation. I found out that Carol was a devout Christian, and she ruminated endlessly about theology. As the nights passed, she and I would stand off together and talk about religion and philosophy. "Do you believe in evil?" she asked me once, holding a basket of bread in her hand.

"No. Not as a thing in and of itself. I believe that you can describe people's actions as evil, but I don't believe in evil as a force."

"I do believe in evil," she said. "But it bugs me because at the same time, if you believe in evil, you take away people's individual responsibility. They can claim to be influenced or possessed by evil, and that washes away their personal guilt."

DURING THE FIRST FEW days of Papineau's class, we were scheduled to take our Fifth Term Cooking Practical. The test would be given daily to six students at a shot, in the same kitchen as the first practical, using

the same protocol, with the exact same menus, except instead of a
soup, we'd be doing a fish course.

There was no reason to be scared, but I was. The first practical had
offered a few difficulties, and even though I knew my skills had blos-
somed in the interim, two and a half hours to do a fish course, a meat,
and three side dishes was almost no time at all. One error—just one—
and the whole thing was shot.

The test would be proctored by Chef DiPeri, who had a hard-assed
reputation for exactitude. Word was already out that any deviations
from procedure—shortcuts, use of improper equipment or plates, mistakes of time—would result in a serious deduction of points. I'd found
out a few times in the past that when you're nervous, when you're panicked, your hands can get stupid. No matter how much you've improved.

I could do any of the potential practical dishes, and I'd done them
each a number of times. Strangely, this made me nervous too. Famil-
iarity could breed carelessness.

Days before the test, I had all the recipes ready. I had gone over and
over the oral exam questions. I had envisioned myself cooking the
dishes, broadcasting the inner eye footage over my own closed-circuit
Food Network.

The night before the test, I stayed up late studying. When I turned
the lights out, sleep hovered just out of reach. When I replayed the
footage of myself grilling a steak, or making french fries, I was including alternate endings of disasters and fire and food burnt to nothing. I
finally drifted off around 1:00. I needed to be at school a little before
6:30. I awoke at 3:00 and, after tossing for half an hour, decided it was
futile, got up, showered, and sat watching the sky lighten until it was
time to go.

At 6:30, all six of us plus DiPeri stood in the kitchen. DiPeri had
us reach into a cup and pull out a slip of paper that indicated which
menu we'd be cooking. I drew shallow-poached flounder with a wine-
reduction sauce, chicken fricassee, glazed root vegetables, rice pilaf,
and green beans. I would go first, with the next testee starting twenty
minutes later.

I was allowed ten minutes to stockpile whatever I needed. Almost every ingredient was gathered for me. I checked them over and supplemented the cache with butter, flour, cream, and oil. I grabbed all the pans I thought I'd need and I turned my oven on to 375.

At 7:00, DiPeri said, "All right, go ahead and start."

I inhaled. I was exhausted. And I was wired. And something in my head said, *Turn off your mind. Turn it off and just cook.* I exhaled.

Two hours and fifteen minutes later, I was done. I'd finished fifteen minutes early. I'd done all the hard stuff first, like making a roux for both a fish and chicken velouté, and filleting the flounder as the roux cooked and concocting a fumet, or broth, with the bones. The rest just flowed—flowed unconsciously, smoothly—from there. I broke the spell just once, stopping at the ninety-minute point to assess where I was. I saw what I had done and I knew I was fine.

At 9:20, I presented my food. I'd made two errors: My sauce for the fish was slightly thick. And I overcooked the rice. That last was just a dumb mistake. Mere forgetfulness. I remembered thinking at one point, *Take care of the rice in about five more minutes,* but the thought didn't reoccur.

I got an 84. DiPeri shook my hand and told me I'd done a good job. I went outside for a few minutes to get some air and call Nelly.

I dialed the number and she picked up on the first ring.

"Jonathan Dixon."

My voice was bright. "Nelly."

"You don't sound like someone who just failed a cooking practical . . ."

Later, I was back inside doing my dishes. I stood next to Diego, the student who'd gone after I did.

"How'd you do?" I asked.

"I did well. I got a ninety."

"Nice."

"I was so nervous going in there."

"Did you tell yourself, 'Turn your mind off and cook'?"

He turned and looked at me. "Yeah. Exactly." He laughed. "And it worked."

13

THE ESCOFFIER RESTAURANT IS the campus showpiece, a small, ornate temple to classical French cuisine. The menu is pricey—$39 for a ragout of lobster, $32 for sliced duck breast set atop cassoulet—and yet there are few nights when the restaurant isn't filled by at least two-thirds. It's an award-winning, Zagat-rated establishment, and it would be our last stop.

Just before our time at St. Andrew's had ended, Jessica, our group leader, had met with the teaching assistant to work out who would be going to which station. The group would be splitting up again. Some would be moving to the American Bounty restaurant, on the opposite end of the building from Escoffier, or E-Room, as it was known. The rest would take over the E-Room afternoon shift, with the addition of a few students who'd been working at the Caterina restaurant.

Jessica wouldn't tell me whom I'd be working with—"You'll find out soon enough," she said—but, one night before dinner service, as she and I sat at a table folding napkins, she let it slip that they had tried to pair strong students with weaker ones. A few moments of silent folding passed until something occurred to me.

"Hey, wait a minute," I said. Jess looked up. "Answer me honestly: Am I one of the weak ones?" She stared for a second, laughed, shook her head, and went back to folding.

"I'm serious," I went on. "It's okay; it'll be character building. Just let me know, so I can really figure out how to approach this."

"You're not the weak one. Let's put it that way. You'll have two other partners. One of them is also pretty strong. Seriously, don't worry about it."

I watched her for a moment to see if her face betrayed her, but she looked as if she could pass a polygraph.

"WHO IS GOING TO be the next Ferran Adrià? Who is going to be the next Thomas Keller? The next Ducasse?" Alain De Coster, chef-instructor of the Escoffier Restaurant, paced the front of his classroom on the first day, half an hour before we'd begin cooking for that night's customers. "Who is going to be the next Girardet? What if it's you?" He pointed at a student up front. Then to the back: "Or you?"

De Coster was a Belgian émigré in his fifties. He looked quite a bit like James Ellroy, and he'd spent his professional life training in the old-school way, starting in restaurants as a thirteen-year-old apprentice and working his way up. He was regarded as an encyclopedia of classical cooking; rumor had it he was a soon-to-be candidate for the title of certified master chef, and yet he was renowned at school for never— *never*—raising his voice.

De Coster told us first thing that not yelling was a new development in his life, that he had, in fact, been a screamer when he was younger. "I was, if you'll excuse my language, a real asshole," he told us. But one day—and he didn't describe exactly what had happened— he'd had an epiphany and vowed never to lose his cool again. He said that a chef needs to have the loyalty of his staff, and that fear was in no way equivalent to loyalty. Therefore, he didn't ever want to inspire fear in anyone who worked for him. Which, at this moment, meant us.

The first day, he lectured in a voice quavering with enthusiasm. "Pay attention to the product, and the product will reward you!" he exclaimed. "Everything you cook should trigger the 'wow!' factor for anyone who eats it! Everything at a peak of refinement! Every detail is crucial! No step matters less than another!"

De Coster talked about the history of French cuisine, from Carême to Escoffier to Fernand Point to the icons of nouvelle cuisine. He spoke about these people and their accomplishments in terms of upheaval and revolution. He made it all wildly exciting.

"Read! Read! Taste! *Learn!*" he implored. "How do you help make revolution? How do you make something *new*? Look at the classics. Look at every single element of a dish—*every one*—and figure out, *What can I do to make each one of those steps contemporary? What can I do to make them new? Make them my own? How much skill and technique and knowledge can I bring to bear on each element?*"

I sat listening, burning with revolutionary fervor, like Bill Ayers in a toque. I wanted to get upstairs in that kitchen, and excel and shine. I wanted to stay glued to De Coster's side and watch him in action, to learn everything, observe everything I possibly could.

This was not in the stars for me, though, because it turned out I wouldn't be cooking any food for customers. The station assignments were called out name by name. I discovered, to my dismay, I had been assigned to the family meal team.

The family meal team's job was to cook vast quantities of food in a very short time for a bunch of moaning, grumbling ingrates. Or, put another way, we would be making a nightly dinner for our classmates. We could occasionally order meat and vegetables but needed to use a lot of what we had on hand in the kitchen—that is, stuff from the walk-in refrigerator that was about to turn bad.

The one thing that made De Coster angry, the one thing that might tempt him to raise his voice, was waste. No matter what it was—an apple core, broccoli stalks, shrimp beginning to throb with rot—there was a use for it.

We had from 3:00 in the afternoon until 4:50 to prepare an entrée, a starch, a vegetable, and a salad for fifty people, which included our group, the E-Room student waitstaff, any security or buildings and grounds people who wandered in at dinnertime, and any instructors who wanted to eat. The kitchen was tiny. You couldn't move without bumping into someone else. The temperature routinely got to 110 degrees. We had the most space of anybody—an entire metal work-table for the three of us—Max, Lou, and me.

Max was about twenty, the son of a Lutheran minister, and shared the same dim view of the world at large that I did. Lou was a pain in the ass—snide, sarcastic, smirking. He was not incredibly industrious, and Max and I didn't really count him as part of the team. It was the Jonathan and Max Show.

We had only a vague idea of what we'd be cooking each day. We had come up with menu ideas in advance—spice-rubbed steak one night, yogurt-braised lamb (ripped off directly from Tabla's menu) on another—but we found out the first two nights that our orders weren't likely to come in. Jon, the teaching assistant who was in charge of phys-ically placing our orders, had a laissez-faire relationship with accuracy. So our initial menu—steak, roasted potatoes, sautéed broccoli rabe, and a salad of spinach and red onion with raspberry vinaigrette—never came into being. Neither the beef nor the potatoes arrived. The spinach was absent too. Plan B: we found several huge pork loins in the refrig-erator, each one on the verge of turning slightly slimy; we found a sack of cornmeal; we discovered a cache of fennel, a bag of Valencia oranges, and a tub of kalamata olives. Max and I trimmed the worst of the pork away, rubbed what was left with a mix of coffee, cayenne, brown sugar, and dried herbs and threw it in the convection oven. We made polenta. We julienned the fennel, sectioned all the oranges, chopped up the olives and mixed everything together with salt, balsamic vinegar, and olive oil. At the last minute, we found some broccoli, hacked it up, boiled it, and tossed it with butter, salt, and pepper. We served dinner five minutes late. And the results were solidly . . . okay. At least, we thought so.

Because we had to do some quick tidying after we served every-thing, we found that the three of us were the last to eat. That first night, we made our way into the dining room where the others were already seated and listened to the comments of "What is this shit?"

and "I think I'm going to go hungry tonight" or "This is terrible" from the student waitstaff and maintenance people. This would go on night after night, like something reflexive, no matter how good or bad our results were. Our group was usually a little more polite. But I came to understand that praise meant not hearing the word "shit" in connection with the food.

I began wondering if De Coster and Jon were messing with the orders intentionally. If it was intentional, they managed a pretty good lesson in improvising and using whatever one had on hand.

I also discovered a good solution to hiding food we just couldn't bear to use out of fear for gastrointestinal safety. I asked the vegetable team to give me all their potato peelings and asparagus scraps—things we were allowed to toss—and hoarded them. When I discarded fish that stank like ammonia, or beef tinted green—both things that had lived too long in the walk-in refrigerator—I'd pull the vegetable scraps and dump them on top of whatever I'd just thrown out. De Coster never noticed.

The decisions we made about our menus weren't arrived at democratically. I grabbed the reins. And for some reason, Max—and Lou—went along. I wound up finalizing the menus, dividing the labor, and saying things like, "Don't worry that we don't have enough milk and cream—just use stock and do a four-to-one ratio of polenta. Cook it in the oven so we don't have to worry about stirring. We're going to need to blanch the green beans in about ten minutes because we won't have the burner space later on. Make sure the pine nuts get browned—don't let them burn. You should add some orange juice to that vinaigrette—you can get the acid and the sweetness that's missing all in one."

I didn't intend to become the foreman. I also didn't intend to get forceful in giving directions, yet at one point, I yelled at Lou for not getting something done on time. It was an uncomfortable moment: I had a sudden and clear insight into why Coyac and Viverito, Ty and Chris and Dwayne, Mullooly, and the other loud chefs raise their voices.

De Coster asked to see me after class. "So I've been watching you the past few evenings. And tonight I *heard* you. You don't need to do that, but, given who you were badgering, I understand. Family meal is a tough station. No one realizes it. But you have very little time to get a lot done. A lot of my classes, things don't get done with that station. But if family meal isn't satisfying, morale is shot for the entire night. You guys are doing well, and I need you to keep taking a leadership role. Even more so than you have. We need to keep the trains running on time."

So I did. It ceased being the Jonathan and Max Show. Max was gracious about it. Our orders began coming in correctly.

Max and I sat next to each other in De Coster's preservice lecture, and we'd arrive a few minutes early to confer about that night's menu. Which meant *my* menu. I found myself simply telling Max what we'd be doing: "Okay, so tonight we're making meatball sandwiches. Jon placed the order for ground beef and I watched him do it, so we know it's in. I'll make the sauce. We'll put bread crumbs, Parmesan, onions, and so on, into the meat and bake them in the convection oven. We'll do the fennel salad thing again. We've got the bread, so we won't need an extra starch. I'll do the broccoli, too. Lou can take care of shredding the mozzarella. Good?"

"Yeah, that's fine."

Discovering your inner asshole is a strange experience. I kept waiting for Max to tell me to shut the hell up, but he never did. So I became more tyrannical, albeit gently. One day Max made a vinaigrette for our salad from soy sauce, rice vinegar, and honey. I tasted it. "Hey, this is good," I said. "Nice. But since we have all these oranges, what would you think of adding some of the juice and zest, just so they don't go to waste?" After the juice and zest was added, I tasted again. "Max!" I exclaimed. "I've got it. We can make this perfect if we add some grated ginger and some mirin. Does that sound right?" Max added the ginger and mirin. I considered that maybe I wasn't truly being an asshole, that maybe, in fact, this was how real kitchens manned by real cooks functioned.

We roasted thirty-five chickens one day. We grilled forty pounds of flank steak and made potato gratin on another. Near the end of our stint, we made fried chicken for seventy people. We bombed badly with a batch of penne alla vodka.

De Coster gave Max and me each an A–.

FROM THE ESCOFFIER RESTAURANT kitchen, we finished the last three weeks of our education in the role of servers. We waited on customers from 6:00 in the evening until about 11:00 at night, when the last of them finished their meals—around two and a half hours for an amuse-bouche, an appetizer, an entrée, and a dessert. A bunch of the dishes were prepared tableside; if someone ordered the mustard-crusted rack of lamb or rack of boar, or the dover sole, we'd wheel a cart, or gueridon, to the customer's table, turn on a heating element, and—taking the sole as an example—debone the fish, plate it, and make a brown butter sauce. We'd spoon the sauce over the fish, add some turned potatoes (also coated with butter) to the plate, and set it down in front of the customer. Several desserts were done tableside too, like crêpes suzette, or strawberry jubilee. At some point during the dessert preparations, we flamed brandy at a presumably safe distance from the customers' heads, sending up a huge plume of fire. People seemed to love the theater of it.

After the novelty of solemnly doing all these tableside dishes wore off, we became quite bored. The customers—especially the older ones—loved asking questions about who we were and where we were from, what we'd do afterward, where we'd go. I think we all had our pat answers that we used ad infinitum, but it just reminded us that the end of school was staring us right in the face, and we were pretty anxious to finish up.

JESSICA GOT A JOB in Chicago. My friend Dan Clawson was going to Nantucket for the summer to work in a restaurant there, then he'd head to New York. He was hoping to wind up at Per Se someday, or Momofuku, or one of Jean-Georges Vongerichten's places. Max was off to a resort in Wyoming, my friend Diego to the Ritz in Miami. Zach was lining something up at a hotel in Vegas.

I hadn't had much contact with anyone from my first group, but Adam had let me know he'd gotten a sous-chef job at Spice Market. Lombardi had never returned from his externship; I asked Adam and he couldn't remember which restaurant it was—some low-key place in Westchester, or maybe Connecticut, Adam thought—but they'd offered him a permanent job and he stayed on. Joe, who'd done his externship at the French Laundry, was moving to San Francisco to help Corey Lee, the French Laundry's former chef de cuisine, open his own restaurant.

Brookshire had taken some time off and come back to school a block after I had; I ran into him from time to time and he'd decided to stay on and complete the bachelor's degree program. A number of people were taking that course; Sitti was staying, as were Margot, Jackie, Rocco, and Gabi.

Everyone asked me: *Where are you going? What are you going to do?* Everyone assumed I'd write.

Almost every graduate moved on to a restaurant kitchen. All of the instructors had taken that path, and the curriculum was built on facilitating it. And I harbored some envy. For two years, virtually every day, I came into school and got to spend hour after hour cooking. *Imagine a life just like this,* I thought. *Imagine doing it day after day, doing what you've been trained to do, how fast you'd get, how efficient. You'd start achieving a serious finesse, real refinement.*

Part of me wondered, *If I could go back to Tabla now, knowing what I know, would it be a totally different experience?*

And what if I found a restaurant to work in here, upstate?

A few days before graduation, I ran into Viverito in the parking lot.

"So what's the next step?" he asked.

"I don't know. I'm working out the details now."

"I'm assuming you're not restaurant bound?"

"I don't think so."

"It's not for everyone. But there's a whole world of things to do out there, you know."

There *is* a world out there beyond the walls of a restaurant kitchen. Although most students chose to stay within them, you heard the occasional story around campus of people who made a different choice. One guy wound up cooking for rock bands on tour. Some people became food stylists. Two of the chefs who used to work in the Martha Stewart test kitchen had graduated from the CIA.

I harbored envy because no matter how great any other situation is, there's nothing like a restaurant kitchen. But I knew it wasn't where I really belonged. Just the amount of talking back I did to people who were in charge of keeping the kitchens running—I knew I was too pigheaded to flourish in a situation where ceding control to others was required to truly learn and succeed. If I went back to Tabla now, the results probably wouldn't be appreciably different. I'd certainly do things differently, learn much more that they had to offer, dive in deeper to the whole culture and experience, but I am who I am, and my focus wasn't entirely aligned with what they needed from me.

I thought about all that one night when I was driving home with only a single day left at school. And I thought intently about my future. I knew I was going to be writing about the experience of learning to cook at school, but I also knew that project wasn't going to sustain the rest of my life.

I wanted—*needed*—the physicality of cooking. I loved working with my hands. I loved working with all my senses.

Dinner parties for me now were a different proposition than they'd been prior to the CIA. I loved having people over now, getting elaborate, knowing I could wow them. I even felt a very vague disappointment when I had to stop cooking, turn off the burners, and take my seat at the table.

In the rare moments when Nelly and I felt a little flush, we'd occasionally go out to eat, but more often we'd splurge on really good ingredients and do something for ourselves at home.

Since being in school a lot of my friends and family would ask me to prepare dinner when we'd visit. I never said no. I loved bringing in my equipment, unpacking it, setting myself up, and cooking for all of us.

There's nothing like a restaurant kitchen, but watching people enjoy food I'd cooked never lost its thrill.

I recalled years ago, when the notion of culinary school was barely germinating, being at a party in an acquaintance's Brooklyn apartment. They'd hired caterers to do Indian food for the guests, and I found myself standing off to the side of the apartment's kitchen for half an hour, nursing a beer, watching the caterers at work, and wishing I was working with them.

And as I drove across the bridge, over the Hudson River, the realization was as much right there in front of me as the swollen moon and its light on the water: *Those caterers weren't conjured up from the ether. They go to people's homes—all the time—and feed them.*

Most catered food is something consumed with weary resignation, to stave off pangs or act like a sponge for cocktails. But I remembered that Indian food being pretty good.

And I asked myself, *Does it really work like that? Can you really do something like that on your own terms?*

One voice answered, *No.*

Another voice countered with, *Why the hell not?*

I liked the second voice much better. Seriously—why the hell not? Now that I thought of it, I'd been at more than a few parties over the years like that one in Brooklyn. And I'd gotten pretty good at the stove. Sometimes when I'd make us dinner, Nelly paid me what I thought of as the ultimate compliment: "If I was served this in a restaurant, I'd be completely happy."

Right then I knew that this idea embodied the best of both worlds for me. It was exhilarating to think about. After I got home, I was up until very late at the dining room table, piles of my cookbooks around me, playing with ideas, planning sample menus. Planning the rest of my life.

I MADE THE DRIVE to school one last time. Graduation began at 10:00 a.m. in the Student Rec Center, where I'd watched the Bocuse d'Or five months prior. From where all the students sat on a dais, I could see my parents and Nelly in their seats. It took about forty-five minutes, from the opening invocation to the moment when Tim Ryan called us each up to a podium where he draped a medal around our necks and shook our hands. At 10:45, he announced, "Consider yourselves graduated."

Later, I guided my parents and Nelly around Roth Hall, taking a last look at the kitchens. I said good-bye to Viverito. I said good-bye to Perillo. I said good-bye to my classmates.

When there were no other places to revisit, no more people to say good-bye to, Nelly and I went to the parking lot and got into my truck. I couldn't bring myself to start it. I turned around in my seat and looked out the back window. I sat once again staring at the buildings. Delivery trucks were pulling in and driving away. Students in uniform were walking to, or home from, their classes. I saw some students in their waitstaff uniforms walking toward Roth Hall. Three weeks from now, it would be their turn. Another minute passed.

Nelly put a hand on my knee. "Let's go home, honey," she said.

"Yeah." I started the truck and drove out of the parking lot.

After we all got back to the house and changed, Nelly, my parents, and I sat at the kitchen table.

"So what do we do about dinner tonight? Is there a restaurant you'd like to go to and celebrate?" my mother asked.

"Any place you want," my father added.

"Let's go hit some of the farm stands, instead. Storey Farm in Catskill has great corn. Sauer Farm has been doing really nice okra. We can go to the market in Kingston and get some good, local meat. I was thinking, why don't we do buttermilk chicken crusted with corn-meal, and some succotash, and a tarragon jus?"

I thought my parents would really enjoy that—and, in the future, other people might too.